Explorations of L

Transfer

SECOND LANGUAGE ACQUISITION
Series Editors: **Professor David Singleton,** *University of Pannonia,*
Hungary and Fellow Emeritus, Trinity College, Dublin, Ireland and
Associate Professor Simone E. Pfenninger, *University of Salzburg, Austria.*

This series brings together titles dealing with a variety of aspects of language acquisition and processing in situations where a language or languages other than the native language is involved. Second language is thus interpreted in its broadest possible sense. The volumes included in the series all offer in their different ways, on the one hand, exposition and discussion of empirical findings and, on the other, some degree of theoretical reflection. In this latter connection, no particular theoretical stance is privileged in the series; nor is any relevant perspective – sociolinguistic, psycholinguistic, neurolinguistic, etc. – deemed out of place. The intended readership of the series includes final-year undergraduates working on second language acquisition projects, postgraduate students involved in second language acquisition research, and researchers, teachers and policymakers in general whose interests include a second language acquisition component.

All books in this series are externally peer-reviewed.

Full details of all the books in this series and of all our other publications can be found on http://www.multilingual-matters.com, or by writing to Multilingual Matters, St Nicholas House, 31-34 High Street, Bristol, BS1 2AW, UK.

SECOND LANGUAGE ACQUISITION: 144

Explorations of Language Transfer

Terence Odlin

MULTILINGUAL MATTERS
Bristol • Jackson

DOI https://doi.org/10.21832/ODLIN9547
Library of Congress Cataloging in Publication Data
A catalog record for this book is available from the Library of Congress.
Names: Odlin, Terence, author.
Title: Explorations of Language Transfer/Terence Odlin.
Description: Bristol; Jackson: Multilingual Matters, [2022] | Series:
    Second Language Acquisition: 144 | Includes bibliographical references
    and index. | Summary: 'This book brings together many insights about the
    influences of one language upon another in language learning. Its
    accessible discussions explore key concerns such as predictions of
    difficulty, the role of translation processes, the relation between
    comprehension and production, and implications for classroom practice' –
    Provided by publisher.
Identifiers: LCCN 2021049933 (print) | LCCN 2021049934 (ebook) | ISBN
    9781788929530 (paperback) | ISBN 9781788929547 (hardback) | ISBN
    9781788929554 (pdf) | ISBN 9781788929561 (epub)
Subjects: LCSH: Language transfer (Language learning) | Second language
    acquisition. | Prediction (Psychology) | Cognitive grammar.
Classification: LCC P118.25 .O34 2022 (print) | LCC P118.25 (ebook) | DDC
    418.0071 – dc23/eng/20211128
LC record available at https://lccn.loc.gov/2021049933
LC ebook record available at https://lccn.loc.gov/2021049934

British Library Cataloguing in Publication Data
A catalogue entry for this book is available from the British Library.

ISBN-13: 978-1-78892-954-7 (hbk)
ISBN-13: 978-1-78892-953-0 (pbk)

Multilingual Matters
UK: St Nicholas House, 31-34 High Street, Bristol, BS1 2AW, UK.
USA: Ingram, Jackson, TN, USA.

Website: www.multilingual-matters.com
Twitter: Multi_Ling_Mat
Facebook: https://www.facebook.com/multilingualmatters
Blog: www.channelviewpublications.wordpress.com

Copyright © 2022 Terence Odlin.

All rights reserved. No part of this work may be reproduced in any form or by any
means without permission in writing from the publisher.

The policy of Multilingual Matters/Channel View Publications is to use papers that
are natural, renewable and recyclable products, made from wood grown in sustainable
forests. In the manufacturing process of our books, and to further support our policy,
preference is given to printers that have FSC and PEFC Chain of Custody certification.
The FSC and/or PEFC logos will appear on those books where full certification has
been granted to the printer concerned.

Typeset by Riverside Publishing Solutions.

Contents

Acknowledgments

This book consists of eight chapters, five previously published by Multilingual Matters and three new ones. The earlier chapters appeared in edited collections:

Odlin, T. (1990) Word order transfer, metalinguistic awareness, and constraints on foreign language learning. In B. VanPatten and J.F. Lee (eds) *Second Language Acquisition/Foreign Language Learning* (pp. 95–117). Clevedon: Multilingual Matters.

Odlin, T. (2006) Could a contrastive analysis ever be complete? In J. Arabski (ed.) *Cross-linguistic Influences in the Second Language Lexicon* (pp. 22–35). Clevedon: Multilingual Matters

Odlin, T. (2008) Focus constructions and language transfer. In D. Gabryś-Barker (ed.) *Morphosyntactic Issues in Second Language Acquisition* (pp. 3–28). Bristol: Multilingual Matters.

Odlin, T. (2016a) Was there really ever a Contrastive Analysis Hypothesis? In R. Alonso Alonso (ed.) *Crosslinguistic Influence in Second Language Acquisition* (pp. 1–23). Bristol: Multilingual Matters.

Odlin, T. (2016b) Language transfer and the link between comprehension and production. In L. Yu and T. Odlin (eds) *New Perspectives on Transfer in Second Language Learning* (pp. 207–225). Bristol: Multilingual Matters.

These chapters have been edited for the new volume to enhance their consistency with the newer chapters. I would like to thank the editors of the earlier collections for their efforts in making my work available to an international audience. Discussions with Larry Selinker proved very helpful for the approach taken in Chapter 7; in the same connection, thanks are due to Scott Jarvis, Marianne Gullberg, and audiences at a number of presentations of material from the same chapter. Laura Wagner provided helpful advice with regard to Chapter 5. I am grateful to David Singleton for encouraging me to undertake this project and to Laura Longworth, Sarah Williams and Rosie McEwan and other staff members at Multilingual Matters. This book is dedicated to the memory of my parents, Aline and Bill Odlin.

1 Introduction

Defining Language Transfer

Over several decades of work on second language acquisition (SLA), the term *transfer* has become the most commonly used shorthand to denote a phenomenon also known as *crosslinguistic influence*. Later in this chapter (and in more detail in the next), the history of the term itself will be considered, but for now it will suffice to say that despite controversies about the term and about crosslinguistic influence, many SLA researchers continue using the word *transfer* or the phrase *language transfer*.

Specialists in other fields have also employed *transfer* in a variety of ways, and, in psychology, different theorists have found different uses for the term, as a comparison of its meanings in psychoanalysis and behaviorism will show. Similarly, the uses of *transfer* in SLA and related fields are not at all the same. Some relevant domains will be compared, but central to the discussion of the term in SLA will be notions addressed in the working definition given here:

> Transfer is the influence resulting from the similarities and differences between the target language and any other language that has been previously (and perhaps imperfectly) acquired. (Odlin, 1989: 27)

The definition deliberately uses 'any other language' instead of 'a second language' since there are many cases of people learning not only a second language but also a third. Two cases of multilingualism are considered in this book: one where English is the target language and Finnish and Swedish the previously learned languages (Chapters 5 and 7), and another where there is again one native language, Polish, and two non-native languages – German and English (Chapter 7). Along with these empirical investigations, other topics involving multilingualism are also considered in various chapters.

Multilingual research has offered new perspectives on the complexity of crosslinguistic influence (e.g. Cenoz *et al.*, 2001; De Angelis & Dewaele, 2011; Gabryś-Barker, 2012; Hammarberg, 2009). There has also been considerable work on reverse transfer in bilingual settings. For example, Porte (2003) analyzed the English spoken by several native speakers of English who were teaching EFL (English as a Foreign Language) in Spain and encountered many cases of L2 → L1 influence: e.g. *I was really shocked when I first saw how molested some teachers got at my criticising the system* (Porte, 2003: 112), where *molested* reflects just the mildly unfavorable meaning of Spanish *molestar* ('annoy') in contrast to the highly pejorative English *molest*, which is often used to denote criminal behavior (e.g. child molester). The teachers in Porte's investigation seem to have been influenced both from some direct knowledge of Spanish and from their relatively long residence in Spain, especially since the *molested* example might just as easily come from a native speaker of Spanish using English (Nash, 1979).

Along with L2 → L1 influences on vocabulary, interesting cases of grammatical transfer are also evident in the literature, as in a chapter by Pavlenko (2003). She found that Russian speakers living in the United Sates sometimes used the perfective/imperfective system of verbs in Russian in ways quite different from monolingual speakers in Russia, with the Russian speakers in America sometimes resembling learners of L2 Russian who were L1 speakers of English. Research on L2 → L1 transfer often overlaps with what is called code-switching, and it has proven difficult in some cases to decide if a particular bilingual utterance should be considered transfer or switching (e.g. Isurin *et al.*, 2009). Chapter 4 of the present volume compares L2 → L1 and L1 → L2 influences involving word order.

Patterns of L2 → L1 and L1 → L2 transfer raise many interesting questions about how much parallelism in crosslinguistic influence there may be in any language-contact setting (Thomason & Kaufman, 1988). Still other forms of parallel influences can be found by comparing acquisition in different settings – for example, Italian children who study English in England, and English-speaking children who study Italian in Italy. Rocca (2007) looked closely at just such cases, with regard to tense and aspect structures in the target language, and she identified clear patterns of transfer.

What researchers regard as typical cases of transfer – and what probably concern language teachers the most – are found in divergences between the target language (e.g. English in EFL settings) and the source language (the native language in L2 acquisition, and either the L1 or L2 in L3 acquisition). Transfer errors in either comprehension or production are often called negative transfer. Such errors frequently appear in vocabulary uses, such as when a native speaker of Spanish chooses *molest* in English as a synonym of *annoy*. Along with negative transfer involving vocabulary, divergences can and do appear in grammar, as in the following sentence from a native speaker of Vietnamese: *She has managed to rise the kite fly over the tallest building* (= *She has managed to fly a kite over the tallest building*) where the pattern *rise... fly* strongly suggests influence from a key pattern Vietnamese syntax known as serial verb constructions

(Helms-Park, 2003). The pronunciation and spelling of learners also indicate many cases of negative transfer. Spelling errors frequently offer a window on pronunciation problems, as in an error of a Finnish student who wrote *crass* instead of *grass*. Thus a Finn's misspelling of *grass* with either the letter <c> or the letter <k> reflects a phonological difference between Finnish and English: the former does not make a phonemic distinction between /k/ and /g/.

Although negative transfer often gets more attention from researchers and teachers, there is also the reality of positive transfer, i.e. a convergence between what speakers of the target language normally do and what non-native speakers succeed in doing because of some similarity between the source language and the target. Examples of positive transfer will appear further on in the discussion of predictions.

The Transfer Metaphor

Although the term *transfer* has become the most commonly used designation for crosslinguistic influence, it has been controversial, as reflected in criticism by Corder, who asserted that 'nothing is being transferred from anywhere to anywhere' (1983: 92). Indeed, transfer is a metaphor when applied to crosslinguistic influence and to other phenomena in linguistics and psychology; in the latter field, for example, researchers have investigated the use of old skills for solving new problems (Singley & Anderson, 1989).

The metaphoric basis of *transfer* comes into sharper focus through a look at its etymology. *Transfer* reflects two Latin forms, *trans* (across) and *ferre* (carry), so that there is a suggestion of something being carried from one place to another. In fact, the English phrase *carried across* has served as an alternative expression for crosslinguistic influence in some discussions of SLA (e.g. Slobin, 1996), and at least one French linguist (Meillet, 1933) used the verb *transporter* in exactly the same way.

The notion of carrying across has also had other extensions, as seen in the very word *metaphor*. Dechert (2006) observes that the etymologies of both *transfer* and *metaphor* literally denote carrying over, *transfer* coming from the Latin forms given above, and *metaphor* from the Greek *meta* (across) and *phor* (carry). The notion of movement implicit in both words makes them (along with *carry over* and *transport*) part of a large set of expressions that Reddy (1979) called 'the conduit metaphor,' examples of which also include expressions such as *get something across* as a synonym for *explain*. The motion implied in *transfer* can also help understand the metaphoric basis of the verb *translate*, which has essentially the same etymology as *transfer*, since the word *latus* is a participial form of the Latin irregular verb *ferre*. Despite the objections of Corder and others, the transfer metaphor as well as the translation metaphor is useful. As Lakoff and Johnson (1980) argue more generally, metaphors offer a tool to try to understand new problems with the help of existing cognitive resources. The phenomena for which *transfer* and *translate* serve as cover terms are complex, but both metaphors rightly hint at interactions between languages or, more precisely, interactions in the minds of bilinguals or multilinguals.

The conduit metaphor expressed by *transfer* and *translate* also has interesting counterparts in German. The word *übertragen* (*über* 'over' + *tragen* 'carry') is sometimes equivalent to *translate* and sometimes to *transfer* in the sense of crosslinguistic influence. Furthermore, a related word – *hinübertragen* – has been used to denote both carrying and crosslinguistic influence. It appears in what may be the earliest discussion of language transfer as a psycholinguistic phenomenon:

> Die erlernung einer fremden Sprache sollte daher die Gewinnung eines neuen Standpunktes in der bisherigen Weltansicht sein, und ist es in der That bis auf einen gewissen Grad, da jede Sprache das ganze Gewebe der Begriffe und die Vorstellungsweise eines Theils der Menschheit enthält. Nur weil man in eine fremde Sprache immer, mehr oder weniger, seine eigne Welt-, ja seine eigne Sprachansicht *hinüberträgt*, so wird dieser Erfolg nicht rein und vollständig empfunden. (von Humboldt, 1836: 59; emphasis added)

> [The learning of a foreign language should thus be the attainment of a new perspective on the worldview already held and indeed it is to a certain degree, since every language contains the entire fabric of concepts and forms of representation of a part of humanity. Still, because one always *transfers*, more or less, one's own worldview and, surely, one's own language-view, this success will not be felt pure and complete.]

This passage, taken from a well-known treatise on language and mind by the philosopher Wilhelm von Humboldt, not only uses *hinübertragen* to refer to transfer but also raises issues that have eventually come to be examined rather closely in modern SLA research, issues sometimes referred to as conceptual transfer (e.g. Jarvis & Pavlenko, 2008; Lucy, 2016; Odlin, 2005). While Humboldt used *hinübertragen*, other intellectuals in the 19th century employed *übertragen* to denote transfer or translation (or both), including Hugo Schuchardt and Hermann Paul, as will be seen in Chapter 2. The same chapter provides detailed evidence that the use of *transfer* in English in discussions of language contact and SLA owes more to the German use of *hinübertragen* and *übertragen* than to the behaviorist theories of learning in psychology that are often cited in the history of transfer research.

The coincidence in German of one word – *übertragen* – denoting both transfer and translation should not, of course, be taken as proof that transferring and translating are really the same thing. Even so, it would also be mistaken to assume that the two phenomena are completely different. Chapter 7 offers what may be the first in-depth look at the overlap between transfer and translation.

Predictions of Transfer

One of the most controversial questions regarding transfer has been whether it is possible to predict when crosslinguistic influence will occur. The chapters in Part 1 consider different aspects of the issue. Chapter 2 looks at predictions through a historical lens, focusing on the so-called Contrastive Analysis Hypothesis, a term which the chapter shows to be quite nebulous. Chapter 3 considers whether a contrastive analysis (i.e. the systematic comparison of two or more languages) could ever be complete, and it also argues that putative constraints on transfer are themselves predictions. For example, one supposed constraint claims that there can be no transfer of basic word-order patterns. Chapter 4, however, offers evidence to the contrary, thus calling into question the prediction of no transfer.

Although the putative constraint on the transfer of word order is contradicted by actual evidence of such transfer (and likewise other supposed constraints discussed in Chapter 3), there is no reason in principle for denying the possibility of some constraints on crosslinguistic influence. By the same token, however, there is also no reason to believe that predictions of transfer are always doomed to failure. Here is one prediction made in a recent discussion (Odlin, 2014: 30):

* Speakers of Finnish as a group will have greater difficulty with the articles of Portuguese than will speakers of Swedish as a group.

The prediction seems plausible, given the existing evidence for a difference in success between Swedish and Finnish speakers in the acquisition of English articles (Chapter 5). The Portuguese article system is, of course, different in some ways but, like English, it does have obligatory articles, some of which signal definite and others indefinite reference.

The prediction considered here, as well as additional ones in Chapter 3, should be understood as expectations of group, not individual, tendencies. That is, positive transfer is predicted for one group whose language shares a structural trait with the target language. Like English, Swedish has an article system whereas Finish does not, and so Swedish speakers should, if the prediction holds true, tend to do better.

Although shared traits such as articles do not guarantee transfer, the comparative group approach suggests that the method can often be used to verify or falsify cases of crosslinguistic influence. A study by Jarvis (2002) of article use shows a further methodological refinement: two L1 groups, Finnish and Swedish, are compared in how they differ in their L1 behaviors as well as in how they differ in their performance in the English target language. By comparing reference strategies used by native speakers of Finnish and Swedish in their own L1s, Jarvis was able to correlate these strategies with the ways that Finnish and Swedish speakers used – or did not use – articles when writing in English. Much of Chapter 5 and also parts of Chapters 6 and 7 of this volume consider cases of Finnish and Swedish influence to be found in the database compiled by Jarvis.

Although controlled comparisons of L1 groups offer an especially useful way to study transfer, other types of investigations can also provide important insights, such as studies of language-contact situations. One example is the so-called *after*-perfect, where *after* marks perfective aspect as in this sentence from a speaker in the Western Isles of Scotland: *The stone is after going through, he says* (Sabban, 1982: 155), which could be paraphrased as *The stone has gone through....* Similar *after*-perfect sentences are also common in Ireland, and there is a close parallel between the Celtic English structure and patterns in both Irish and Scottish Gaelic. In a survey of worldwide varieties of English, Kortmann and Szmrecsanyi (2004: 1151) found that the *after*-perfect appeared only in the Celtic lands or in areas where speakers of Irish and Scottish English lived, especially certain parts of Canada. In contrast, the same global survey found some verb forms to be extremely widespread, such as verbs that are traditionally irregular being made into regular forms, as where the past tense of *catch* becomes *catched* instead of *caught*; this pattern is common among both native- and non-native speakers of English. Although it would be hard to argue for transfer in the case of *catched*, the *after*-perfect does indicate contact-induced change due to transfer.

In recent decades the academic fields often labeled as language contact and second language acquisition have drifted apart, even though some researchers remain active in both fields (e.g. Mufwene, 2010). However, all cases of SLA involve some kind of language contact, and pioneers in the study of transfer such as Hugo Schuchardt and Uriel Weinreich (Chapter 2) recognized the value of both classroom-based and naturalistic research. The wide domain of language contact seems all the more important to acknowledge if researchers wish to get a good grasp of the problem of predictions. Because the various proposed constraints on transfer have generally come from research done in school settings, work in naturalistic settings can bring to bear a wider range of data from second language users, as in a number of studies of word-order transfer cited in Chapter 4. Many regions of the world offer potential opportunities to study contact-induced variation and change due to transfer, but only a small number have received much attention, such as the Celtic lands of the British Isles and the Andes region of South America (e.g. Filppula *et al.*, 2008; Klee & Ocampo, 1995; Muysken, 1984). There seems little doubt that if research can be carried out in more diverse settings, a wider range of findings about transfer will emerge.

Transfer and Language Processing

Issues related to predictions inform the chapters of Part 1, while in in Part 2 issues of language processing are prominent, specifically, comprehension and production (Chapter 5), using and understanding focus constructions (Chapter 6), and translation (Chapter 7). Transfer researchers have long acknowledged the importance of processing. Weinreich (1953a) and Selinker (1969, 1972) recognized the value of predictions, but they also saw a need for going beyond expected patterns of transfer to understand how crosslinguistic influence formed part of what Selinker called 'the latent psychological structure' underlying second language acquisition. The topics in Part 2 certainly do not exhaust the range of processing concerns, but they do overlap with concerns raised in Part 1. The most interesting predictions are arguably those that have implications for processing. Accordingly, part of Chapter 3 considers predictions relevant to the production and comprehension of focus constructions.

However controversial they may be, predictions of transfer are usually language-specific. Yet, if it is true that some predictions have implications for processing, a paradox seems to arise. Various SLA theories have addressed linguistic processing, including Processability Theory (e.g. Pienemann et al., 2005), Universal Grammar (White, 2003), and the Competition Model (MacWhinney, 2008). All three approaches seem to assume that processing in a first or second language will occur not in a language-specific but rather in a language-neutral way, somewhat as many computers prove compatible with different kinds of software. Nevertheless, some psycholinguists who focus on native-speaker performance have argued that processing routines are language-specific to some extent, and that the routines may vary between even highly similar languages. Work by Caramazza et al. (2001) indicates that native speakers of French, Spanish, and Italian show significant inter-group differences in how they select appropriate determiners in picture-naming tasks; moreover, group differences are also evident between speakers of Dutch and German. Caramazza and his colleagues see considerable crosslinguistic variation in how categories such as gender and number interact in the determiner selection process.

The chapters of Part 2 explore certain language-specific character-istics of transfer relevant to processing. Chapter 5 is an empirical study finding that the link between comprehension and production is, at least in part, language-specific with evidence of large differences between native speakers of Finnish and native speakers of Swedish in how they process input in L2 English. One of the findings of this chapter is a statistically significant difference in the two groups' use of cleft-focus sentences (e.g. *It was the girl who stole the bread*), with many more native speakers of Swedish using them in comparison with native speakers of Finnish.

Focus constructions more generally are the concern of Chapter 6, which looks at evidence in various contexts – such as the influence of Yiddish on English in New York City and of Celtic languages on focus patterns in Wales, Scotland and Ireland. The chapter examines the problem of language-specificity in various domains such as translation, especially German → English and English → German renderings of focus constructions.

Chapter 7 considers the relation between transfer and translation introduced earlier in this chapter. There is a detailed look at problems involving crosslinguistic equivalence, individual variation, and cognitive processing. Among the topics considered are the language-specific ambiguities that can arise when one language, such as English, has an article system and another, such as Polish, does not. Translation is also relevant to Processability Theory, as part of the chapter shows.

Parts 1 and 2 inevitably leave numerous questions unanswered, some of which are raised in Chapter 8. These questions suggest directions that future transfer research could usefully take, and the discussion reflects on why explorations of transfer matter for teachers and other people who may not be engaged in SLA research. Readers curious about the historical context of such research will find it helpful to turn next to Chapter 2.

Part 1: Predictions and Constraints

The three chapters in this section examine matters as diverse as the history of SLA and word-order transfer, but a common thread runs through them, namely, the problem of predicting transfer. The problem has a long if misunderstood history, some of which will be clarified in Chapter 2. Predictions about transfer depend on crosslinguistic comparisons, aka contrastive analyses, yet there has been relatively little discussion of whether a contrastive analysis could ever be complete, the question posed in the title of Chapter 3. This same chapter also considers some predictions of when transfer will *not* occur, aka constraints on transfer, and cites evidence contradicting some supposed constraints. Chapter 4 examines in depth the evidence refuting alleged constraints on word-order transfer. The following paragraphs offer more detailed summaries of each of these chapters.

One key point in Chapter 2 is that, contrary to some claims, the use of *transfer* as a term for crosslinguistic influence has its origins in linguistics and not in behaviorist psychology. The earliest known uses appear in work from two American linguists in the 1880s, William Dwight Whitney (Whitney, 1881) and Aaron Marshall Elliott (Elliott, 1886). They may have had in mind two German terms already in use at the time: *hinübertragen* and *übertragen*. The use of *transfer* by Edward Sapir and Otto Jespersen in the1920s shows continuity between the 1880s and the 1950s, the decade that saw the publication of Uriel Weinreich's *Languages in Contact* and Robert Lado's *Linguistics across Cultures*. The term *contrastive* goes back at least to 1941, appearing in the work of Benjamin Lee Whorf. The phrase Contrastive Analysis Hypothesis (CAH) came into widespread use only after the appearance of an article by Ronald Wardhaugh in 1970. Accordingly, the phrase is anachronistic when it is ascribed to Robert Lado or his mentor Charles Fries. Inconsistencies abound in how the CAH is defined by contemporary SLA researchers. The original characterization by Wardhaugh is often ignored, and some discussions focus on Wardhaugh's strong version whereas others focus on his weak version of CAH, these two versions differing in their stance on contrastive predictions.

With regard to the psychology of transfer, structural linguists varied in how much they espoused behaviorist ideas. Regardless of their views, many freely employed the words *habit* and *habitual*. Post-behaviorist research offers useful constructs to help unpack the notion of habits: activation, automaticity, and entrenchment can all aid in understanding specific patterns of transfer. Despite attempts to disassociate Lado's work from Weinreich's, the latter did in fact consider many cases of L1 → L2 transfer. Moreover, Weinreich and Lado did not differ substantively in their analysis of what underlies transfer: crosslinguistic similarities and differences. Taken together, the historical facts laid out in the chapter make it natural to wonder if there really ever was a CAH. The term seems too nebulous to be useful, and it can create a misleading impression that the alleged hypothesis has been tested and found to be false.

Chapter 3 looks closely at contrastive problems, such as the challenge of reconciling general linguistic descriptions with individual behaviors. Despite the problem, viable predictions are possible as long as they address group instead of individual behaviors. Especially desirable are predictions comparing two groups of learners and ones derived from known tendencies in other groups having somewhat similar languages. Such predictions can lead to better generalizations about transferability. No contrastive analysis can be comprehensive without a viable theory of transferability. Furthermore, no theory of transferability can be entirely satisfactory without a viable account of relevant affective factors. Focus constructions illustrate the challenge of formulating a complete set of comparisons in even a limited grammatical domain. The transferability of constructions resembling the English *it*-cleft pattern depends on both structural similarity and on the frequency of the L1 structure in specific contexts. Focus constructions also raise questions as to whether affective stances are fully comparable across languages and whether adults can comprehend all affective stances in the target language. Completeness in contrastive analysis may be viewed as a satisfactory set of predictions. However, with regard to constraints, existing research shows the unsoundness of some predictions about when transfer will *not* occur.

Supposed constraints on the transfer of basic word-order patterns prove unsound in the light of research discussed in Chapter 4. Several counter-examples indicate that there is no strong universal constraint on basic word-order transfer. Attempts to explain such counter-examples as evidence of language-neutral discourse strategies such as topicalization cannot account for all the data. Word order is susceptible both to L1→ L2 and to L2→ L1 transfer (referred to in the chapter as *substratum* and *borrowing transfer* respectively). Despite the existence of basic word-order transfer, examples of it do seem to be somewhat rare. Possible explanations for the scarcity include: (1) probabilistic effects of universal grammatical constraints;

(2) observational problems, including insufficient attention to the speech of individuals with low proficiency; and (3) metalinguistic awareness, which makes the basic word order of the native and target languages accessible and which encourages the monitoring of negative transfer. Negative word-order transfer seems most likely in situations involving little focusing, i.e. situations in which metalinguistic awareness is relatively low.

2 Was There Really Ever a Contrastive Analysis Hypothesis?

Introduction[1]

The terms *contrastive analysis* (CA) and *language transfer* abound in discussions of crosslinguistic influence, but even a cursory reading of these discussions shows a wide range of definitions, characterizations and historical claims about the origins of these notions and terms. Discussions of the so-called Contrastive Analysis Hypothesis (CAH) likewise show considerable variation, as in the examples below.

> The CA hypothesis held that where structures in the L1 differed from those in the L2, errors that reflected the structure of the L1 would be produced. (Dulay *et al.*, 1982: 97)

> With the eclipse of descriptive linguistics and its concept of language learning, Robert Lado is now best remembered as the author of *Linguistics across Cultures*. In particular, he is represented as the architect of the Contrastive Analysis Hypothesis – essentially, the claim that whenever a learner's native and target languages differ, the learner will face difficulty and delay in acquiring the target language. (Thomas, 2006: 302)

> Lado (1957) developed the Contrastive Analysis (CA) approach to L2 acquisition. Under the Contrastive Analysis Hypothesis, learning a new language involves identifying and learning differences between the L1 and the L2. Similarities between the L1 and L2 are predicted to facilitate acquisition. L2s with more differences are predicted to take longer to learn. (Foley & Flynn, 2013: 98)

Still another characterization of the CAH equated it with the following conditions:

> Where two languages were similar, positive transfer would occur; where they were different, negative transfer, or interference, would result. (Larsen-Freeman & Long, 1991: 53)

Along with Robert Lado (1915–95), some other names are also invoked in discussions of the history of transfer research, such as Uriel Weinreich (1926–67), whose 1953 book *Languages in Contact* is referred to in the following passage:

> Adopting a general view of transfer as the use of knowledge or skills from one context in a different linguistic context, Weinreich (1953) introduced the concept of *transfer* in L2 acquisition: use of the L1 that leads to 'correct' usage in the L2. Interference, in contrast, involves use of the L1 that leads to 'incorrect' language use. (Foley & Flynn, 2013: 98)

Although Foley and Flynn do not give any source as an example of the 'general view' that they ascribe to mid-20th-century notions of psychology and language, Nick Ellis (2008) does offer a very specific source: the behaviorist construct of proactive inhibition (PI):

> Much of this [behaviorist] work was succinctly summarized in Osgood's 'transfer surface' that draws together the effects of time of learning, similarity of material, and retention interval on negative (and positive) transfer (Osgood, 1949) ... . PI underpins a variety of fundamental phenomena of language learning and language transfer, as Robert Lado proposed in his CAH... The CAH held that one could predict learner difficulty by reference to utterance-by-utterance comparison of a learner's L1 and L2. (Ellis, 2008: 384)

The six quotations given above vary considerably in what they address, including the issues of errors, of prediction, of positive and negative transfer, and of proactive inhibition. Even so, it would be a mistake to conclude that the characterizations of transfer and CA are completely different. There is arguably a gestalt interpretation of the history of transfer research that many readers might construct from these or other sources. For those completely new to SLA, the gestalt history might consist in part of the following statements:

- It was Lado who formulated the Contrastive Analysis Hypothesis.
- The notion of language transfer has its origins in behaviorist psychology.
- Weinreich introduced the term *transfer* into L2 research.

Moreover, it seems likely that not only neophytes but, indeed, a wide segment of the SLA community – professors and students alike – would agree with at least one of these three statements. However, *none* of the three is true. Intellectual interest in crosslinguistic influence goes back many decades before Lado, and probing that earlier history is necessary in order to understand transfer research in the mid-20th century and to scrutinize the historiography of transfer in research and in textbooks on SLA. As in other domains of intellectual history, complications arise in trying to untangle the strands of the story. This chapter will untangle some of the strands involving the so-called Contrastive Analysis Hypothesis. Doing so will require not only much attention to transfer research long before Lado and Weinreich but also much attention to those two figures. The results of the investigation suggest that the phrase *contrastive analysis hypothesis* is nebulous and contributes little to understanding the intellectual history of transfer. Beyond the critique of a questionable term, the chapter can provide, albeit in a very limited space, encouragement to members of the SLA community who care to reflect on when SLA research actually began. It can also provide them with encouragement to reflect on where the field might be going.

The chapter proceeds from definitions of two key terms, *language transfer* and *contrastive analysis*, to exploring the origins of the term *transfer* independent of any work in psychology. It then considers the term *contrastive analysis* and proceeds from there to a critique of the so-called Contrastive Analysis Hypothesis. The word *habit* is also relevant to the intellectual history of transfer, and considerable attention is paid to the uses of the term in linguistics and psychology and to recent notions such as automaticity that involve similar concerns. The concluding section of the chapter summarizes the main points and discusses the implications of the findings.

Preliminary Definitions

Throughout the chapter, the following definitions will serve as a reference point for the diverse ideas considered:

Transfer is the influence resulting from the similarities and differences between the target language and any other language that has been previously (and perhaps imperfectly) acquired. (Odlin, 1989: 27)

Contrastive analysis: Systematic comparison of two or more languages. (Odlin, 1989: 165)

The above definition of transfer also appears in Chapter 1 and is repeated here for convenience. As the discussion in the preceding chapter shows, the definition needs to be understood in relation to several notions, such as multilingual transfer, positive vs. negative transfer, etc. Likewise, the comparisons that contrastive analysis involves raise complex questions as to what counts as different, the same or similar, and some of these problems of crosslinguistic equivalence are considered further in Chapters 6 and 7.

The definition of CA departs from uses of the term as a historical designator and certainly from uses of the phrase *contrastive analysis hypothesis*. Moreover, the definition of transfer characterizes it as influence, but what *influence* might actually mean remains a major research question. Even so, the notion of influence has a long history. In 1884 the German linguist, Hugo Schuchardt (1842–1927), used *Einfluss* (influence) in his classic study (1971 [1884]) of German and Italian in contact regions inhabited by speakers of various Slavic languages (especially Slovenian, Czech and Polish). Schuchardt had already considered language contact in pidgin and creole settings (see Chapter 4), and many linguists today remember him as a founder of the field of creolistics. In his work on contact in Central Europe, Schuchardt focused on what he considered to be examples of L1 influence, but he also occasionally commented on the psychology of SLA. Work on language contact in the decades after Schuchardt also reported crosslinguistic influence but, as the discussion in Weinreich's *Languages in Contact* will show, the psychology of bilingualism remained an under-explored area. As interest in transfer grew among contemporaries of Weinreich, such as Lado, so did the controversies over the general psychology of language and the specific psychology of L2 acquisition. Before the discussion of controversies, however, the origins of the term *transfer* require attention.

Transfer and its Independent Origins in Linguistics

In English, the use of *transfer* to denote crosslinguistic influence goes back at least to the 19th century, well before the behaviorist research cited by Ellis in the quotation in the introduction to this chapter. The term appears in the writing of two American linguists, William Dwight Whitney (1827–94) and Aaron Marshall Elliott (1844–1910). Both had studied in German universities, the former in Berlin and Tübingen and the latter in Munich, and both were probably influenced by German terms to be considered in the next paragraph. In a discussion of language contact in historical linguistics, Whitney declared: 'By universal consent, what is most easily transferred from one language to another is a noun' (1971[1881]: 184). This assertion might suggest that Whitney considered crosslinguistic influence to be widespread, but in fact he shared the skepticism of many linguists of his time about the extent of such influence. Elliott used a variant of the term (*transference*) in an 1885 review of Schuchardt's book in the *American Journal of Philology* (and the review is reprinted in the 1971 edition of Schuchardt's work). Elliott employed *influence* as well as *transference* in the review, and he also used *transfer* in an 1886 article on language contact in Canada (Elliott, 1886).

Since Whitney and Elliott had studied linguistics (aka philology) in Germany, they probably adopted *transfer* and *transference* as translations for two words used by German linguists: *hinübertragen* and *übertragen*, both of which can also translate as 'carry over' and the latter term can be glossed as 'translate'. As noted in Chapter 1, *hinübertragen* goes back at least to 1836, appearing in a famous study of mind and language by Wilhelm von Humboldt (1767–1835), and the metaphoric notion of carrying over is the same as in the Latin word *transferre* (see also Chapter 1). With regard to *übertragen*, it goes back at least to 1875, appearing in an analysis of loanwords by a Finnish linguist, August Ahlqvist (1826–89); although some uses of *übertragen* in his book involve simple cases of semantic extensions not related to language contact, other uses clearly refer to crosslinguistic influence (e.g. Ahlqvist, 1875: 51) in the language-contact setting of Finland.[2] Schuchardt used *übertragen* at least a year before his book on language contact in Central Europe, as the term denotes crosslinguistic influence in one of his creolist studies (Schuchardt, 1883a), and it also appears a number of times in his 1884 book as well as in an 1885 review of the book, the historical linguist Hermann Paul being the reviewer (also reprinted in the 1971 edition of the Schuchardt work). That the use of *transfer* comes from German linguistics rather than from any work in psychology seems all the more likely because neither Whitney nor Elliott discusses any psychological research, behaviorist or otherwise. Indeed, behaviorism was in its infancy in the late 19th century (Graham, 2010; Levelt, 2013; Singley & Anderson, 1989). Weinreich, it should be added, cites both the Whitney article and the Schuchardt book, and he calls the latter 'unexcelled' (1953a: 111).

In the several decades between Whitney and Weinreich, the term *transfer* did not disappear. Both Edward Sapir (1884–1939) and Otto Jespersen (1860–1943) used the term in their introductions to linguistics:

> We may suppose that individual variations arising at linguistic border-lands – whether by unconscious suggestive influence of foreign speech habits or by the transfer of foreign sounds in the speech of bilingual individuals – have gradually been incorporated into the phonetic drift of a language. (Sapir, 1921: 200)

> …it is, of course, a natural supposition that the aboriginal inhabitants of Europe and Asia were just as liable to transfer their speech habits to new languages as their descendants are nowadays. (Jespersen, 1922: 192)

While Jespersen's use of 'transfer' clearly involves the influence of a language already known on learning or speaking a new one, Sapir's use is a little ambiguous. One may wonder, for example, whether those susceptible to the 'suggestive influence of foreign speech habits' are monolingual speakers of a target language that foreigners are attempting to speak (e.g. monolingual speakers of Cockney English in a modern London neighborhood having many Pakistani or Polish immigrants) or native speakers of a language (e.g. Middle English) attempting to learn the language of a conquering class (e.g. Norman French). In any case, there is no doubt that *transfer* in this passage refers to some kind of crosslinguistic influence. As with Whitney and Schuchardt, Sapir had a clear effect on Weinreich, who cites this passage (1953a: 24). Also noteworthy is the use by both Sapir and Jespersen of the word *habits*. While the word might suggest that both men were behaviorists, in fact neither one was. The differing stances on behaviorism that linguists have taken will be discussed in various parts of this chapter.

Weinreich's *Languages in Contact* frequently uses *transfer*, which the author deems to be 'one form of interference' (1953a: 7), and the notion of transfer as a type of interference is likewise evident on page 50 of the book. These instances squarely contradict the claim of Foley and Flynn (quoted in the introduction to this chapter) that Weinreich viewed transfer as 'use of the L1 that leads to "correct" usage in the L2'. Although the adoption of *transfer* by Whitney, Elliott, Sapir and Jespersen shows that the term appeared long before *Languages in Contact*, Weinreich may well be the originator of a related term, *transferability*, which appears occasionally in the book (e.g. 1953a: 31, 34).

While *transfer* means some kind of crosslinguistic influence in all the sources discussed in this section, the role of actual bilingual individuals in the phenomenon is frequently more implicit than explicit. For instance, Elliott wrote, as linguists often do even now, of the transfer of forms across linguistic boundaries as if they have a life of their own independent of actual bilinguals:

> ...these alien forms, when taken up into one dialect, sometimes pass to others, and at each transfer undergo certain phonetic or morphological changes necessary to adapt them to easy use in the dialects, respectively, where they find a new home. (Elliott, 1886: 154)

Here the use of *transfer* is not in the more restricted sense found in SLA research and does not explicitly refer to any bilinguals at all. Even so, the psychology of bilingualism and multilingualism was a topic that some 19th-century linguists at least touched on; moreover, Schuchardt was very specific about the 'Einfluss der Muttersprache' (influence of the mother language) as the source of the many examples of Slavic influence he found, and he made occasional remarks about the psychological dimensions of transfer and language learning, including the need of the learner to risk making errors (1971[1884]: 150). In fact, Schuchardt used as the epigraph of his book a Slovenian proverb to the effect that blunders are necessary in learning a language. This awareness of the relation between the psychological and structural dimensions of language contact is even more evident in Weinreich and in much work on language contact in recent decades (e.g. Thomason & Kaufman, 1988; Winford, 2003).

The word *transfer* as a psycholinguistic term in SLA thus has its origins more in 19th-century ideas in linguistics than in the use of *transfer* in psychology either in the behaviorist period or beyond. On the other hand, the distinction between positive and negative transfer does suggest an eventual effect of behaviorist psychology, but only long after the initial appearance of the term *transfer* itself.

Contrastive Analysis and its Varied Meanings

Nick Ellis (2008: 384) reports a database search for the keyword entry 'contrastive analysis' which produced 1,268 results. As this finding suggests, the term *contrastive analysis* remains widely used, especially since the search that Ellis reports was limited to the occurrences of the term in the research literature of the previous thirty years (hence, back to the 1970s, when there was a growing skepticism about the usefulness of CA). Nevertheless, some caution is necessary. *Contrastive analysis* is not just a term in SLA: it is sometimes used by specialists in fields such as translation theory (e.g. Chesterman, 1991) and anthropological linguistics (e.g. Lucy, 1992) for concerns other than those of acquisition and pedagogy, albeit concerns compatible with the definition of CA given in the second section of this chapter.

When the term is used for the problems of SLA, it often takes on a very special cast, where Selinker (1992, 2006), for instance, uses it mainly as a historical label, e.g. '...though it predicted a lot of language transfer, CA generated a lot of "residue" and, as we know, CA is not a good acquisition theory' (2006: 202). This point will be considered further in the next section, which discusses the so-called Contrastive Analysis Hypothesis.[3]

References such as Selinker's to a CA period should not obscure two historical facts. First, the term *contrastive* predates Lado's *Linguistics across Cultures*: it appeared at least as early as 1941 in an article by Benjamin Lee Whorf (1897–1941), who wrote of 'contrastive linguistics' (1956[1941]: 240), by which he meant the comparative study of languages and cultures. Moreover, passages from Weinreich and Lado quoted in the next section show that they regarded contrastive analysis very much in the same way.

The Contrastive Analysis Hypothesis

Ever since an article by Ronald Wardhaugh was published in *TESOL Quarterly* in 1970 entitled 'The Contrastive Analysis Hypothesis', the term has remained in use. The CAH, as Wardhaugh characterized it, is 'the claim that the best language teaching materials are based on a contrast of the two competing linguistic systems' (Wardhaugh, 1970: 123).

Wardhaugh, it should be emphasized, distinguished between what he termed the 'strong' and 'weak' forms of the hypothesis, with the author using the two adjectives in an explicit analogy to what has often been called the Sapir-Whorf Hypothesis of linguistic relativity (Hoijer, 1954). The strong and the weak versions of the CAH are not defined explicitly by Wardhaugh, but he does suggest two ways in which they differ:

(1) predictions of difficulty in learning a second language are essential in the strong version but are merely possible in the weak version (1970: 127); and
(2) nothing beyond a thorough comparison of two languages is needed to make predictions in the strong version, while the weak version 'starts with the evidence provided of linguistic interference and uses such evidence to explain the similarities and differences between systems' (1970: 126).

It is worth noting that Wardhaugh's characterization of the weak version seems odd; analyzing similarities and differences between systems to explain the evidence would be more plausible than using the 'evidence to explain the similarities and differences'.

For Wardhaugh, the strong version was 'unrealistic and impracticable' (1970: 124); however, he judged the weak version potentially useful (even though he did express reservations about this version also). The putative untenability of the strong version arises, in Wardhaugh's estimation, from the problems of deciding how to describe and compare languages in cases where real differences are evident: for instance, the phoneme /p/ in French is not phonetically identical to English /p/. The question of what the best comparisons might be is *not* resolved, Wardhaugh judged, just by changing theoretical approaches: for him, the difficulties persist regardless of whether the analysis adopted is structuralist or generative. Uncertainties about linguistic theories themselves remain and could thus affect estimations of difficulties. Wardhaugh also saw a need for ranking degrees of difficulty, noting that although instructors often take seriously the possible influence of, for instance, Spanish phonology on how a learner tries to pronounce English sounds, many teachers also have a sense that some parts of a language can be more easily acquired than others. Nevertheless, how one might best construct a pedagogical sequence remains problematic, Wardhaugh believed, due to the theoretical uncertainties.

The general characterization of CAH offered by Wardhaugh is in fact a paraphrase of an assertion made in 1945 by Lado's mentor, Charles Fries (1887–1967), that 'the most efficient materials are those that are based upon a scientific description of the language to be learned, carefully compared with a parallel description of the native language of the learner' (Fries, 1945: 9). Something close to the 'strong' version of

CAH inferred by Wardhaugh appears in a statement by Lado himself in his preface to *Linguistics across Cultures*:

> The plan of the book rests on the assumption that we can predict and describe the patterns that will cause difficulty in learning, and those that will not cause difficulty, by comparing systematically the language to be learned with the native language and culture of the student. (Lado, 1957: vii)

Discussions of CAH often invoke this quotation from Lado, but far less frequently cited is an earlier and similar assertion of Weinreich: 'The contrastive analysis of the phonemes of two languages and the way they are used yields a list of the forms of expected interference in a particular contact situation' (1953a: 22). The main difference from Lado in Weinreich's use of *contrastive analysis* is not the absence of the word *predict* – the use of 'expected' is obviously similar. Instead, Weinreich's concerns are those of language-contact specialists, who typically focus on linguistic change and cases of 'interference' rather than on those cases which, as Lado put it, 'will not cause difficulty'. Throughout *Languages in Contact*, Weinreich seems to have regarded historical linguists and dialectologists as his primary audience. In *Linguistics across Cultures*, Lado's focus on an audience of teachers is certainly clear.

Some of the historical accounts in SLA textbooks (e.g. Rod Ellis, 1985) do cite Wardhaugh's article, though others do not (e.g. Dulay *et al.*, 1982), and, in the latter case, the distinction proposed by Wardhaugh between a strong and a weak CAH is ignored. In fact, the quotation from Dulay *et al.* in the introduction suggests a focus on what Wardhaugh deemed the weak – and for him the more credible – version of the putative hypothesis. Foley and Flynn do not cite Wardhaugh or the strong/weak distinction either, yet in contrast to Dulay *et al.* their definition of CAH (also quoted in the introduction) clearly focuses on what Wardhaugh saw as essential to the strong version, i.e. predictions. What the supposed CAH says about difficulties also differs in the two characterizations: for Dulay *et al.*, difficulty means errors, while for Foley and Flynn it means the length of time needed for acquisition. Although error rates and acquisition times would no doubt strongly correlate in many studies, they are distinct variables, and so the two characterizations of CAH disagree in yet another way.

Such inconsistency in the way that CAH is defined contributes to the gestalt impression of the history of transfer discussed in the introduction. Another contributing factor is the neglect in noting the anachronism of Wardhaugh's term: that is, neither Fries nor Weinreich nor Lado actually used the term Contrastive Analysis Hypothesis. The relation of Weinreich to some supposed CAH is also inconsistently covered in accounts such as those cited in the introduction. Even so, some historical accounts do note important similarities between Lado and Weinreich; for example, Larsen-Freeman and Long (1991: 53) cite both of the following passages:

> The greater the differences between systems [languages or dialects], i.e. the more numerous the mutually exclusive forms and patterns in each, the greater is the learning problem and the potential area of interference. (Weinreich, 1953a: 1)

> Those elements that are similar [to the] native language will be simple... and those elements that are different will be difficult. The teacher who has made a comparison of the foreign language with the native language of the students will know better what the real learning problems are and can better provide for teaching them. (Lado, 1957: 2)

What led researchers to link Lado yet not Weinreich to some supposed CAH is probably the difference in focus between the two noted above, with Lado concentrating on educational concerns and with Weinreich on change and variation; even so, the psycholinguistic assumptions of both linguists are essentially the same. Another reason for the relative inattention to Weinreich may be the efforts of Dulay *et al.* (1982) to deny the relevance of *Languages in Contact* to SLA research. Before those efforts are discussed, however, it will help to consider the historical relation between linguistics and psychology.

Habits and Behaviorism

The skepticism in textbooks about contrastive analysis arose not only from empirical problems about what CA might actually predict (as in Wardhaugh's critique) but also from the impression that CA inevitably relied on behaviorist assumptions about the psychology of learning, as suggested in the quotation from Nick Ellis in the introduction to this chapter. Authors of textbooks such as those of Dulay *et al.*, Rod Ellis, and Larsen-Freeman and Long have associated behaviorism with CA and the supposed CAH (although Wardhaugh did not address behaviorism in his article). As seen already, confusion over the origins of the term *transfer* in SLA contributed to the association, but another problematic term has been *habits*. In the foreword to Lado's book, Fries claimed that adult SLA is quite different from child language acquisition because of the 'special "set" created by the first language habits' (Lado, 1957: v). The word *habit* was certainly prominent in behaviorist psychology; even so, the notion of *habits* proves more complicated, largely because linguists who distanced themselves from behaviorism nevertheless saw fit to use the word *habits* – and among them was Fries (whose beliefs will be contrasted with those of Lado on behaviorism).

However much or little linguists might agree about the psychology of language, it is necessary to consider just what behaviorism is. One might reasonably use the plural form *behaviorisms* instead, since not all behaviorists have thought alike, and since the history of behaviorist ideas involves notions from earlier intellectual movements, such as the British empiricism of David Hume and John Locke as well as the logical positivism of the 19th century (Blumenthal, 1985; Graham, 2010). Still, three recurring traits seem to be most significant, especially for the kind of behaviorism that influenced some linguists, including Leonard Bloomfield and Robert Lado: (1) belief in the applicability of a stimulus–response (S–R) model to the study of language; (2) rejection of 'mentalist' terms and assumptions in such study; and (3) advocacy of empirical methods that made experimental results the standard for evaluating theories.

For American behaviorists of the early 20th century (though not for Ivan Pavlov (1849–1936), who is often seen as the first behaviorist), the stimulus–response paradigm seemed applicable to the human species as well as to other mammals. The influence of behaviorism (aka verbal learning) on some linguists seems quite evident in an introductory textbook by Bloomfield (1933), who foregrounds S–R relations. The notion of habits proved easy to incorporate into behaviorism, as seen in a definition of *habit* in one behaviorist textbook of psychology which equates it with a 'learned response' (Morgan & King, 1971: 740).

In the verbal learning tradition, a crucial distinction was made between mentalist and mechanist theories, with the former being condemned as unscientific and the latter held up as the proper framework for attempting to understand the psychology of language. An article by Albert P. Weiss shows quite clearly the behaviorist commitment to an anti-mentalist philosophy, heralding the progress of verbal learning research and seeing the burden of proof to be not on those who look at language as simply another behavior but rather on those who hypothesize 'the existence of a special mental force' (Weiss, 1925: 56). At that time, Weiss and Bloomfield were colleagues at Ohio State University, and Bloomfield was a founder of the Linguistic Society of America, the sponsor of *Language*, the (then) fledgling journal in which the Weiss article was published. Like his colleague in psychology, Bloomfield eschewed terms such as *thought*, *belief*, *concept* and *idea* as inaccessible to scientific observation and therefore unacceptable as terms in developing a theory of meaning.

Partly because of Bloomfield, who is often seen as the most influential American linguist of the first half of the 20th century, and partly because of the growth of behaviorist psychology in that period, there arose a strong emphasis on experimental methods in the hybrid field of psycholinguistics (as it came to be known), especially after 1950. A volume expressly designed to foster greater collaboration between linguists and psychologists (Osgood & Sebeok, 1965), shows a growing awareness in the1950s and 1960s of the need for experimental or quasi-experimental research in several fields, including language acquisition and bilingualism. Moreover, many of the discussions (e.g. a chapter by Susan Ervin on language acquisition) formulate the theoretical issues in terms of S–R relations.

The third characteristic of behaviorism discussed here – the emphasis on experimental frameworks – has endured more robustly than the other two in the psychology of language in the post-behaviorist era. A critique by Noam Chomsky (1959) of a key book in the verbal learning tradition (Skinner, 1957) proved very influential among linguists in rejecting the S–R framework, and this rejection affected the perception of transfer in books such as that of Dulay *et al.* (1982). Chomsky also proved influential in restoring confidence in mentalism, although many of the cognitive linguists and psychologists who nowadays accept mentalist constructs part company with Chomsky on key issues in the study of meaning (e.g. Lakoff & Johnson, 1999; Langacker, 2008; Slobin, 1996).

Habits and Structural Linguistics

The movement in linguistics known as structuralism included a wide variety of linguists, some of whom, such as Bloomfield, took behaviorist stances, while others such as Sapir and Whorf did not reject mentalism. Whether behaviorist or not, many structuralists used the word *habit* to describe certain dispositions in language. Sapir (1929), for instance, made clear his sympathies for Gestalt psychology, not behaviorism (1929: 212), yet asserted too that 'the language habits of our [speech] community predispose certain choices of interpretation' (1929: 210). As noted already, Sapir also used *habits* in a passage in his introduction to language. Quite similarly, Whorf used *habitual* in the title of one of his most detailed discussions of relativity: 'The Relation of Habitual Thought and Behavior to Language' (1956[1941]), with the title showing a remarkable mix of terms accepted by behaviorists (*habitual* and *behavior*) with a mentalist one (*thought*). Still, in another (undated) essay, Whorf said, 'behaviorism does not show us which lines to work upon in order to be fully in accord with human intangibles, except by way of announcing in behavioristic terms things already obvious to common sense' (1956[1941]: 41).

Reservations about behaviorism are also evident in the views of Weinreich, who nevertheless did not shy away from the word *habit*, as seen in his phrase 'separate subphonemic habits' (1953a: 24). Weinreich also showed some interest in the contributions of behaviorism to the developing field of psycholinguistics, but *Languages in Contact* contains a mix of behaviorist terms (e.g. 'stimuli', on p. 64) and mentalist ones (e.g. 'aware', on p. 8). Most crucially, his analysis of crosslinguistic influence remained agnostic as to what the best psychological account might be. His book cites as evidence both mentalist and non-mentalist research, and in other writings, Weinreich states his conviction that the anti-mentalist stance of some structural linguists was impeding progress in linguistics, especially in regard to the study of meaning (Weinreich, 1953b, 1963).

However much (or little) credence structural linguists gave to behaviorism, there was a great deal in human language that seemed to call for words such as *habit* or *habitual*. Although behaviorists might claim that by invoking *habits*, Whorf and others were tacitly accepting the relevance of stimulus–response relations, one could just as easily argue that the word *thought* in Whorf's phrase 'habitual thought' shows a mentalist agenda. Yet what matters most in assessing the positions of Sapir, Whorf, Weinreich and others is the reality that they were linguists looking at psychology from the outside. Just as psychologists who explore language can hardly avoid making some assumptions about linguistic structure when they use terms such as *sound, form* or *word*, linguists can hardly avoid psychological assumptions if they delve into topics such as language acquisition. In the structuralist era, many linguists strove for precision in how they used grammatical terms such as *morpheme* and *constituent*, but they tolerated more ambiguity in using *habit* and other terms on the borders of their field.

Fries, Lado and Weinreich

More often than not, both Fries and Lado are represented as behaviorists in historical accounts of transfer (e.g. Odlin, 1989), although one analysis (Thomas, 2006) argues that neither Fries nor Lado was a behaviorist. The reality turns out to be more complicated, however, in the light of recent observations from Larry Selinker, who studied with Lado at Georgetown University and with Fries, who did some guest teaching there:

> Lado was a behaviorist in that he openly believed (and told us in class) in the habit-formation theory, strength of stimulus-response, dominant in the behavioristic linguistics of the time... Fries, on the other hand, believed deeply in semantics and never seemed to be a believer in the dominant theory of stimulus-response learning. (Selinker, 2006: 209)

Despite the differences between Fries and Lado over the general psychology of language, both used the word *habit* in their discussions of language learning, and, as suggested above, such ambiguity does not seem to have troubled anybody. By the same token, the non-committal stance of Weinreich toward behaviorism did not keep Lado from citing *Languages in Contact* as support for his assertion that linguists 'report that many linguistic distortions heard among bilinguals correspond to describable differences in the languages involved' (Lado, 1957: 1). In this regard, Lado cites two books, *Languages in Contact* and Einar Haugen's (1953) *The Norwegian Language in America*.

Lado thus considered his approach to transfer to have considerable empirical support. His assumption was challenged, however, by Dulay *et al.* (1982), who claimed that the contact research of Haugen and Weinreich was not relevant to the discussion of second language acquisition. The strategy of Dulay *et al.* for contesting Lado's interpretation was to compare the definitions of *interference* by Weinreich and *borrowing* by Haugen with the 'CA hypothesis' which they ascribe to Lado (1982: 99). The critique offered by Dulay *et al.* proves valid with regard to Haugen, who was in fact more concerned about L2 English influence on American Norwegian than about L1 Norwegian influence on English in immigrant communities. Even so, Dulay *et al.* fail to offer a convincing analysis with regard to Weinreich, whose position on interference differs from their characterization; most crucially, several of the studies that Weinreich discusses are ones that focus on L1 influence on L2 (along with studies less relevant to such transfer, including some of Haugen's earlier research on L2 → L1 influence). Interestingly, among the L1 → L2 studies that Weinreich cites (1953a: 20) is one of phonetic transfer that has Lado as a co-author (Reed *et al.*, 1948). Moreover, Weinreich frequently cites Schuchardt's study of how native speakers of Slavic languages use German and Italian. While Schuchardt considered different kinds of bilingualism, he focused on the mother tongue or 'Muttersprache' as a key factor in what he termed imperfect bilingualism, 'unvollkommene Zweitsprachigkeit' (1971[1884]: 150). Along with his interest in L1 → L2 transfer, Schuchardt was also aware of possible multilingual influences (e.g. L2 → L3), as he mentions the possible influence of a language that stands in place of the mother tongue ('einer anderen welche an ihre Stelle getreten ist' (1971[1884]: 150).

Other examples of studies cited by Weinreich which involve L1 → L2 transfer have been noted elsewhere (Odlin, 1989: 24), and there are others as well in *Languages in Contact*. By the mid-20th century, a wealth of relevant contact research existed, yet, as Selinker (1992: 26) suggests, many SLA researchers from the 1960s to the 1980s tended to ignore Weinreich's insights. If they had read *Languages in Contact* with more care, several would have probably rejected the extreme and rather widespread skepticism about transfer that was fashionable at the time.

The Notion of Habits in a Post-Behaviorist Era

As noted above, Chomsky had a considerable impact on SLA researchers such as Dulay *et al.*, who linked their skepticism about transfer to wider theoretical changes, especially the shift from theories of learning as habit formation to theories of rule-governed behaviour (1982: 140). However, the reality of the change seems somewhat problematic in view of an assertion by John Carroll, an early psycholinguist with an interest in SLA. Carroll recognized the ostensible challenge of Chomskyan linguistics, yet he voiced doubts about how much of a theoretical shift had really occurred: 'I am not convinced... that there is any real difference between a "habit" and a "rule" or between a "response" and a "rule-governed performance"' (Carroll, 1968: 114). He used his training as a psychologist to review a wide range of studies in psychology involving many kinds of transfer, but he remained pessimistic about their relevance to transfer insofar as the materials and learning conditions in those studies usually differed from the circumstances of learning a second language. Carroll did suggest, however, that the behaviorist construct of proactive inhibition (PI) was 'the kind of interference... we are probably dealing with in connection with contrastive linguistics' (1968: 119). He viewed PI as especially relevant to the question of how particular forms of guidance might overcome negative transfer. Some research in subsequent decades (e.g. Kupferberg & Olshtain, 1996; Otwinowska-Kasztelnic, 2010) supports his optimism.

As seen in the introduction to this chapter, Ellis has also affirmed the usefulness of PI, which he defines as the 'effect of prior learning inhibiting new learning' (Ellis, 2008: 384). It is not the only learning factor that Ellis deems relevant to SLA or, indeed, to transfer. Even so, he cites examples of work on transfer that he views as support for PI. His attempt at rehabilitating PI is especially noteworthy since he looks to the behaviorist tradition, yet does not – in contrast to Bloomfield and Weiss – reject mentalism, as is evident in the use of mentalist terms such as *conceptual schema*, *language knowledge* and *awareness* by Ellis and Robinson (2008). The relevance of some PI research for cognitive linguistics thus suggests that structuralist intuitions about habits warrant further reflection. It seems appropriate to consider how post-behaviorist research might help unpack the notion of habits in relation to transfer.

Recent work on transfer does suggest that much in the notion of habits can be analyzed in terms of three widely used constructs: activation, automaticity, and entrenchment. Activation patterns that differ crosslinguistically occur in a wide range of cases, as when a target-language word evokes more than one meaning in the native language lexicon yet not for monolingual speakers of the target. For instance, Elston-Güttler and Williams (2008) found that the English noun *bag* evokes the joint meanings of pouch and container among bilingual Germans whose L1 has a word (*tasche*), which can denote either a pocket or a bag. Automaticity is certainly a goal to strive for in acquiring a new language, serving as it does the needs for speed and economy in language processing; even so, what is automatic in the native language can contribute to a foreign accent. Hammarberg and Hammarberg (2009) determined that a learner of L3 Swedish relied more on L2 German similarities with Swedish in earlier stages of acquisition yet experienced greater difficulty in avoiding L1 English phonetic interference as she grew more proficient in the L3. Hammarberg and Hammarberg attribute this problem to the automaticity of L1 articulatory patterns. Entrenchment may arise from an L1 influence that persists and impedes – or perhaps even makes impossible – successful acquisition of structures such as English articles, which despite their formal simplicity involve great semantic and pragmatic complexity (Han, 2010; Odlin, 2012). The constructs of activation, automaticity and entrenchment are no doubt interrelated, but a precise understanding of the relationships seems possible only with much more research.

Conclusion

This chapter has raised several points about the history of the idea of language transfer in relation to the so-called Contrastive Analysis Hypothesis:

- The earliest known uses of *transfer* to denote crosslinguistic influence did not come from behaviorist psychology but rather from two American linguists in the 1880s, William Dwight Whitney and Aaron Marshall Elliott, both of whom had studied in Germany.
- The use of *transfer* by Edward Sapir and Otto Jespersen in the1920s indicates continuity between the 1880s and the 1950s, the decade that saw the publication of Uriel Weinreich's *Languages in Contact* and Robert Lado's *Linguistics across Cultures*.
- The use of *transfer* probably arose as translations of German terms, *hinübertragen* and *übertragen*, the former going back at least to the 1830s and the latter to the 1870s.
- The term *contrastive* goes back at least to 1941, appearing in the work of Benjamin Lee Whorf.
- The term Contrastive Analysis Hypothesis came into widespread use only after the publication of an article by Ronald Wardhaugh in 1970. In that sense the term is anachronistic when it is ascribed to Robert Lado or his mentor Charles Fries.
- Inconsistencies abound in how Contrastive Analysis Hypothesis is characterized. The original characterization by Wardhaugh is often ignored, and some discussions of CAH focus on Wardhaugh's strong version whereas others focus on his weak version. Inconsistencies as to what indicates learning difficulty are also evident.
- Structural linguists varied in how much or little they espoused behaviorist ideas in psychology. Some (e.g. Bloomfield and Lado) did indeed subscribe to behaviorism, yet others (e.g. Sapir, Whorf

and Fries) did not. Regardless of their views on psychology, many structural linguists freely employed the words *habit* and *habitual*.

- While Lado was a behaviorist, Fries was not, according to Larry Selinker.
- Despite attempts to disassociate the concerns of Lado's *Linguistics across Cultures* from those of Weinreich's *Languages in Contact*, the latter work did in fact consider many cases of L1 → L2 transfer. Moreover, Weinreich and Lado did not differ substantively in their analysis of what underlies transfer: crosslinguistic similarities and differences.
- Post-behaviorist research offers useful constructs to help unpack the notion of habits: activation, automaticity, and entrenchment can all aid in understanding specific patterns of transfer.

Taken together, these points call into question much of the conventional wisdom about the intellectual history of language transfer. As such, the findings may encourage readers to reflect on a pair of questions:

(1) Was there really ever a Contrastive Analysis Hypothesis?
(2) When did the study of second language acquisition begin?

The two questions are interrelated since conventional answers to the second question often invoke some version or other of an assumed CAH. If, however, the answer to the first question is negative, the second question needs to be reconsidered.

An easy but not totally satisfying way to answer the first question would be to say that there was indeed a CAH: namely, the assertion by Fries in 1945 that 'the most efficient materials are those that are based upon a scientific description of the language to be learned, carefully compared with a parallel description of the native language of the learner' (which was quoted above and is repeated for convenience here). It was this assertion that Wardhaugh paraphrased in his own overall characterization of CAH. However, none of the quotations of SLA specialists given in the introduction mentions materials in their characterizations of CAH (and their inconsistency with regard to Wardhaugh's strong/weak distinction has already been noted).

Those who would hold that the CAH did indeed exist might argue that what it really involved was the psychology implicit in Fries' 1945 assertion: i.e. an assumption about the importance of crosslinguistic similarities and differences in guiding L2 acquisition. This assumption was in fact explicitly stated in 1957 by Lado in the first chapter of *Linguistics across Cultures* and by Fries himself in the foreword. Even so, any defense invoking implicit psychology has a clear weakness. One can just as easily find the same psychological assumption in Weinreich's position on crosslinguistic similarity and, indeed, much earlier in, for example, Hugo Schuchardt's use of *Einfluss der Muttersprache* in his 1884 book, which is full of comparisons of the two target languages, German and Italian, with various Slavic languages, especially Slovenian, Czech and Polish, being the native languages. If implicit psychological assumptions about crosslinguistic differences are taken as the criterion, one can just as logically give the date 1884 as the genesis of CAH, thus long before 1945, 1953 or 1957.

If the transfer metaphor were to be invoked instead of crosslinguistic correspondences as the basis for CAH, one can argue that the putative hypothesis arose in the 1830s with Wilhelm von Humboldt's use of *hinübertragen* (see Chapter 1). There is, of course, another possibility still: namely, that Humboldt was not the first to use the transfer metaphor and that it goes back to linguistic thinking in French or Latin, the latter having the word *transferre*. Unless defenders of some historically real CAH ever manage to agree on just what it was, and exactly when it was formulated – and by whom– the notion will continue to be as nebulous as it has been.

The nebulousness of the term CAH argues for reconsidering the second question, i.e. when the study of SLA began. The problem of historical beginnings is not unique to SLA. Even though many beginnings are clear (e.g. the day that Abraham Lincoln became President of the United States – March 4, 1861), there is ample room for debate about when the Middle Ages began, or the Romantic era of literature. Textbooks introducing the field of SLA have often recounted discussions from the 1950s to the 1970s as the starting point, but authors of future texts would do well to heed the warning in a recent history of psycholinguistics:

> It is a widely shared opinion that the new discipline of psycholinguis-
> tics emerged during the 1950s. Nothing could be further from the truth.
> The purpose of this book is to sketch a history of psycholinguistics, the
> psychology of language, going back to the end of the 18th century, when
> empirical research began in earnest. (Levelt, 2013: 3)

Despite this warning, however, Chapter 1 of Levelt's history is titled '1951'. In effect, he recognizes a major milestone in the field in that year: namely, the interdisciplinary activities of John Carroll and others. In the preface, moreover, Levelt characterizes his book-length examination of developments before 1951 as a 'prehistory'.

Some discussions of SLA and/or language teaching offer glimpses of an intellectual history of SLA before 1957 (e.g. Jarvis & Pavlenko, 2008; Kelly, 1969; Thomas, 2004) but there seem to be few if any discussions of, for example, Humboldt and transfer, or very few indeed of Schuchardt, even though his work strongly influenced Weinreich's. In any case, future textbooks should acknowledge the 19th-century uses of the term *transfer* (and also the corresponding German terms) in linguistics independent from any ideas in psychology.

However one construes the prehistory and history of SLA, it is no coincidence that the field rapidly grew at virtually the same time that the broader field of psycholinguistics did. The increasing interest in language acquisition among figures as different as Susan Ervin, Roger Brown and Noam Chomsky attracted the attention of SLA researchers committed to using empirical methods that would contribute to understanding the special problems of L2 and multilingual acquisition. Moreover, it was in this same period that the field of language contact showed a stronger sense of the relevance of psychology. In various parts of Weinreich's book, one can detect the author's awareness of the limits of linguistics in isolation from psychology, e.g. 'How firmly the patterns of linguistic interference become habitualized is already a matter beyond strictly linguistic causation' (1953a: 105). In the third chapter of *Languages in Contact*, 'The Bilingual Individual', Weinreich surveys what he could find in psychological research, but even though the number of studies is small, it shows a growth of interest since the discussion of Schuchardt about psychological factors (1971[1884]: 150–152).

This earlier independence (or isolation) from psychology should not obscure the longstanding need for linguists to invoke psychological constructs, however vaguely conceived. Schuchardt, for example, used *Einfluss*, Whorf *habitual thought*, and Weinreich *habitualized*. As empirical psychology thrived ever more, there grew a tendency – and hardly a surprising one – for linguists such as Bloomfield or Lado to adopt some behaviorist notions. The adoption of the terms *positive transfer* and *negative transfer* in SLA seems to follow the same pattern. Although the linguistic term *transfer* predates behaviorism, the positive/ negative distinction seems to have resulted from linguists such as Stockwell *et al.* (1965) paying at least some attention to the verbal learning enterprise. Yet in the same contrastive analysis of Spanish and English grammatical patterns, Stockwell *et al.* devoted considerable attention to generative analyses of the then-new Chomskyan approach. Such eclecticism shows that linguists have not always felt constrained to ally themselves exclusively with just one psychological theory.

In SLA, as in other areas of linguistics, it is often easy to find objections to the use of some term or another, as in the disapproval of Corder (1983) of the term *transfer*. However, neither his objections nor those of other critics seems to impede the use of *transfer* among many specialists, and likewise quite a few other terms seem to maintain a life of their own. Despite the critique of the phrase Contrastive Analysis Hypothesis in this chapter, the term may survive for quite a while to come. Like the use by Selinker of *contrastive analysis* cited above, invoking the supposed CAH at least offers a convenient label to direct attention back in time to the mid-20th century. Nevertheless, anyone who employs CAH should be aware of its deficiencies.

Despite the nebulousness of the term CAH, SLA specialists using it probably have the impression of there being a common and consistent understanding of the term. Such impressions are not unique to SLA; Lehrer (1983) has found that referential illusions arise in conversations about wine among non-specialists and has noted more serious problems of referential consistency among psychiatrists and phoneticians (though, in the latter case, instrumental studies have helped reduce the ambiguities). The nebulousness of CAH is reason enough to make it suspect – but there are other liabilities as well.

In the phrase *Contrastive Analysis Hypothesis*, the words *contrastive analysis* seem to suggest a questionable notion to many specialists, quite possibly as a result of using CA in historical references to earlier controversies. Yet no alternative term has been widely adopted when discussing language transfer. Crosslinguistic comparisons are indispensable in doing transfer research, whatever the theoretical orientation of the researcher. In Universal Grammar studies, for instance, analysts frequently invoke *parameters* (e.g. verb-object versus object-verb word order), but parameters obviously imply a contrastive analysis in the sense of the definition used in this chapter, i.e. a crosslinguistic comparison. The phrase *crosslinguistic comparison* could, of course, work as a synonym for *contrastive analysis*, but the latter is a bit more economical. Furthermore, the idea that languages can and should be compared in second language research and second language teaching is *not* one of the problems in the assumptions of Fries and Lado. Whatever else may be questionable in their positions, their advocacy of comparisons has always made sense.

The word *hypothesis* in Contrastive Analysis Hypothesis seems, if anything, even more problematic than the first two words. Thesis and dissertation students are often required to state hypotheses in their research and to state them as precisely as possible. Any student guided to think of hypothesis formulation as a precise enterprise might well expect the Contrastive Analysis Hypothesis to be just as unambiguous as their own hypotheses and just as unambiguous in terms of any empirical testing used to evaluate it. Yet the nebulousness of the term CAH as actually used can occasion misunderstandings, including a mistaken belief that some imagined hypothesis about the importance of transfer was tested and found to be false. Reading surveys of recent transfer research (e.g. Jarvis & Pavlenko, 2008; Odlin & Yu, 2016; Ringbom, 2007) can forestall such misunderstandings, of course, but the word *hypothesis* does invite misconceptions.

The progress of transfer research in recent decades as well as in earlier ones shows that Fries and Lado did not err either in ascribing great importance to crosslinguistic influence or even in believing that contrastive predictions are possible, although there remains the challenge of identifying the kinds of prediction most likely to succeed (Odlin, 2014; see also Chapter 3). That said, some assumptions of Fries or Lado (or both) will not be shared by many SLA researchers at all nowadays, including Lado's belief in behaviorism or Fries' skepticism about parallels between child language learning and L2 acquisition. It is fair to say, moreover, that the great attention to crosslinguistic comparisons in the mid-20th century has given way, quite rightly, to an interest in conceptions of SLA, such as interlanguage, which take transfer into account yet also recognize complex processes like overgeneralization that are sometimes independent of crosslinguistic influence (Selinker, 1972, 1992, 2014). Nevertheless, anyone interested in SLA should be aware that the study of transfer in L2 and multilingual acquisition has (like psycholinguistics more generally) a prehistory as well as a history, with both indeed relevant to the understanding of the human capacity for more than one language.

Much of the current chapter has offered a historical perspective on contrastive predictions. Predictions also get considerable attention in the next chapter, which focuses on the question of whether a contrastive analysis could ever be complete.

Notes

(1) I would like to thank Marianne Gullberg and Camie Hamans for their help in regard to this project. Thanks also to Rosa Alonso Alonso for encouraging me in the project. Naturally I take sole responsibility for any errors in the chapter.

(2) The 1875 version of the Ahlqvist book is a translation of a work originally published in Swedish in 1871 (Ahlqvist, 1871). In the foreword to the German edition, Ahlqvist notes that the translator was a native speaker of German.

(3) Selinker (personal communication) notes that contrastive analysis is not in itself a theory of learning, so in effect it is unrealistic to see any crosslinguistic comparison as a model of acquisition even though such comparisons can contribute much to a sound model.

3 Could a Contrastive Analysis Ever Be Complete?

Many linguists have referred to key problems in language transfer under the rubric of the so-called Contrastive Analysis Hypothesis (see Chapter 2). Other problems in second language acquisition (SLA) have likewise been referred to with the moniker *hypothesis* – for example, the Critical Age Hypothesis. In all cases, it is important to remember that the label used for any phenomenon can affect what someone expects to find. The word *hypothesis* does have the advantage of reminding investigators or curious readers that they should view problems such as transfer and age of acquisition as research concerns accountable to actual data. However, *hypothesis* can also be misleading. Birdsong (1999) has noted, for instance, that there is actually more than one possible hypothesis connected with the notion of age-related differences in SLA. And, as seen in Chapter 2, the so-called Contrastive Analysis Hypothesis should not imply a monolithic hypothesis – or a litmus test that could show the hypothesis to be true or false.

The influential article by Ronald Wardhaugh (1970), discussed in detail in Chapter 2, tacitly acknowledged that his own conception of CAH is not monolithic. Indeed, he distinguished a strong version of CAH from a weak version, with the main difference between them being the role of predictions (see also Odlin, 2014). As this chapter will show, however, one question not addressed by Wardhaugh or most other commentators is the one posed in the title of the chapter: could a contrastive analysis ever be complete? One problem to recognize at the outset is the question of what the criterion is for completeness. A tentative answer to that as well as to the larger question will be offered at the end of this chapter. Other answers seem conceivable, of course, but there can be no doubt that enormous challenges arise in trying to understand all the implications of a thoroughgoing comparison of languages.

Difficulties of Contrastive Predictions

Although transfer researchers have good reason to question the distinction Wardhaugh made, the difficulties of contrastive analysis should not be underestimated. For one thing, a great deal of research indicates that transfer plays little if any role in some cases. Moreover, even when transfer does play a role, it can be evident in different ways, some easier to detect than others. In an important challenge to Wardhaugh, Jacquelyn Schachter (1974) argued that learners' avoidance patterns sometimes arise from differences between the native and target language: thus, speakers of Chinese and Japanese may have an especially hard time with the relative clauses of English because relativization in these languages is so different. Although there have been empirical challenges to Schachter's analysis (e.g. Kamimoto *et al.*, 1992), there is other evidence both for avoidance and for its interaction with crosslinguistic differences (Odlin, 1989, 2003). In effect, then, avoidance can sometimes be considered a covert kind of language transfer.

A somewhat similar case of covert transfer is evident in a study by Jarvis and Odlin (2000) of prepositions – and the absence of obligatory prepositions – in the acquisition of English in Finland. Finland has two official languages, Finnish and Swedish (see also Chapter 5). The latter is, like English, a prepositional language, whereas Finnish uses a mixed set of structures for the same purposes. The primary type of structure is the nominal case inflection: Finnish nouns can inflect for 15 different cases, often translatable into Swedish and English as prepositions. For example, the word *nurmikolle* consists of a stem *nurmiko-* for grass and an inflection *-lle*, which typically signals movement to or onto a location; thus *nurmikolle* can translate as 'on(to) the grass'. Along with noun inflections, there are postpositions and even a handful of prepositions in Finnish. Both Finnish and Swedish speakers often choose an English preposition that reflects the influence of their native language. In addition, however, Finnish but not Swedish speakers often omit prepositions that are obligatory in the target language, as in *C[harlie] C[haplin] and the woman go to sit the grass*. Because cases such as the absence of *on* before the noun phrase *the grass* occurred only among the Finnish learners and never among Swedish learners with comparable backgrounds, zero prepositions should be viewed as an interaction of two processes often thought to be mutually exclusive: simplification and transfer.

The example of zero prepositions among Finns thus suggests that the absence of something can be implicated in crosslinguistic influence, and so contrastive analysts face the very formidable problem of predicting when they will find a covert as well as an overt behavior. Two other problems in making predictions about transfer should also be noted here. First, individual variation matters in the study of transfer. Although contrastive analysis normally involves group rather than individual patterns of usage, the latter must be taken into account. Thus it is a fact that different speakers of Finnish show different patterns of transfer, as do the Swedish speakers.

The second point to be noted is that a highly significant concomitant of individual variation is the fact that *all* crosslinguistic influence arises through the subjective assessments of individual learners (see also Chapter 7). Indeed, many transfer researchers have taken subjective assessment into account, as seen in the work of Kellerman (1977, 1995) and others (e.g. Abdullah & Jackson, 1998). Closer attention will be paid to the problem of subjective assessment later in this chapter.

Constraints as Predictions

Skeptics about crosslinguistic influence have often invoked constraints on language transfer yet they have often ignored the close resemblance between predictions and constraints or the difficulties entailed by both. If it is hard to predict when language transfer will occur, it is no easier to predict when it will *not* occur. Indeed, there is no compelling reason to argue that a constraint is any different from a contrastive prediction. At least four constraints on grammatical and/or lexical transfer have been proposed, yet all four have turned out to be empirically unsound. From at least as early as the 19th century some linguists have viewed bound morphology as a structural subsystem that is immune to crosslinguistic influence. However, a wealth of evidence contradicts any blanket claim about the non-transferability of bound morphology (e.g. Dušková, 1984; Jarvis & Odlin, 2000; Orr, 1987; Thomason & Kaufman, 1988; Weinreich, 1953a). Another constraint sometimes proposed would have it that basic word order is never transferable (e.g. the use of an SOV sentence pattern in an SVO language). Once again, however, there is considerable evidence suggesting that basic word order is not immune to transfer (see Chapter 4).

The third constraint/prediction involves idioms. An early claim of Kellerman (1977) about Dutch idioms was that they are not transferable, although he later scaled back his constraint (se also Chapter 7). In any case, language-contact research indicates that second language learners sometimes have few if any inhibitions about transfer and sometimes take idioms from their native language and create translation equivalents in their own version of the target language (see also Chapter 7). For example, the Irish English idiom *We could not knock any rights of each other* (meaning 'We could not agree') has a clear parallel in Irish (aka Gaelic), and there seems to be no evidence of influence from idioms used in British dialects (Odlin, 1991).

The fourth structural constraint involves what advocates of Universal Grammar research have called the 'functional projection'. This construct includes a wide variety of grammatical morphemes including articles, and Vainikka and Young-Scholten (1998) argued that functional projections are not transferable. However, a great deal of evidence indicates that this supposed constraint on transfer will not hold for articles (Odlin, 2003, 2014).

Somewhat different from the four alleged structural constraints just reviewed is a 'developmental constraint' claimed by proponents of Processability Theory (e.g. Pienemann *et al.*, 2005). Space does not permit an extended discussion of this claim, but two points should be noted. First, the putative developmental constraint does not rule out the possibility of transfer of a structure but, rather, the timing of such transfer in relation to what has and has not been acquired by a learner. Second, the alleged constraint does not take into account the reality of individual variation among learners (Odlin, 2013). A related (and unwarranted) assumption in Processability Theory involves the connection between transfer and translation and will be considered at length in Chapter 7.

To show the inadequacy of some constraints does not, however, mean that there are no constraints at all on transfer. Researchers do well indeed to avoid sweeping claims, such as the one holding that bound morphology is not transferable. Nevertheless, some kinds of morphological transfer seem to occur rarely if ever. For example, it is probably safe to predict that speakers of a synthetic language will not often try to use nominal case inflections or person/number markers when trying to speak or write a target language that is analytic (and this prediction is consonant with conditions suggested by Weinreich (1953a)). It would be surprising, for instance, if many native speakers of Polish used the first-person plural suffix *-my* on English verbs to produce interlanguage forms such as *readmy* for *we read* or *gomy* for *we go*. Yet though these errors seem very improbable, it may well be true that Polish learners of an East or South Slavic language would be tempted to use some bound morphology from their native language. The discussion by Dušková (1984) of Czech learners of Russian suggests that whatever constraints there may be on bound morphology, they depend very much on both the languages in contact, and on learners' perceptions of the crosslinguistic distances.

Predictions and Transferability

Just as some predictions about when transfer will not occur seem reasonable to make, so do some predictions about when transfer will occur. In some cases, the evidence against a supposed constraint can, if used carefully, offer the basis for predictions about positive as well as negative transfer. Such evidence can indeed help formulate related predictions, as in the following case (Odlin, 2014: 30):

(1a) Speakers of Finnish as a group will have greater difficulty with the articles of Portuguese than will speakers of Swedish as a group.

(1b)   Speakers of Estonian as a group will have greater difficulty with the articles of Portuguese than will speakers of Danish as a group.
(1c)   Speakers of Korean as a group will have greater difficulty with the articles of Portuguese than will speakers of Albanian as a group.

The prediction in (1a) draws on results of a study by Jarvis (2002), which found that Finnish speakers as a group had far more difficulty with English articles than did speakers of Swedish, a language similar to English in many ways, including the use of definite and indefinite articles, whereas Finnish has neither. Portuguese, like English, has both definite and indefinite articles (e.g. *o barco* 'the boat' and *um barco* 'a boat'). Thus it seems likely that a study of Portuguese as the target would produce results similar to those of the Jarvis study if the learners were native speakers of Finnish and Swedish.

Prediction (1b) also seems plausible since Estonian is a Uralic language closely related to Finnish, and Danish is a North Germanic language similar to Swedish. Prediction (1c) is arguably more interesting because it involves two native languages not closely related to those in (1a) and (1b). Yet, like Swedish and Danish, Albanian has definite and indefinite articles, whereas Korean has neither type; thus, this prediction, if accurate, would indeed support a putative generalization that the absence or presence of articles in the native language is a good predictor of how easy or difficult articles may be to a particular group of learners.

Such predictions are among the desiderata of a more general theory of transferability, a concept long discussed in the literature but still not achieved (e.g. Jarvis & Pavlenko, 2008; Kellerman, 1995; Odlin, 2003; Selinker, 1992; White, 2000). Even so, the remarkable consistency of findings such as those on articles gives real hope for ever-better contrastive predictions.

Completeness in Contrastive Analysis

Affirming the robustness of some contrastive predictions does not, however, address the question that is the title of this chapter: could a contrastive analysis ever be complete? The question should not be taken to mean that existing contrastive analyses lack value. On the contrary, there are many reasons to continue consulting several crosslinguistic comparisons (e.g. Fisiak *et al.*, 1978; Stockwell *et al.*, 1965). Moreover, teachers who can carefully compare the native and target languages are especially qualified to help their students, as seen, for example, in a study by Han (2001). Yet for all the theoretical and practical value of contrastive research, much remains to be done. Some of the necessary work will involve a search for evidence to support or refute the following two claims:

- No contrastive analysis can be comprehensive without a viable theory of transferability.

- No theory of transferability can be entirely satisfactory without a viable account of relevant affective factors.

Much of the rest of this chapter will consider focus constructions because they well illustrate problems related to transferability and affect. Furthermore, the discussion will preview certain topics, such as translation and comprehension, that are foregrounded in the subsequent chapters of the book.

Transferability and Focus Constructions

Readers will find a formal definition of focus in Chapter 6, but for now it will suffice to consider focus constructions as attention-getting devices that typically signal a speaker's or writer's feeling that something in the information focused on is especially important for the hearer or reader to note. Chapter 6 also discusses examples of focus patterns in several languages. One pattern common in English is the *it*-cleft sentence, which typically begins with a non-referential *it* followed by *is* (or some other form of the verb *be*) and then a focus element followed in turn by a relative clause. Both the following examples show those characteristics:

It is the man who took the bread.
It is the woman who took the bread.

In the first example, *the man* is in the focus position (and characteristically has the heaviest stress when spoken) whereas in the second, *the woman* is the information in focus. Cleft sentences often contrast the elements in the focus position. By adding the word *No* to the second cleft, a dialogue writer could construct an argument between two speakers as to who took the bread, with the second speaker contradicting the first with the assertion *No, it is the woman who took the bread.* However, cleft sentences also serve other functions, as discussed in Chapter 6. It should also be noted that several languages have formal patterns of clefting similar to English, including French, German, Swedish and Finnish.

Despite the robust use of cleft structures, not all languages have formal patterns closely resembling the clefts of English. Japanese, for example, has a basic word order that works against similarity to English clefts (see also Chapter 4) and, unlike English, Japanese relative clauses do not follow nouns. One common pattern in Japanese uses a focusing particle *ga* that sometimes corresponds in meaning to the *it*-cleft pattern of English, as in an example given by Kuno (1973: 51):

John ga gakusei desu
John-ga student is
It is John who is a student.

Other translations of the Japanese sentence are sometimes more appropriate, but Kuno states that when John is the only person who is a student in a relevant group, the cleft translation is appropriate.

The Japanese example is by no means the only case of where a partial crosslinguistic correspondence will complicate a contrastive analysis. Part of Chapter 6 considers the asymmetry of translating English cleft sentences into German (and also German clefts into English). Even though formal patterns of clefting are similar in the two languages, skilled translators do not always regard a cleft in German as the best possible translation.

Crosslinguistic correspondences in focus constructions are often only approximate. And what holds for cleft sentences holds for other kinds of crosslinguistic correspondences as well. Negative transfer can arise in such cases. Chapter 7 considers negative transfer sometimes found among both professional translators and less accomplished bilinguals, while Chapter 6 looks at cases where an L2 use of a cleft pattern indicates translating an L1 construction in ways that professional translators would certainly eschew.

A complete contrastive analysis ought to predict a vast range of partial correspondences that would prove difficult for language learners. However, a thorough analysis would also have to do even more than predict difficulty (or ease). It would also have to offer satisfactory explanations for why one group tends to use a structure more than another group despite both groups having structures similar to one in the target language. Chapter 5 provides evidence that Swedish speakers tend to use English cleft sentences in a particular discourse context much more than do Finnish speakers even though both languages have cleft patterns similar to English. The findings indicate that transfer is manifested in the differing frequency of cleft sentences in Swedish and Finnish in the same discourse context. The following prediction would therefore be worth testing:

(2a)   Speakers of Finnish as a group will not produce as many French cleft sentences as will speakers of Swedish as a group.

This prediction is similar in some ways to prediction (1a) discussed above in that there is a difference predicted between L1-Finnish and L1-Swedish speakers. There is, however, an obvious difference from the earlier prediction since French, not Portuguese, is now the target language. Moreover, the new prediction refers to frequency of production, not to linguistic difficulty. As already noted, Finnish does have cleft patterns similar to those in English, French, and other languages.

The transferability of focus constructions thus involves questions of not only structural similarity but also of frequency of use. Both structure and frequency can be elements in contrastive predictions, and, in fact, such predictions can include other factors as well. For example, Ringbom (2007: 121–122) considers the possibility that knowledge of Finnish as a second language, not as a first, could lead to easier acquisition of Swahili, a language that resembles Finnish in some ways. Other predictions related to multilingual abilities are also conceivable, but in any case, contrastive predictions may sometimes involve more than just structure.

Focus Constructions and Affect

The preceding section cited formal similarity and frequency of use in the native language as factors in the transfer of focus constructions. The discussion considered these factors mainly in relation to linguistic *production*. However, any thorough contrastive analysis also has to take *comprehension* into account. The informal characterization of focus at the beginning of the preceding section noted the feeling of a speaker or writer that something put into focus is especially significant for the hearer or reader. Understanding what that feeling is often means more than just comprehending referential information: in many cases a listener will also have to judge the speaker's certainty or confidence about the information put in focus, and similar judgements are required, of course, for any reader. Confidence and certainty are two affective states that may or may not be 'emotions' comparable to love, fear, joy, and so on, but, in any event, they figure prominently in linguistic focus.

Focus constructions are emphatic statements, but emphatic expressions also include other patterns including some kinds of negation as well as language-specific structures such as the use of *do* in *Your parents do love you.* To the extent that a common meaning underlies all emphatic expressions, emphasis signals some affective commitment by the speaker or writer to the statement made. For listeners or readers, then, much of the challenge of comprehension involves understanding a particular commitment in a particular context.

As noted above, some emphatic patterns are language-specific and examples from Irish and Spanish in Chapter 6 suggest cases where any translator would be hardpressed to communicate the affective stance of the original focus construction – assuming, of course, that the translator has understood the affective stance. Such difficulties raise questions as to whether affective stances are the same in all languages and whether adult learners of a new language can understand the entire range of stances expressed in the target language.

The observations here about the link between affective stances and focus constructions are not the first to consider the link. There have been language-specific analyses in, for example, Wolof and Mandarin Chinese (Guo, 1999; Irvine, 1990), as well as efforts to integrate affect into a general theory of focus (e.g. Firbas, 1992).

The case of Wolof will be considered further in Chapter 6; for now, though, the implications of research for crosslinguistic comparisons warrant closer attention. It seems likely that anyone who accepts the usefulness of these comparisons will agree that comparing meanings is a part of any thorough analysis. Even so, the problem of affective meaning arguably constitutes the greatest impediment to any complete contrastive analysis.

Part of the problem of comparing meanings involves understanding the relation between affect and cognition. Although some in cognitive studies have given little attention to the relation, others (e.g. Lane & Nadel, 2000; Ortony *et al.*, 1988; Pavlenko, 2005) have viewed it as a central challenge. Any satisfactory theory of affect must be pan-cultural in order to provide a basis for crosslinguistic comparisons, yet how feasible such a theory is remains controversial (Pavlenko, 2005). If a consensus can be achieved about a pan-cultural basis for comparing languages in terms of how emotions are communicated, it may prove possible to compare in full detail the variations in affective stances found in the focus constructions of pairs of similar languages such as English and German and also pairs of dissimilar languages such as English and Japanese.

Conclusion

The discussion in this chapter has led to several generalizations:

- Even though crosslinguistic comparisons may suggest the possibility of transfer in many cases, contrastive analysts face a formidable problem of predicting covert as well as overt cases of transfer, as found with zero prepositions. Individual variation likewise poses serious challenges since contrastive analysis normally involves group rather than individual patterns of usage.
- If predictions are problematic, so are constraints, which indeed often predict (rightly or wrongly) when transfer will *not* occur. Existing research shows the unsoundness of some proposed constraints, including ones on basic word order and bound morphology. Even so, there are reasons to believe that some constraints will be sound as will some predictions about when transfer will actually occur.
- Predictions of group tendencies seem viable when at least two groups of learners are contrasted and when the predictions derive from findings of similar tendencies in other groups. Such predictions offer a useful way to develop better generalizations about transferability.
- No contrastive analysis can be comprehensive without a viable theory of transferability. Furthermore, no theory of transferability can be entirely satisfactory without a viable account of relevant affective factors.

- The transferability of constructions resembling the English *it*-cleft pattern depends on both structural similarity and on the frequency of the source language structure in a particular discourse context.
- Focus constructions raise questions as to whether affective stances are fully comparable across languages and whether adults learning a new language can comprehend the entire range of stances expressed in the target language.

None of the generalizations expressly answers the question of whether or not a contrastive analysis could ever be complete. A definitive answer may well seem problematic, especially since agreeing on a criterion for completeness could prove elusive, with different theorists proposing different criteria. Tentatively, however, the criterion can be stated in terms of predictions. That is, a complete contrastive analysis would be one that resulted in a satisfactory set of predictions. These would involve not only ease and difficulty in acquisition but also patterns of frequency of use. While a complete set seems a remote goal at best, there is no reason to deny the hypothetical possibility of such a set.

With a set of predictions as the criterion for completeness, a plausible answer to the question would be a qualified *yes*. Yet although no theoretical objection may rule out the possibility, the difficulties involved in any attempt at completeness are formidable indeed, as much of the discussion in this chapter suggests.

Even a complete contrastive analysis would not succeed in predicting all cases of ease or difficulty; to argue otherwise would require making dubious assumptions, like those that critics imputed – in contradictory ways – to the so-called Contrastive Analysis Hypothesis (see Chapter 2). Nevertheless, transfer does play a key role in ease and difficulty. A thorough contrastive analysis could predict the full subset of successes and failures specifically due to transfer within the larger set of cases of ease or difficulty encountered in SLA.

One methodological problem inherent in the notion of completeness involves the form of predictions. If they refer to two different L1s, as with Finnish and Swedish in prediction (1a), two different contrastive analyses are required: one for Portuguese and Finnish, and one for Portuguese and Swedish. In this sense, complete contrastive analyses would have to come in pairs of descriptions. Predictions involving a target that is a third language prove even more of a challenge in cases such as the one involving a Swahili target and Finnish as the L2, predicted to facilitate acquisition.

Despite the complexities that any thorough comparison would require, researchers and teachers will profit from predictions involving new language-contact situations. For example, teachers of Portuguese may not yet have any reason to wonder about the problems that Estonian or Danish speakers are likely to encounter, but commercial, political, or cultural circumstances might someday make even a limited comparison of Portuguese and the two languages of the Baltic region desirable to develop.

Insightful comparisons of languages, including comparisons of paralinguistic traits such as gestures and facial expressions, may also offer useful perspectives on bilingualism or multilingualism. At times the comparisons may foreground similarities, not just differences, across cultures. For example, research on paralanguage by Hearn (1989) suggests that facial expressions of Poles and Americans tend to be mutually intelligible to people from English- and Polish-speaking countries. This result contrasts with subjective impressions reported by Eva Hoffman (1988: 146) in her memoir of her immigration from Poland to North America. The author recalled that her mother worried that her daughter was becoming 'English', which was a maternal way of saying emotionally cold. Hoffman herself had a sense that her paralinguistic repertory was changing and that her gestures were more subdued as a result of using English. The research by Hearn does not, of course, justify doubting the subjective convictions of Hoffman and her mother, but such empirical work does offer a valuable caution that no one should underestimate the complexities of crosslinguistic and cross-cultural differences.

Much of the discussion in this chapter has focused on contrastive predictions and on the related issue of constraints on transfer that are tantamount to predictions. The next chapter addresses a particular constraint proposed more than 30 years ago involving word order and considers related questions including how bilinguals' awareness of word order may affect transfer.

4 Word-order Transfer, Metalinguistic Awareness and Constraints on Foreign Language Learning[1]

Introduction

Of the many problems in second language research, the role of language transfer in the acquisition of syntax has been one of the most intractable.[2] In comparison with attitudes in the 1960s and 1970s, there is now less skepticism that knowledge of one language can greatly influence performance in another language, but controversy over the extent of syntactic transfer has by no means disappeared (e.g. Dulay *et al.*, 1982; Meisel, 1983). Much of the controversy is related to the interest in language universals. While some research suggests that transfer and universals can and do interact in the acquisition of syntax (e.g. Gass, 1979; Zobl, 1980), there is no consensus about how much interaction there is or about the role of transfer and universals (and other factors) as independent influences on acquisition.

The interest in universals has no doubt made clearer the range of questions that research on second language acquisition must answer, but universalist analyses are just as problematic as contrastive analyses. While contrastive analyses often fail in predicting when transfer will occur, there is an obvious pitfall in predicting when transfer will never occur (see also Chapter 3). A putatively universal constraint on some kind of transfer cannot be universal if a single clear-cut case of such transfer exists. The literature on language attrition is instructive on that point. With regard to what may be termed *borrowing transfer*, there have been many claims by eminent scholars denying that transfer of bound morphology is possible in any bilingual milieu. However, as Thomason

(1981) has observed, there are unambiguous cases of just such transfer: some dialects of Anatolian Greek, for instance, have incorporated many Turkish bound morphemes (Dawkins, 1916). In this type of transfer, speakers' knowledge of a second language (Turkish) influenced their native language (Greek). Such cases suggest that putative constraints on other kinds of transfer may also be illusory (see also Jarvis & Odlin, 2000; Thomason & Kaufman, 1988).

Counter-examples to any would-be universals might come either from data on borrowing transfer or from data on *substratum transfer*, i.e. the influence of a native language (or some other previously learned language) on the acquisition of another language (Thomason & Kaufman, 1988). In this chapter, evidence from both substratum and borrowing transfer is relevant to the problem of crosslinguistic influences on word order. Studies with a universalist orientation have purported that there are structural constraints on the transfer of word order (Rutherford, 1983, 1986; Zobl, 1986a, 1986b). Yet like purported constraints on morphological transfer, the supposed constraints on word-order transfer are dubious on empirical grounds. This chapter will cite cases of word-order transfer that violate the constraints. Whatever value universalist analyses may have, there exist other factors relevant to the phenomenon of word-order transfer. Among those factors is *metalinguistic awareness*, i.e. individuals' awareness of language. If such awareness has an effect on the development of second language syntax, then the study of syntactic transfer and the study of Foreign Language Learning, i.e. acquisition of a second language influenced by instruction, are interrelated. The chapter first considers the universalist positions of Zobl and Rutherford and the counter-examples to their claims, it then considers various factors relevant to word order, and finally considers the relations between transfer and metalinguistic awareness with regard to Foreign Language Learning.[3]

The Analyses of Zobl and Rutherford

Although different in some respects, the interpretations of word-order acquisition given by William Rutherford and Helmut Zobl are similar in two important ways. First, neither denies that word-order transfer plays some role in the acquisition of syntax. Zobl sees transfer as a real influence in, for example, the placement of adverbs in English, as documented by Selinker (1969) and others. Rutherford finds transfer occurring at a rather abstract level involving typological properties or 'parameters'. For instance, the rigidity of word order in some languages (e.g. English) is, Rutherford claims, a transferable parameter. The other major similarity in the positions of Zobl and Rutherford is that both scholars are skeptical that negative transfer of basic word order takes place: i.e. that there are any simple cases of linguistic interference in which the canonical declarative pattern of the syntactic constituents subject, verb phrase

(VP), and object in one's native language is anomalously used in lieu of the canonical pattern of the target language. For example, in an examination of syntactic patterns of Japanese ESL students at an American university, Rutherford (1983: 367) emphatically claims that transfer of the subject-object-verb (SOV) pattern of Japanese never occurs: 'Japanese learners of English do not at any time produce writing in which the verb is wrongly placed sentence finally'. Although English uses a subject-verb-object (SVO) pattern, one might expect to find occasional SOV sentences in the speech or writing of Japanese ESL students. Rutherford, however, found no evidence of such transfer. While the quotation just given might suggest that Rutherford's analysis is restricted to one aspect of ESL performance (i.e. writing), the substance of the claim found in his analysis is clearly universalist: Japanese and other learners are likely to rely on other native-language 'parameters' but not on the basic SOV pattern.

Citing evidence in Rutherford's study as well as other evidence, Zobl (1986a: 178) is skeptical about the occurrence of transfer of word-order traits that are 'central' to the syntactic typology of a language: 'learners are sensitive to the principle that defines the central traits of a word order type and that the L1 does not lead to transfer in the central traits'. Although he sees basic word order as one of those 'central' traits, Zobl does believe that basic word-order transfer is possible in one very restricted case: when a language makes use of more than one basic word order as in Dutch, which uses SOV in subordinate clauses and SVO (as well as other patterns) in main clauses. His analysis thus takes into account some European research, such as a very detailed study of the acquisition of Dutch by speakers of Moroccan Arabic (an SVO language) and Turkish (an SOV language) that shows that transfer was quite common (Jansen *et al.*, 1981). However, it is clear that Zobl regards such cases of typological ambiguity as exceptional and not as ones that call into question his hypothesized universal principle on the non-transferability of basic word order.

Both Zobl and Rutherford thus make claims about the non-transferability of basic word order in *all* 'unambiguous' second language contexts. As both analyses are thus universalist in the strictest sense of the word, both can be falsified if there exists a single 'unambiguous' counter-example of basic word-order transfer. The claims of Zobl and Rutherford are in fact untenable since counter-examples do exist: 11 will be presented in this chapter. These counter-examples show that universalist claims about the non-transferability of basic word order cannot be true in any absolute sense although universalist analyses might point to interesting statistical tendencies (cf. Comrie, 1981).

General Patterns Seen in Basic Word-order Transfer

Table 4.1 summarizes four attested cases of basic word-order transfer in the acquisition of a second language (i.e. substratum transfer). In

Table 4.1 Attested cases of basic word-order transfer in second language acquisition

Target Language	Native Language	Interlanguage
English (SVO)	Japanese/Korean (SOV)	Hawaiian Pidgin English (SOV)*
English (SVO)	Korean (SOV)	Bamboo English (SOV)*
Spanish (SVO)	Quechua (SOV)	Andean Spanish (SOV)*
Fijian (VOS/SVO)	Hindustani (SOV)	Pidgin Fijian (SOV)*

* SVO order is also used.

Hawaiian Pidgin English, Bamboo English, Andean Spanish and Pidgin Fijian there are documented cases of the use of an SOV pattern that in all likelihood is due to influence from the native language, as discussed below. Table 4.2 summarizes three other cases of word-order transfer that are instances of borrowing transfer in which change in the word order in the native language can be attributed to the acquisition of a second language having a different basic word order. For example, Young People's Dyirbal, the drastically altered form of Traditional Dyirbal, an Australian language, employs a word order that shows the effects of Dyirbal/English bilingualism in an aboriginal community. All the cases in Tables 4.1 and 4.2 show other influences in addition to transfer. In the case of Andean Spanish, for example, both SOV and SVO patterns are used. While the SOV patterns show an influence from the native language, Quechua, the SVO patterns indicate the effects of exposure to the target language, Spanish.

Table 4.3 indicates four language-contact situations that occurred in earlier times and that show a strong likelihood of basic word-order

Table 4.2 Attested cases of basic word-order transfer in language attrition due to bilingualism

Traditional Language	Second Language	Language Shift
Bhojpuri (SOV)	Mauritian creole (SVO)	Mauritian Bhojpuri (SVO)**
Dyirbal (OAV, AOV)	English (SVO)	Young People's Dyirbal (AVO)**
Nubian (SOV)	Egyptian Arabic (SVO)	Cairo Nubian (SVO)**

**SOV order is also used (in Young People's Dyirbal: AOV).

Table 4.3 Historical cases of basic word-order transfer

Contact Language 1	Contact Language 2	Result
Portuguese (SVO)	Tamil (SOV)/ Gujarati (?) (SOV)/ Hindustani (?) (SOV)/ Malayalam	Indo–Portuguese (SOV)*
Ethiopic (SVO)	Cushitic (SOV)	Amharic (SOV)
Cushitic (SOV)	Bantu (SVO)	Ma'a (SVO)
Sintitic (SVO)	Altaic (SOV)	Hui (SOV)

* SVO order is also used.

transfer having taken place. In these cases, however, there are uncertainties about the exact nature of the contact situation, and so the languages involved are simply referred to as Contact Language 1 and Contact Language 2, with the result of that contact listed in the third column.

Cases of Substratum Transfer

The cases listed in Table 4.1 warrant extended description since they pertain most directly to syntactic transfer affecting the acquisition of a second language. Two of the cases (Hawaiian Pidgin English and Andean Spanish) have been discussed elsewhere in connection with basic word-order transfer, but there are facts relevant to both that have not received sufficient attention.

Hawaiian Pidgin English

Hawaiian Pidgin English (HPE) is commonly characterized as having a basic SVO order, but there are attested examples of other word orders and these examples indicate transfer. Nagara (1972) characterized the HPE of Japanese speakers as having both SVO and SOV. The SOV pattern he attributed to Japanese influence, as in Example (1) (Nagara, 1972: 300–01):

Example (1)

mi: cu: stoa gécc
Me two store get
I got/acquired two stores.

Bickerton and Givón (1976) provide detailed quantitative evidence of transfer-based differences in basic word order in HPE. Their statistics indicate that verb-final utterances are by no means unusual among Japanese speakers of HPE. They found, moreover, that verbs sometimes preceded subjects in the utterances of speakers of verb-initial Philippine languages (e.g. Ilocano), as in Example (2) (Bickerton & Givón, 1976: 27):

Example (2)

samtaim kam da shak
Sometime come the shark.
Sometimes sharks came.

As in the case of the Japanese speaker, Bickerton and Givón attribute the Philippine English word order employed to the native-language patterns (here VSO). Both HPE studies make it clear that SVO is an alternative order to the transfer-based pattern. In the case of the Japanese and Filipinos studied by Bickerton and Givón, the evidence indicates that the most proficient speakers of HPE used SVX patterns the most, while the least proficient speakers used SVX patterns the least and instead used a sizeable number of SXV or VSX patterns in keeping with word order in their native languages.[4] Similar instances of a relation between word-order transfer and language proficiency will be seen in the discussions of Andean Spanish and Young People's Dyirbal below.

Aside from the SOV and SVO patterns in the HPE syntax of Japanese speakers, another frequent pattern is OV, as in Example (3) (Nagara, 1972: 303):

Example (3)

hawai kám

Hawaii come.

(I) came (to) Hawaii.

While the example just given suggests that XV phrases are reduced variants of the SXV pattern, some linguists who have been skeptical about the existence of basic word-order transfer have suggested that XV patterns may result from other factors besides native language influence. In a critique of transfer cited by Mühlhäusler (1986: 125), Meisel claims that OV patterns merely reflect syntactic movement rules that are motivated by a (putatively) universal pragmatic mode.[5] In other words, what seems to be syntactic transfer could be an instance of topicalization or some other language-neutral discourse function (see also Chapter 6). For example, the phrase *hawai kám* does have an XV pattern, but one might still claim that the word order reflects discourse considerations such as a desire on the part of the speaker to introduce Hawaii as the setting for subsequent discourse.

Although the language-neutral (or universal) discourse explanation may account for some of the word-order patterns seen in HPE, there are at least three reasons to be skeptical about the value of such an explanation for most of the HPE data. First, that explanation does nothing to account for the existence of SOV sentences such as *mi: cu: stoa gécc*. Second, a language-neutral discourse explanation probably cannot account for such verb-final phrases as in Example (4) (Bickerton & Givón, 1976: 18):

Example (4)

œn luk-laik-punkin-kain get

And look-like-pumpkin-kind get.

And there's the kind that look like pumpkins.

As Bickerton and Givón note, the use of *get* seems to function as an existential marker somewhat like *there is* or as a possessive somewhat like *have*. However, this clause-final position of the existential/possessive marker may be less frequent in some other varieties of HPE. For example, in the HPE of a Hmong refugee – Example (5) – described by Huebner (1979, 1983), VO order involving existential/possessive constructions seems to have been more common than OV order (Huebner, 1979: 23):

Example (5)

bat kaemp nam pong haeva sowjer

But there was a soldier at Camp Nam Phong.

In all probability, then, the clause-final position of *get* in œn *luk-laik-punkin-kain get* reflects Japanese influence.

A third reason to reject a language-neutral discourse explanation is that it probably cannot account for differences in HPE word order produced by speakers of VSO and SOV languages. Transfer-based differences in the use of OV and VO patterns are in fact evident in a study of discourse functions in the early stages of L-2 acquisition (Givón, 1984a). A speaker of Korean, which like Japanese is SOV, produced many more instances of OV patterns than did a speaker of a VSO Philippine language, as seen in Table 4.4.

Table 4.4 Comparative frequency of VO/OV patterns in two texts in Hawaiian Pidgin English[6]

	Definite NP Objects		Indefinite NP Objects	
	VO	OV	VO	OV
Philippine–English text	26	2	32	0
Korean–English text	11	22	17	28

Figures are adapted from those in Tables I–IV in Givón (1984a).

Korean Bamboo English

Similar instances of transfer are evident in Bamboo English, a trade jargon that developed through contact between American soldiers and Japanese and Korean civilians in the 1940s and 1950s. While there is little written about the use of Bamboo English, one study of Korean Bamboo English (Algeo, 1960) indicates that by the 1950s it showed signs of developing into something quite like a pidgin. Algeo illustrated that development with a few sentences that follow the SOV and OV patterns of Korean, as in Example (6):

Example (6)

You number one washee-washee catchee, number one present hava-yes.

If you do a fine washing, you'll get a fine tip.

As with HPE, Korean Bamboo English also employed SVO patterns, but the verb *hava-yes* probably occurred more often in clause-final position than in any other environment (John Algeo, personal communication). An instance of semantic transfer in Korean Bamboo English makes all the more plausible the occurrence of basic word-order transfer: the use of *number one* reflects a Korean (and Japanese) tradition of indicating satisfaction through the use of a number. There is also historical evidence suggesting that basic word-order transfer would be likely. American soldiers generally were not in Korea for more than 16 months, and so what norms there were in Bamboo English probably developed more among Koreans who used the jargon frequently than among the American military (John Algeo, personal communication).

Andean Spanish

Spanish, an SVO language in most dialects, does not normally use an SOV pattern except when the object noun phrase (NP) takes the form of a pronoun. However, in the Spanish spoken in Peru and Ecuador there are verb-final patterns in which the object is a noun: Lujan *et al.* (1984) studied the Spanish of several Peruvian children who sometimes used SOV patterns, such as in Example (7):

Example (7)

Y mi hermano aquí otra paloma hembra había chapado
and my brother here another dove female had caught
And my brother had caught another female dove here.

Lujan *et al.* also found numerous OV patterns, such as in Example (8):

Example (8)

Volantín antes hacían
somersault before did
They used to do somersaults.

According to Lujan *et al.*, the OV as well as the SOV patterns reflect influence from Quechua, an SOV language.

Skepticism about basic word-order transfer in Andean Spanish has, however, been expressed by another investigator (Muysken, 1984). In his study of the variations in the Ecuadorean Spanish of adults of different social classes, Muysken found no examples of SOV sentences although there were some occurrences of SXV sentences (he does not specify the exact number) and frequent occurrences of OV patterns. Using an argument like that of Meisel about HPE, Muysken does not see the OV patterns as evidence of transfer but rather of movement rules that reflect 'stylistic' (i.e. discourse) considerations. Yet, just as there were in the case of HPE, there are reasons to question the discourse-based explanation of the OV patterns in Andean Spanish. First, although Muysken appeals to 'stylistic' considerations, he provides no discourse analysis (such as that developed by Givón, 1983, and others), which could determine just how often discourse factors encourage the placement of object nouns before verbs. Second, the data in both his study and that of Luján *et al.* (1984) suggest that the least proficient speakers of Spanish use OV patterns the most. This statistical tendency is very similar to that seen in the study of HPE by Bickerton and Givón (1976). One explanation for that tendency is obviously transfer. Another explanation – and one that Muysken would presumably favor – is that the least proficient speakers would be the most likely to make use of 'stylistic' OV patterns even if OV patterns are rare in their native language. However, that explanation is dubious in the light of the data in Table 4.4 showing that the speaker of basilect Philippine English made almost no use of OV patterns. Another difficulty with Muysken's 'stylistic' explanation is seen in statistics provided by Luján *et al*. The speakers who used OV patterns the most were 5-year-old children. If their use of those patterns was primarily 'stylistic', that would contradict other findings indicating that learners around the age of 5 show a great deal of 'syntactic conservatism', i.e. such learners are not likely to use word-order shifts such as from VO to OV for 'stylistic' reasons (Zobl, 1983).

Pidgin Fijian

A pidginized variety of Fijian seems to have been spoken from the mid-19th century onwards (Siegel, 1987). First used as a *lingua franca* among Fijians, Europeans, and islanders from other parts of the Pacific, it assumed new forms when used by immigrants from India, who started coming to Fiji about a century ago. Some descriptions of Fijian characterize the basic word order in the language as VOS, although Siegel sees word order in Fijian as highly variable. On the other hand, the pidginized form of Fijian spoken by most groups has had, according to Siegel, a rigid SVO order. SVO is probably the order that Indians would most frequently hear (and thus take to be the syntactic target). Siegel found that Fijians prefer to communicate with Indians in a form of Pidgin Fijian. The Pidgin Fijian of Indians uses SVO, but SOV sentences also occur, such as in Example (9):

Example (9)
koau dua na bisniss Sa rawa tiko
I one business can have
I can have a business.[7]

Siegel attributes the SOV pattern to the influence of the Hindustani spoken in Fiji. The status of both Fijian and Hindustani reflects a rather complex language-contact situation, and space does not permit an extended discussion. However, Siegel's description of the contact situation suggests that other types of substratum (and perhaps borrowing) transfer involving word order are not unusual in the languages spoken in Fiji.

Other Cases of Basic Word-order Transfer

Borrowing transfer

The cases of basic word-order transfer listed in Table 4.2 pertain more to issues of language attrition and thus are less directly relevant to transfer in SLA and Foreign Language Learning. Nevertheless, the word-order changes evident in these cases show effects of transfer in bilingual communities and thus have implications for second language research. The case of Dyirbal will serve as a useful illustration of how some changes proceed. Schmidt (1985) presents a very detailed analysis of the changes that have taken place in Dyirbal, and among these shifts is an increasing use of word order that reflects influence from English. In Traditional Dyirbal, subjects of transitive verbs normally are marked with an ergative case inflection, and this case-marking of transitive subjects (such inflected subjects are designated with the letter A in the sentence patterns) is sometimes seen in Young People's Dyirbal. However, while the more proficient Dyirbal children continue to make frequent use of the AOV pattern (Example (10)) common in Traditional Dyirbal, the less proficient speakers have come to use AVO much more, as well as to drop the ergative inflection (Example (11)).

Example (10)
jugumbil-du nyalnga bura-n
woman-ERG child see-NONFUT
The woman sees the child.

Example (11)
jugumbil bura-n nyalnga
woman see-NONFUT child
The woman sees the child.

Another sign of word-order change due to influence from English is that young speakers depend much more on AOV and AVO. In Traditional Dyirbal, word order was rather flexible, with OAV and AOV being the most common but by no means the only possible word orders (cf. Dixon, 1972; Schmidt, 1985). The dependence on rigid word order that has developed in Young People's Dyirbal may support Rutherford's claim that word-order rigidity is a transferable property.[8]

The use of SVO order in Mauritian Bhojpuri reflects the influence of the creole spoken in Mauritius. Speakers of Bhojpuri who emigrated from India in the 19th and 20th centuries have increasingly come to use the creole, which has a basic SVO order. As a result of bilingualism the traditional SOV pattern of Bhojpuri has weakened (Domingue, 1971). A similar change seems to be taking place in Cairo Nubian, an SOV language, although details provided by Rouchdy (1980) are rather sketchy. Nevertheless, Rouchdy offers evidence that the SVO patterns seen in Cairo Nubian show the influence of Arabic/Nubian bilingualism.

Other cases of language contact

The cases in Table 4.3 are also examples of word-order change due to transfer, although the historical circumstances of the language contact leading to transfer are not entirely clear. Indo–Portuguese was a creole that developed on the coasts of India and Sri Lanka during the centuries of contact between Asians and Europeans in several colonial enclaves. In two descriptions of local varieties of Indo–Portuguese, Schuchardt (1883b, 1889) noted examples of SOV and other verb-final sentences. In his account of one of these varieties, the Indo–Portuguese spoken in Diu in Gujarat, Schuchardt (1883b) was hesitant about attributing to transfer the peculiarities of grammar and pronunciation that he found; nevertheless, his description in that article of the SOV word order in Hindustani indicates that he considered basic word-order transfer a likely explanation for the SOV sentences that he listed. One problem with Schuchardt's data is an uncertainty about who the speakers were. They may have been native speakers of Indo–Portuguese, or Hindustani, or Gujarati, or Malayalam, the latter being a probable source of the SOV examples from Mahé and Cannanore cited by Schuchardt (1889). Other evidence, however, gives much support to Schuchardt's intuitions about transfer.

A detailed investigation by Dalgado (1906) of the Indo–Portuguese of Diu and other northern enclaves also turned up SOV sentences. According to Dalgado, such sentences were especially common in spontaneous speech. Other evidence comes from an investigation by Smith (1977) of a dialect of Sri Lankan Portuguese Creole. Although the focus of his study was phonology, Smith cited SOV order as an instance of grammatical transfer occasioned by speakers' knowledge of Tamil (an SOV language). Neither in Smith's investigation nor in the earlier studies is it clear whether the instances of SOV order reflect substratum or borrowing transfer – or both. However, the evidence from as far north as Diu and as far south as Sri Lanka points to the effects of crosslinguistic influence in Indo–Portuguese.

Evidence from Amharic also points to crosslinguistic influence on word order. Most scholars who have worked on Amharic and other

Semitic languages of Ethiopia, which are known as Ethiopic languages, believe that the SOV order in those languages reflects a change due to contact centuries ago between speakers of Ethiopic and Cushitic languages (Leslau, 1945). Modern Cushitic languages, such as Galla, are generally SOV whereas most of the ancient and modern Semitic languages outside Ethiopia have been SVO or VSO. Accordingly, Amharic seems to be a textbook case of structural change due to language contact (Comrie, 1981). Nevertheless, extremely little is known about the people, the specific languages they spoke, or the nature of the language-contact situation that led to the development of Amharic word order (Leslau, 1945). As in the case of Indo–Portuguese, it is not clear whether the instances of SOV order reflect substratum or borrowing transfer. Thomason and Kaufman (1988), however, suggest that the Ethiopian contact situation involved both types of transfer.

Further south in East Africa is a contact zone between the Cushitic and Bantu languages. In some areas of this zone, speakers of Cushitic languages have learned Bantu languages, and it appears that some of the ensuing bilingualism has led to a hybrid known as Ma'a (also known as Mbugu). Though there has been some controversy over the classification and origins of Ma'a, there is little question that Ma'a shows many characteristics of both the Cushitic and Bantu languages (Goodman, 1971). Its basic word order (SVO) is that of neighboring Bantu languages whereas much of its basic vocabulary is Cushitic. According to Thomason (1983) borrowing transfer can best account for the language mixture. Her argument is essentially that Ma'a is the modern version of an earlier Cushitic language that became increasingly influenced by the word order and morphology of the surrounding Bantu languages as a result of Cushitic/Bantu bilingualism.

Hui is a variety of Chinese spoken by Moslems in several parts of China. A variety of Hui spoken in Gansu province reflects a mixture of Sinitic and Altaic features, including SOV order, which Li (1984) considers to be the result of substratum transfer from an Altaic language. Although Mandarin does make use of SOV as well as SVO patterns, SVO is still the predominant order according to Li and also according to Sun and Givón (1985). In contrast, the Gansu variety of Hui relies primarily on SOV and on morphological and phonological devices much more characteristic of Altaic than of Sinitic languages. Little is known, however, about the specific Altaic language(s) involved in the contact situation.

Explanations for the Infrequency of Word-order Transfer

The counter-examples presented thus suggest that there is no universal constraint on the transfer of basic word order. In the light of so many counter-examples, there might seem to be little reason for doubting that basic word-order transfer is a very common phenomenon in language-contact situations. Nevertheless, the vast amount of research on bilingualism shows relatively few examples of such transfer. There is more than one possible explanation for the apparent scarcity. Metalinguistic awareness seems to be a constraint on the frequency of word-order transfer, as suggested earlier, but there are at least two other possible explanations (and these explanations are not mutually exclusive). Accordingly, before metalinguistic awareness is discussed, the other two possibilities will be considered.

Language universals

Universals may indeed play a role similar to what Rutherford and Zobl have hypothesized. Research on language universals contains many instances of 'universal tendencies' where data from most but not all languages corroborate a generalization, e.g. the tendency for SOV languages to employ postpositions (Greenberg, 1966). Refinements of Greenberg's analysis by Hawkins (1983) have proven useful not only for a general understanding of word order but also for an understanding of basic word-order transfer in Andean Spanish (cf. Luján *et al.*, 1984; Zobl, 1986a). It is indeed possible that a similar analysis would be useful for understanding word-order change seen in languages such as Cairo Nubian. Nevertheless, the fact that there is no absolute bar to any kind of word-order transfer indicates that it is desirable to consider other possible explanations for the infrequency of basic word-order transfer. The explanatory value of universalist analyses cannot be ascertained until the merits of other explanations are also understood.

Observational problems

In comparison with universalist approaches, a second explanation is more prosaic, but perhaps more important. The seeming infrequency of basic word-order transfer may simply reflect insufficiencies in the data available to linguists. One aspect of this problem is related to language proficiency. In the studies of Bickerton and Givón and of Lujan *et al.*, the least proficient speakers showed the greatest use of native-language SOV and OV patterns. If there is a definite relation between proficiency and basic word-order transfer, observers may have to make a special effort to detect the phenomenon: speakers with minimal second-language proficiency are often shy and ashamed of the way they speak. (Schmidt, moreover, notes a similar difficulty in working with speakers of a drastically altered language like Young People's Dyirbal.)

Another aspect of the observational problem is the dearth of research on some important aspects of second language acquisition. In the many decades of study of language contact both inside and outside the classroom, adult speakers with extremely little proficiency in a language have only recently received much attention. Even now the number of studies that have looked at basic word-order transfer in the early stages of acquisition is very small. Researchers often lack access to a large, homogeneous group of individuals who have only minimal proficiency in the target language. Rutherford (1983), for example, seems to have based his claim about the non-transferability of basic word order on the writing of Japanese college students in California whom he considered to be beginners. However, English is a required subject for all pre-college students in Japan (Conrad & Fishman, 1977); it thus is probable that the Japanese students observed by Rutherford were not really beginners, despite their relative lack of proficiency in English.

Still another observational problem is related to the fact that many languages have relatively flexible word orders. In cases where both the native and target language allow a great deal of flexibility, documenting any transfer might prove difficult even though basic word order in the two languages differs. For example, both Turkish and Serbian make use of most of the six permutations of basic word order: VSO, SVO, SOV, OSV, OVS and VOS (Slobin, 1982). While the basic word order of Turkish is SOV and that of Serbian is SVO, the extreme flexibility of word order in both languages would make it difficult to document negative transfer in a case, for example, of a Turk learning Serbian. A study of differences in the frequency of each of the six permutations, or a study of violations of discourse constraints on word order in the target language, might show negative transfer but the difficulties of such a study should not be underestimated: aside from the problems created by the complex relations between syntax and discourse, such a study would require a very large data base. While positive transfer is also possible – indeed likely – it would also be hard to establish since success in acquiring word order could also be attributed simply to exposure to the target language.

Metalinguistic awareness

Aside from universals and observational problems, metalinguistic awareness may be a very important reason for the apparent scarcity of basic word-order transfer. That is, learners may be somewhat conscious of basic word order both in their native language and in the target language, and that consciousness could aid in the acquisition of the target-language word order, or at least in the avoidance of native-language word order if that order is different. There does exist some evidence that word order is a structural characteristic rather *accessible* to consciousness. This does not mean that word order, or any other accessible structure, is always automatically available as *explicit knowledge* (Odlin, 1986): in many cases training may be necessary. Many native speakers of English are probably not consciously aware, for example, of the difference often found in the position of the modal auxiliary in declarative and interrogative word-order patterns (e.g. *You can swim* versus *Can you swim?*). Yet while some training would probably be necessary to make native speakers aware of this difference, it seems likely that such training would require less time than, for example, training people to be aware of the differences in the prescriptive usage of *who* and *whom*.

There is a diverse array of evidence pointing to the accessibility of word order under certain conditions. A study of the metalinguistic awareness of children (Hakes, 1980) indicates that children as young as five can reliably judge as ungrammatical sentences that violate English word-order rules; at the same time, children of that age have difficulty with sentences that require some awareness of sub-categorization rules and selectional restrictions. In a study of adults in a non-literate society, Heeschen (1978) noted that individuals generally made unreliable judgements about sentences that involved violations of verb morphology but that the same individuals proved quite capable of making reliable judgements about sentences that involved violations of word order. In at least one case, the use of a transfer-based word order has become a marker of negative social prestige: Spanish speakers in Lima sometimes use SOV order to mimic and deride Indians and mestizos in the Quechua-speaking hinterlands of Peru (Carol Klee, personal communication).

The accessibility of word order is also evident in a study of individuals' awareness of transfer-based errors in ESL (Odlin, 1996). Korean/English bilinguals in the study were very successful in identifying English word-order errors characteristic of Korean speakers, and Spanish/English bilinguals were very successful in identifying word-order errors characteristic of Spanish speakers. For example, a stereotypical Korean word-order error might be *She fell in love with a different country man*, 'a man from a different country'; a stereotypical Spanish word-order error might be *The car is the transportation system most popular*, 'the most popular transportation system'.[9] Significantly, very few Koreans thought that the Spanish errors were characteristically 'Korean' and very few Spanish speakers thought that the Korean errors were characteristically 'Spanish'. Moreover, the judgements that Korean and Spanish speakers made of word-order errors were more consistent than, for example, their judgements of article errors.

While the evidence thus suggests that word order is highly accessible, there are constraints on accessibility. For example, in languages such as Dutch and German the number of word-order rules is large, with some rules involving intricate structural detail. The complications that multiple rules of any kind engender are formidable, and, as Bialystok (1979) has shown, rules involving a substantial amount of structural detail are not very accessible. Not surprisingly, then, studies of the acquisition of Dutch and German show frequent examples of word-order errors with many of the errors attributable to crosslinguistic influence (Andersen, 1984; Jansen *et al.*, 1981).

There may also be typological constraints, and Zobl's analysis of 'central' and 'peripheral' traits may thus have implications for accessibility. It seems plausible that peripheral traits in a word-order typology (e.g. the placement of adverbs) would be less accessible and that errors involving the placement of adverbs or other peripheral constituents would therefore prove harder for learners to monitor. Yet while there may be some relation between typology and accessibility, word-order accessibility is not simply a function of formal parameters. Empirical work by Bock and Warren (1985) suggests that the accessibility of word order is not rooted in formal principles such as serial order but in the functional role of constituents in basic clause structure. That is, people may easily access patterns such as SOV and SVO because the semantic information in subjects and objects is generally crucial to discourse processing (see also Odlin, 1986).

Another reason why formal principles alone cannot explain accessibility is the considerable variation in individuals' metalinguistic abilities. Individuals who know two languages are likely to show more awareness than individuals who know only one (Galambos & Goldin-Meadow, 1983; see also Chapter 8). Individuals who can read are likely to show more awareness than individuals who cannot (Scribner & Cole, 1981). And individuals who are in classes where explicit knowledge is often presented will likely know more 'about' language than will individuals acquiring a second language in informal contexts that involve little Foreign Language Learning. No matter what methods are used or how effective the methods are, the pedagogies found in second-language classrooms are likely to involve at least some, and often a great deal of, 'consciousness-raising' (Sharwood Smith, 1981).

One type of awareness that is especially likely to develop in Foreign Language Learning settings is the notion of negative transfer. Even when that term is unknown to language teachers, the concept that it represents is often familiar. Whether through overt correction, or through paralanguage functioning as covert correction, or through questions eliciting clarifications, or through other means still, teachers frequently provide negative feedback. Such feedback does not always deem the cause of an error to be transfer – and, of course, many errors are not due to transfer. Nevertheless, teachers frequently speak or at least know something about the native language of their students and are therefore in a position to identify and warn about transfer errors. In many second-language classrooms, then, one important characteristic of the pedagogy is the teacher's effort to warn students about those structures liable to negative transfer. In the light of the evidence presented earlier on the accessibility of word order, it is likely that the pedagogies used in Foreign Language Learning can make basic word order even more accessible.

The consciousness-raising that occurs in formal instruction may thus put constraints on the possibilities for native-language influence. A study by Trévise (1986) provides evidence of just such constraints on word-order transfer. Trévise notes that while spoken French has quite flexible word-order patterns, French students speaking English are rather conservative in the variety of patterns they use. Some patterns do seem to be the result of transfer: e.g. *I think it's very good the analysis between the behavior of animals and the person*, which has a close translation equivalent in French. However, many of the French patterns that might be transferred did not show up in the conversations recorded by Trévise. The reason why students used only a narrow range of patterns may lie in 'their more or less conscious feeling for the French written standard they were (intensively) taught in school' (Trévise, 1986: 197).

The cautiousness of the students described by Trévise seems related to the formality of linguistic contexts in which standard languages are used. Just as formality may discourage negative transfer, informality may encourage it. Evidence for that possibility is seen in the observation made by Dalgado (1906) that Indo–Portuguese sentences were especially likely to have an OV order in spontaneous language use. Dalgado's observation accords well with the findings of various sociolinguistic studies summarized elsewhere (Odlin, 1989, 2003). Social factors especially relevant to word-order transfer will now be considered.

The Social Context of Transfer

The cases of basic word-order transfer discussed above offer important evidence for the relation between negative transfer and metalinguistic awareness. Table 4.5, which is a synthesis of the information in Tables 4.1 and 4.2, shows the strong likelihood of basic word-order transfer occurring in language-contact situations in which speakers have relatively little metalinguistic awareness. (Since terms such as 'target language' are not appropriate to all seven cases, the languages

Table 4.5 Attested cases of basic word-order transfer

Contact Language X	Contact Language Y	Result
English (SVO)	Japanese/Korean (SOV)	Hawaiian Pidgin English (SOV)*
English (SVO)	Korean (SOV)	Bamboo English (SOV)*
Spanish (SVO)	Quechua (SOV)	Andean Spanish (SOV)*
Fijian (VOS/SVO)	Hindustani (SOV)	Pidgin Fijian (SOV)*
Bhojpuri (SOV)	Mauritian Creole (SVO)	Mauritian Bhojpuri (SVO)**
Dyirbal (OAV, AOV)	English (SVO)	Young People's Dyirbal (AVO)**
Nubian (SOV)	Egyptian Arabic (SVO)	Cairo Nubian (SVO)**

* SVO order is also used.
** SOV order is also used (in Young People's Dyirbal, AOV).

in the first two columns are simply labelled 'Contact Language X' and 'Contact Language Y'.) The social contexts in which learners acquired a knowledge of HPE, Bamboo English, Andean Spanish and Pidgin Fijian were generally informal. Although speakers may have had some formal instruction in the target language, the descriptions of those four contact varieties suggest that informal second-language acquisition prevailed. In the case of Cairo Nubian, Mauritian Bhojpuri and Young People's Dyirbal, the descriptions indicate that there was virtually no formal instruction in the native language. Thus in all seven cases speakers received little or no formal instruction in Contact Language X, and in all seven cases there is evidence of basic word-order transfer due to knowledge of Contact Language Y.

If basic word-order transfer occurs most in contexts involving relatively little metalinguistic awareness, the distinction between *focused* and *unfocused* systems proposed by Le Page and Tabouret-Keller (1985) may be relevant to the distinction between Second Language Acquisition and Foreign Language Learning.

Le Page and Tabouret-Keller claim that in some communities the notion of what constitutes a language is not very sharply defined. For example, in Belize speakers often mix elements of Spanish, English and creole in varying proportions with relatively little concern for what is 'grammatical' or 'ungrammatical'. In contrast, the language of some communities − most typically, communities with a standard language − is highly focused, and the notion of what constitutes grammatical utterances can assume considerable importance. It would be mistaken, however, to equate focused languages and standard languages. In multilingual Indian communities of the Vaupés region in South America studied in the 1960s (Jackson, 1974; Sorenson, 1967), there do not seem to have been distinct linguistic varieties corresponding to the standard-nonstandard oppositions found in many places; nevertheless, members of the Vaupés communities evinced a considerable effort to speak 'correctly' according to norms that had developed despite the absence of formal schooling. For members of the Vaupés communities, 'correctness' included taking great care to avoid mixing languages. As Jackson (1974) notes, speakers often had a strong aversion to using words from several languages; in formal contexts speakers would object to the employment of forms that were not characteristic of a particular focused variety being used. The aversion that Vaupés Indians had to language mixing was due to the close relation between language, kinship systems, and marriage: Indians may only marry speakers of certain languages. Accordingly, linguistic focusing can occur in contexts besides formal language instruction.

In the analysis of Le Page and Tabouret-Keller, the distinction between focused and unfocused varieties is not a dichotomy: some forms of language behavior are simply more focused than others. Accordingly, many of the types of language-contact situations discussed in this chapter can be distinguished in the following manner:

More focus
Foreign Language Learning
Vaupés multilingualism

Less focus
Unstable pidgins
Language attrition

In contrast to Foreign Language Learning, Second Language Acquisition is not classified as either focused or unfocused. While the term 'Foreign Language Learning' is applicable only to contexts that involve considerable metalinguistic awareness, the term 'Second Language Acquisition' is applicable to contexts as diverse as unstable pidgins, multilingualism in the Vaupés region, and also to classroom contexts in which learners acquire some mastery of the target language (i.e. Foreign Language Learning). As one process or strategy in Second Language Acquisition, transfer can occur both in focused and unfocused contexts. However, since negative transfer (including transfer of word order) often leads to language mixing, it may occur more in unfocused contexts in which speakers are not as concerned about linguistic variation.[10]

Summary

Rutherford and Zobl have made strong claims that unambiguous cases of basic word-order transfer do not exist. However, 11 counter-examples suggest that there is no strong universal constraint on the occurrence of basic word-order transfer. Attempts to explain some of the counter-examples as evidence of language-neutral discourse strategies such as topicalization cannot account for all the data (e.g. SOV sentences in Hawaiian Pidgin English) and such attempts do not even seem to account well for many of the tokens that might have a discourse-based explanation (e.g. OV sentences in HPE). Word order is susceptible both to substratum and to borrowing transfer: that is, transfer of basic word order is possible not only in second language acquisition but also in cases of native-language attrition due to language contact.

Despite the existence of basic word-order transfer, examples of it do seem to be somewhat rare. There are at least three explanations, which are not mutually exclusive, for the scarcity of examples of such transfer: probabilistic effects of universal grammatical constraints; observational problems, including insufficient attention to the speech of individuals with low proficiency; and metalinguistic awareness, which makes the basic word order of the native and target languages accessible and which encourages the monitoring of negative transfer. There is evidence suggesting that negative word-order transfer is most likely in situations involving relatively little focusing, i.e. situations in which metalinguistic awareness is relatively low. While Foreign Language Learning involves focused language behavior, Second Language Acquisition may not be inherently focused or unfocused.

Notes

(1)   I would like to thank several people for their valuable comments on the substance and form of this chapter in some of its earlier versions. I am especially indebted to Sarah Grey Thomason for her extensive comments. The chapter has also benefited from comments and other help from John Algeo, Sara Garnes, Elaine Horwitz, Brian Joseph, Carol Klee and Bill VanPatten. Naturally, I take full responsibility for any errors that remain.

(2)   Chapter 1 provides a definition of transfer.

(3)   When the terms *Second Language Acquisition* and *Foreign Language Learning* appear with word-initial capital letters in this chapter, they represent a theoretical distinction in which the former term refers to acquisition that may or may not be guided, while the latter term refers only to contexts involving guided instruction. When these terms are not capitalized, there is no theoretical distinction implied. Similarly, the terms *acquire* and *learn*, not capitalized, do not imply any of the theoretical distinctions often found in the literature.

(4)   The use of X instead of 0 allows for a description of sentence patterns involving other constituents besides objects. For example, the SVX abbreviation can represent certain sentential complements in English, e.g. *I believe that you're right*.

(5)   Mühlhäusler's bibliographical citation of the article by Meisel is inaccurate, and I have not been able to determine what paper by Meisel is the source of the long quotation about word order that Mühlhäusler gives.

(6)   Since no examples of object pronouns occurred in the Korean–English text, Table 4.4 only lists occurrences of nominal objects. Ironically, Givón's analysis downplays the possibility of transfer and instead emphasizes the importance of discourse universals. I do not believe, however, that the data in his tables invalidate any of his claims except for one, namely, that the word order found in basilect pidgins is asyntactic.

(7)   The special (and complex) functions of *na* within the noun phrase and of *sa* within the verb phrase are not marked since discussion of them is not relevant to the issue of basic word order.

(8)   There is, however, another possible explanation for the rigid word order, namely, the declining reliance on bound morphology in Young People's Dyirbal. Word-order rigidity may simply be a compensatory strategy that develops as the reliance on morphology dwindles.

(9)   The two examples given represent the format used in the survey of bilinguals' intuitions. Each sentence with an error was preceded by another sentence to establish a context and each was followed by a correction so that informants would focus on the error in the underlined sentence.

(10)   Positive transfer may occur just as much in focused as in unfocused contexts since such transfer involves a convergence of the source and target languages.

Part 2: Language-specific Processing and Transfer

The notion of a 'transfer process' appears regularly in SLA research but the precise nature of that process remains only partially understood. The presumed process must interact with comprehension, with production, with verbal memory, and with other cognitive processes as well. Theorists in various fields have offered many explanations for these processes, often with models that are (at least in theory) language neutral. A paradox inevitably arises, then, since an adequate model must also accommodate language-specific traits, and, in the case of transfer, those language-specific characteristics deeply interact with presumably pan-linguistic processing patterns. Comprehension and production patterns differ in some respects according to the L1 groups involved. Chapter 5 presents evidence supporting this assertion. Chapter 6 also explores the interaction of cognitive processes but with a particular set of linguistic structures known as focus constructions as the point of departure. Chapter 7 explores a process that often overlaps with transfer: translation. As with the introduction to Part 1, the next three paragraphs summarize in more detail each of these chapters.

In exploring the link between comprehension and production, Chapter 5 compares the written EFL performance of L1 Finnish and L1 Swedish speakers. The analysis identifies very different reproductions of the same input, and the differences indicate crosslinguistic influence. The input, two titles in English in a silent movie, varied in length, with one of the titles being rather short and the other considerably longer. Although the length factor is clear in the case of the longer title, which no one reproduced verbatim in their written synopses of the film scene, very few individuals reproduced verbatim even the much shorter title. Accordingly, the reproductions of the short (and the long) title should not be viewed as attempts at mimicry but rather as reconstructions – and as reconstructions influenced by distinct grammatical patterns in the native languages of the participants. For example, almost none of the reconstructions of the L1-Swedish speakers showed omissions of English articles, but those of the L1-Finnish speakers often did, thus a performance difference consistent with the grammatical facts about Swedish and Finnish. The results offer support for Slobin's theory known as Thinking-for-Speaking which, despite the emphasis on production in the label, also accounts well for transfer-affected comprehension patterns.

Psycholinguistic theories of comprehension inform much of the analysis of Chapter 5, whereas Chapter 6 considers the effects of focus constructions on comprehension largely in terms of Relevance Theory, which allows for insights about pragmatic commonalities in how focus constructions are processed. Even so, the meanings of the constructions vary both within and between languages, and L1-specific meanings sometimes appear in bilinguals' use of the L2 (as seen, for instance, in a word-order shift often termed Yiddish Movement). Considerable typological variation in focus constructions exists; clefting, word-order shifts, and focus particles are three major formal types. All three are involved in specific cases of crosslinguistic influence. Studies of monolingual performance indicate that focus constructions can have special cognitive effects involving attention and memory. Accordingly, certain effects may well also appear in language-contact situations. Crosslinguistic similarity is an important factor encouraging the use of focus constructions in L2 even while transfer in such cases sometimes results in errors. However, the frequency of particular focus structures in L1 discourse also strongly affects transfer, as seen in structures in the English in Celtic lands and in the English of many Swedish speakers. The comparability of focus constructions across languages is a major problem for translators, as well as for linguists and language learners. In some cases, learners may be skeptical about the equivalence of such structures in two languages, and they may therefore be reluctant to use them – and such reluctance may delay or even make impossible the ultimate attainment of the target language. On the other hand, some learners do attempt to use radically different structures of the L1 in the L2, as seen in a remarkable word-order shift in the English of an L1-German speaker.

The relation between transfer and translation has gotten relatively little attention even though the German linguist Hugo Schuchardt recognized its importance in the late 19th century. Chapter 7 focuses on typical instances of translation from one language to another, but a classification by Jakobson acknowledges related behaviors such as rewording within just one language. Most of the chapter considers three topics involving transfer and translation: crosslinguistic equivalences, individual variation, and cognitive processing. With regard to equivalence, certain problems that have dogged machine translation also show the fallibility of some widespread assumptions about translation: e.g. that there are always simple one-to-one correspondences that invariably make finding translation equivalents a straightforward task.

Everyday intuition will give experienced human translators some great advantages over computers for a long time to come. Even so, the pitfalls of transfer-induced misjudgements remain a hazard for translators, who may be imperfect learners of a second language.

With regard to variation, highly proficient bilinguals sometimes differ in how they understand and translate a source text. Variation is also evident among less proficient individuals, who sometimes produce interpretations much too close to the structure of the source language. Even so, some bilinguals contradict the claims in Processability Theory about transfer. The PT model does not allow for the possibility that some learners will first formulate an entire utterance in their L1 and then translate it into the target language. Examples from highly proficient and from less proficient individuals show the reality of transfer and translation intersecting. Experience and proficiency do matter, however, in the way individuals judge whether the forms of one language are practically equivalent to forms in another language. Focus on meaning proves especially important for highly experienced interpreters, and even young bilingual children practicing translations show a growing awareness of relations between languages. Along with evidence from actual learner productions, survey results suggest that translation strategies are very common among L2 learners in school settings.

5 Language Transfer and the Link between Comprehension and Production

Introduction

Understanding a language and using it are the typical practical goals of second language acquisition (SLA). Sometimes, of course, learners may settle for a minimal knowledge of L2 that will enable them, for example, to read it (and perhaps even then only certain kinds of texts). Conversely, users of a foreign language phrasebook may learn just enough to be able to speak a little of the L2, which could help these users sometimes even when they do not understand a spoken reply but do understand gestures or other paralinguistic cues. Yet apart from such cases, the practical goals of listening and speaking and of reading and writing are complementary: that is, comprehension should normally help production, and production can foster encounters with users of the target language that lead to better comprehension. Not surprisingly, the interaction of comprehension and production has prompted interest among researchers looking closely at how proficiency develops (e.g. Izumi, 2003).

While the practical goals are complementary, the complex processes involved in comprehension and in production remain only imperfectly understood, and in the study of the exact ways in which comprehension interacts with production there remains much unexplored territory. One important dimension of the interaction is the role that crosslinguistic influence may play, and a recent study of transfer by Ringbom offers an interesting assessment of the relation:

> Similarity of grammar appears to be especially important in facilitat-ing *learning*..., both learning for comprehension and learning for pro-duction. Lexical similarity, which facilitates the learner's linking words to other formally similar words, is also basic for learning, but may not

work in exactly the same way for comprehension, as comprehension can be merely approximate, and comprehension does not leave a permanent mark in the mental lexicon. (Ringbom, 2007: 17; emphasis in the original)

The similarity that Ringbom alludes to is the set of resemblances seen between two languages, and for Ringbom a high degree of crosslinguistic similarity makes an especially important contribution to the kinds of transfer seen in SLA.

In this chapter, the exact claims seen in the above quotation will not be tested, but the evidence will indeed support Ringbom's position that crosslinguistic similarity in grammar and vocabulary can enhance both comprehension and production, and thus promote learning.

Comprehension and Manifestations of it in Production

Before considering the empirical study of certain consequences of lexical and grammatical similarity, some aspects of comprehension and production warrant attention. As Ringbom notes, comprehension can be less than full, and, apart from imperfect knowledge of a second language, there can be a wide range of reasons for only 'approximate' comprehension, even when the context involves only native speakers. Foss and Hakes (1978: 100–101) make a useful distinction between three levels of comprehension: *structural* (What has the speaker (S) said?), *intentional* (What does S actually want?), and *motivational* (Why does S want it?). One can understand the structural product yet have no clue as to a speaker's (or writer's) intentions or motivations; an obvious example is where two people (be they spies, lovers or bankers) communicate with sentences that say one thing yet actually 'mean' another. The three levels imply that listeners must have the capacity to analyze meanings communicated in relation to all three questions. Such capacity involves both individual mental processes and cultural norms of interpretation (e.g. *Bon appetit!*, which is often used in France before starting a meal). Also relevant to the three-level notion is the complex interaction of the levels (e.g. understanding the intentional correlates of a syntactic pattern). Some work in pragmatics has looked closely at such interaction (e.g. Kortmann, 1991; Wilson & Sperber, 1993; Sperber & Wilson, 1995), and there are certainly implications for transfer research (see also Chapter 6).

Another key aspect of theories of comprehension is the relation to memory. Although memory and comprehension are distinct capacities in many respects, they interact a great deal also. Especially important for this chapter will be the reconstructive nature of some memory processes. A classic psycholinguistic experiment by Loftus and Palmer (1974) well illustrates some aspects of the role of reconstruction in remembering. Participants were shown a film of an accident and later asked, 'About how fast were the cars going when they smashed into each other?' or

'About how fast were the cars going when they hit each other?' or other questions where only the verb denoting the collision was different. In the case of *smash* and *hit*, the former verb elicited significantly higher estimates of the speed of the cars, even though everyone had seen the same film. The different verbs clearly encouraged somewhat different reconstructions of the nonverbal event witnessed.

The notion of cognitive construction also applies when what is to be recalled is linguistic input, whether it is speech or writing. As with the recall of non-linguistic input, productions in response to linguistic input can be seen as reconstructions, and here they may involve both linguistic comprehension and linguistic production. In fact, work on child language and L2 acquisition has employed techniques such as repetition testing and (in the case of literate individuals) dictation. Assessing empirical work on repetition in child language research, Slobin and Welsh conclude that 'sentence recognition and imitation are filtered through the individual's productive linguistic system' (Slobin & Welsh, 1973: 496). In a discussion of both L1 and L2 research, Natalicio likewise stresses that repetition and dictation require 'the full comprehension and production processes—the internalized grammar of expectancy' (Natalicio, 1979: 169). By such analyses, the techniques often elicit more than just mimicking the spoken or written input: changes in the repetitions from what language learners have heard show that the input is not so much copied as reconstructed, and the same result is evident in the difference between the spoken input and written output of dictation. For Natalicio and for Slobin and Welsh, the products evident in dictation and repetition often reflect comprehension processes, and the errors seen in the products can offer insights about how the developing language system interacts with what learners understand. To extend the 'filter' metaphor of Slobin and Welsh to L2 contexts, the interlanguage is the filter (Natalicio's 'grammar of expectancy'). Apart from the testing research, there has also been some attention in SLA to the constructive nature of the comprehension process, where listeners or readers recreate, to some extent, what seems to them to be the form and meaning of what they have heard or read (e.g. Grabe, 2002).

If an interlanguage filter affects how the input to comprehension is used, it quite plausibly has language-specific dimensions whereby the particular target language and native language (and perhaps other previously encountered languages) affect the path from input to comprehension to re-creation and production. In fact, there is already some evidence of the interlanguage having language-specific processing characteristics in various stages of comprehension, from the apprehension of word forms to the re-creation of syntactic structure (e.g. Fender, 2003). The research to be discussed in this chapter accordingly considers the question of whether or not crosslinguistic influence affects the path from input to output. The evidence will show that such influence is strong.

Background on the Two Main Languages of Finland

To demonstrate crosslinguistic influence a variety of methods can be employed but work on the language-contact situation involving Finnish, Swedish and English in Finland has led to an especially promising methodology (Jarvis, 2000; Odlin, 2012). Finland has a bilingual language policy for many purposes, although the relation between Finnish and Swedish is certainly one of a majority language (around 93% native speakers of Finnish) and minority language (around 6% native speakers of Swedish). In the schools, both are taught as first and second languages, and English is normally a required foreign language, even though the details of who may study what language and for how long have varied in the past twenty or thirty years (Ringbom, 1987, 2007).

The main evidence used in this chapter will be data collected in Finland by Jarvis (1998). The methodology that Jarvis used has a number of strengths. His study compared speakers of two quite different languages: Swedish, a Germanic language similar to English in many ways (despite some divergences), and Finnish, a non-Indo–European language showing numerous points of contrast with English. Moreover, the speakers in the Jarvis study had similar social backgrounds, all the participants being students attending schools in Finland. (For brevity, the native Finnish speakers will be called 'Finns' and the native Swedish speakers 'Swedes', although it should be kept in mind that the participants were Finnish citizens.) A third strong point of the Jarvis study is that the data elicited come from performances of a task given to all the participants (details of that task are provided in the next section). Finally, the fact that Jarvis collected data from Finns and Swedes who varied in the number of years they had studied English allows for some inferences about interlanguage development. Table 5.1 summarizes the relevant characteristics of the different groups.

As noted above, there have been changes in when and how long particular languages are studied as second or third languages, and groups such as F9B (Table 5.1), who had an early start with Swedish relative to

Table 5.1 Experimental participant groups

Group	n	L1	Ages	Grade	English instruction	Swedish instruction
F5	35	Finnish	11–12	5	3rd year	None
F7	35	Finnish	13–14	7	5th year	1st year
F9A	35	Finnish	15–16	9	7th year	3rd year
F9B	35	Finnish	15–16	9	3rd year	7th year
						Finnish instruction
S7	35	Swedish	13–14	7	3rd year	5th year
S9	35	Swedish	15–16	9	5th year	7th year

Source: Jarvis (1998).

English, are not so common as they were in earlier decades, as details given by Ringbom (1987, 2007) indicate. Ringbom, a member of the Swedish-speaking minority, considers the socioeconomic and cultural differences between Finns and Swedes to be minimal, and so the results of comparisons that he, Jarvis, and others have made of the two groups' performance in English seem largely due to the linguistic differences and not to socio-cultural factors. The role of these linguistic differences can be assessed in detail because Jarvis collected data not only from the groups described in Table 5.1 but also from native speakers of Finnish, Swedish and English writing in their native languages, and some examples of constructions used by native speakers will be considered in the discussion of the results.

Task and Procedures

The main language task was the same for the non-native speakers of English as well as for the three native-speaker groups. All wrote accounts of certain episodes in the Charlie Chaplin film *Modern*, *Modern Times*, starring himself and Paulette Goddard. The groups described in Table 5.1 wrote their narratives in English, and, as noted, the other native speaker groups wrote narratives in Finnish, Swedish and English (in the latter group, students in the state of Indiana participated). Two scenes of the film were presented in separate segments, first a 5-minute sequence and later a 3-minute sequence. After each sequence, participants were given intervals of about 30 minutes (for the first sequence) and 14 minutes (for the second) to write their narratives. Additional details about the elicitation procedure and materials are provided by Jarvis (1998: 85–93).

The entire film is a silent movie even though it was produced in the 1930s, when sound was available; and in fact there is some music heard but no spoken language. In the two segments viewed there were nine titles with the words of the characters printed on the screen. The two scenes will be referred to as the Rich Lady Scene (RLS) and the Dream Scene (DS). Synopses of the main details appear below.

Rich Lady Scene

Goddard looks in a bakery window and then turns to see the bakery truck, which the baker is just leaving. As Goddard takes a loaf from the truck and runs away, a rich lady comes round the corner and sees what has happened, and she seems to tell the baker (although there is no title yet). In her dash away, Goddard collides with Chaplin. When the baker goes after Goddard, he tells a policeman (in a title) that she took the bread. Chaplin then says (in a title) that he himself did. After the policeman starts to take Chaplin away, with Goddard being left free, the rich lady says to the baker, 'It was the girl, not the man.' The baker and the lady approach the policeman and both seem to tell him this (although no title is used at this point). The policeman then releases Chaplin and takes Goddard.

Dream Scene

After Chaplin as well as Goddard got arrested, they managed to escape. As they sit on a grassy space, they dream of a happy life together, complete with a house and orange trees. At the end of this reverie, Chaplin says in a title, 'I'll do it! We'll get a home even if I have to work for it.'

Results

In both the scenes just described, the words of the titles made an impression on many Finns and Swedes, who attempted to quote them or to use at least some of the words in reported speech (often preceded by words such as *said that*). The actual words of the titles in question are these:

RLS: 'It was the girl, not the man.'
DS: 'I'll do it! We'll get a home even if I have to work for it.'

As will be seen, the attempts at using words or paraphrases are often not successful in terms of verbatim accuracy, but virtually every attempt offers insights. If comprehension and production of the information in the titles were completely independent of the native language of the writers, there should be no difference in the grammatical patterns used by the Finns and Swedes in supplying the information. However, the results of the analysis indicate that there are in fact considerable differences, differences that correspond to particular patterns in Finnish and Swedish. By the same token, the results indicate that reproducing the information of the titles was not a mere parroting of the words. In the case of the RLS only two Finns and two Swedes reproduced the words of the title verbatim, and in the case of the DS no one at all did. A more detailed discussion of the implications of this result will follow later in the chapter but, in general, the finding of so few verbatim reproductions will serve as preliminary evidence that the reproductions of the vast majority of Finns and Swedes were reconstructing – not copying – what they had read.

In analyzing the learner-supplied information in the titles, the first step was to determine who used the RLS title or the DS title information at all. In general, identifying the use of such information proved easy, but an illustration of some of the decisions that had to be made will prove helpful. The following comes from the first part of the narrative of a ninth-grade Finn (F9A 04), with misspellings and other errors retained:

Young girl walk a town.
She gomes to the breadshop.
She is hungry.

She see how man take bread at the breadbil [the bakery truck] and go in.
She steal a bred.
Old woman see everything and tell a shopkeeper.
Shopkeeper tell a polis ho [who] goes stoping a rober.
Girl run stright on Chaplin.
They fall, and polise rest a rober.
Girl say police att [that] she isn't a rober.
Chaplin say, 'She didn't do it, I did.'
Polie rest Chaplin men old woman tell shopkeeper, 'That's not a man, it's woman.'

The first italicized line in the narration does not contain information derived from the title 'It was the girl, not the man' but rather from an earlier one ('She stole a loaf of bread'). However, the second italicized line does constitute a reproduction (albeit with lexical and grammatical errors) of the information in 'It was the girl, not the man'. Only those cases were counted where the information given by the student indicated a use of that particular title. In the example, the errors involving *a man* and *woman* with no article are, incidentally, characteristic of many reproductions of the Finns and will be discussed later in this chapter.[1]

Analysis of the use of the information in the RLS title

In the case of the RLS, the information used thus involved reports about who really stole the bread: Goddard, not Chaplin. Table 5.2 details, according to group, the use of the information. With the exception of the F5 learners, who had only two years of English, the various groups showed a high use of the information: about 80% or more of the individuals in the other L1-Finnish groups, and both of the Swedish groups showed almost identical rates of use. As for those who did not use the information in any of these groups, it would be unsound to conclude that they did not understand the information in the title although, of course, there is not any evidence either that they did understand. In any event, the title in the RLS proved accessible for most of the learners in most of the groups, and so it proves relatively easy to compare what these groups did with the same information.

Table 5.2 Information from title in the RLS used or not used, by number of Finns and Swedes

	F5	F7	F9A	F9B	S7	S9
Used	23	27	28	28	28	30
Not used	12	8	7	7	7	5

Table 5.3 Cleft sentences used, by number of Finns and Swedes

F5	F7	F9A	F9B	S7	S9
1	3	2	3	11	12

One indication that the Finns and Swedes made different use of the information is the different rates of occurrence of cleft sentences such as *It was the girl, who stole the bread* (S7 04). Swedish learners frequently produced them in using the title information to indicate contrast in the RLS, and the results in Table 5.3 are consistent with analyses of transfer and focus constructions (see also Chapters 3 and 6). The high proportion of cleft sentences among Swedes is especially striking in view of the difference of years of study: the S7 group had only two years of English yet the students in this group who produced clefts outnumbered by more than five to one the F9A group, who had had six years of English.

As noted earlier, native speakers wrote accounts of the same episodes in their native languages. Interestingly, the native speakers of English rarely used cleft sentences in the RLS. Out of 66 individuals, 47 used the information in the RLS, but only two opted for cleft sentences. In contrast, the Swedes often used cleft sentences in their native language. Out of a total of 44 individuals writing in Swedish, 36 used the information in the RLS, and of these 36, some 24 used a cleft pattern to identify who stole the bread: e.g. ...*det var kvinnan som stal brödet*... (it was the woman who stole the bread, SX 12) and ...*det var flickan som tog det och inte mannen* (it was the girl who took it and not the man, SY11, with the SX and SY designating different native speaker groups, and the numbers referring to different individuals in these groups). The formal patterning and also the pragmatic functions of clefts in Swedish are similar to what is found in English clefts, and so the crosslinguistic similarity is consistent with a transfer explanation for the Swedes' use of the structure. Further support for seeing the results as evidence of transfer comes from occasional errors in specific forms used by certain Swedes (see Chapter 6).

Although formal similarity helps explain the Swedes' use of clefts in the English accounts of the RLS, frequency of the cleft pattern in L1 Swedish also matters a great deal. One sentence in the L1 Finnish accounts of the RLS shows that Finnish also has an appropriate cleft pattern that can be used: ... *kyllä se oli se nainen joka sen leivän varasti*... (indeed it was that woman who the bread stole, FY 20). However, this use proved the exception, not the rule, in the L1 Finnish accounts. Out of a total of 66 Finns writing in their native language, 53 individuals reported the details of the RLS about who stole the bread, and yet only one person used a cleft – the case cited above. Perhaps the extremely rare appearance of the cleft pattern should not seem surprising, given that Finnish relies heavily on other devices, especially

Table 5.4 Rich Lady Scene: NP types used in pairs contrasting Chaplin and Goddard

Proper noun	...the girl stole a bread, not *Chaplin*
Pronoun	...'*she* stole the bread'
Demonstrative and noun	It wasn't *that man*, it was the girl.
Definite article and noun	It wasn't that man, it was *the girl*.
Indefinite article and noun	'It wasn't *a man*. It is *a lady*'.
Zero and noun	It wasn't *man*. It was the girl!

word order, to achieve focus. In any case, the difference in the use of clefts by Finns writing in Finnish and Swedes writing in Swedish proves statistically significant ($\chi^2 = 47.8$, df 1, $p < .001$).

It should be noted that the native-speaker groups did not consist of the same individuals as the groups writing in English. Even so, the results in Tables 5.2 and 5.3 show that three of the four Finnish groups used the information about as much as the Swedes did, but they used the cleft pattern far less. As with the difference between Finns and Swedes writing in their native languages, a chi-square test indicates that the distribution of results in Table 5.3 is statistically significant ($\chi^2 = 22.1$, df 5, $p < .001$), and the lopsided pattern is thus attributable to frequent influence from L1 Swedish on individuals in the S7 and S9 groups.

Besides clefts, another way to indicate the contrast between Chaplin and Goddard in the RLS is through pairs of noun phrases (NP) juxtaposed in the same clause or contiguous clauses (and indeed the actual wording of the RLS title is one example: 'It was the girl, not the man'): Finns and Swedes used a variety of NP types (including erroneous ones), as seen in Table 5.4: a proper noun (usually *Chaplin* or *Charlie*), a pronoun, a noun with a demonstrative determiner, a noun with either a definite or (erroneously) an indefinite article, or a noun with the article erroneously omitted (the omission being termed a *zero article*).

Finns and Swedes differed greatly in the use of zero and indefinite articles. In Table 5.5 the number of pairs of NP references to Chaplin and Goddard used in each group of Finns appears in the first row while

Table 5.5 NP types used by Finns in pairs contrasting Chaplin and Goddard

	F5	F7	F9A	F9B	Total
NP pairs	19	14	9	17	59
Proper	2 (5%)	2 (7%)	1 (5%)	4 (11%)	9 (7%)
Pronoun	2 (5%)	1 (3%)	0 (0)	2 (5%)	5 (4%)
Demonst.	6 (15%)	2 (7%)	3 (16%)	1 (2%)	12 (10%)
Def. Art.	10 (26%)	14 (50%)	8 (44%)	20 (58%)	52 (44%)
Indef.	8 (21%)	6 (21%)	4 (22%)	3 (8%)	21 (17%)
Zero	10 (26%)	3 (10%)	2 (11%)	4 (11%)	19 (16%)
NP total	38	28	18	34	118

in the last row a figure twice the value appears. For example, in the F5 group 19 individuals produced referential pairs (e.g. *It wasn't that man, it was the girl*), and so there were 38 references (19 to Chaplin and 19 to Goddard). There were two proper noun references in this group, thus about 5% of the total 38, while there were 10 references with a definite article (which thus correctly reproduce the determiner in the title), and thus about 26% of the total. Errors with an indefinite article constituted 21% of the total while zero articles constituted 26%. The F7 and F9A groups used fewer zero articles, and the percentages for tokens showing the correct definite article are larger: 50% and 44%. Remarkably, the percentage is even higher in the F9B group (who had only two years of English but six years of Swedish), with a figure of 58%. This group also had a much lower error rate in using an indefinite article (8%) than did the other three groups.

As Table 5.6 indicates, the Swedes far more often produced the correct definite article in the same references, and their sentences almost never show errors involving either indefinite articles or zero articles.[2] Like English, Swedish has definite and indefinite articles whereas Finnish has neither, and so positive transfer from Swedish seems clear. The Swedes' greater success also suggests a role for positive transfer in the greater success of the F9B group (who had six years of L2 Swedish) in comparison with the other Finns in producing definite articles and avoiding indefinite articles. As for zero articles, the incidence among the F9B group is no different from the F7 or F9A groups although it shows greater success compared with the F5 group, who had likewise had only two years of English.

The frequent use by Finns of indefinite articles in the title information of the RLS suggests that these learners have not yet understood the meaning difference between *a* and *the*. However, the incomprehension does not arise from any absence of definiteness as a meaning category in Finnish (Chesterman, 1991), and so it is doubtful as to whether any kind of conceptual transfer is involved (cf. Han, 2010; Jarvis, 2002; Jarvis & Pavlenko, 2008; Odlin, 2008). The use of zero

Table 5.6 NP types used by Swedes in pairs contrasting Chaplin and Goddard

	S7	S9	Total
NP pairs	16	6	22
Proper	1 (3%)	1 (8%)	2 (4%)
Pronoun	3 (9%)	0 (0)	3 (6%)
Demonst.	1 (3%)	0 (0)	1 (2%)
Def. Art.	26 (81%)	10 (83%)	36 (81%)
Indef.	1 (3%)	0 (0)	1 (2%)
Zero	0 (0)	1 (8%)	1 (2%)
NP total	32	12	44

likewise does not indicate any absence of definiteness in the Finns' L1 but rather insufficient awareness of the usually obligatory mapping of definiteness meanings onto articles in English. In contrast, the Swedes nearly always prove sensitive to the mapping requirements, which are similar in their native language.

Analysis of the use of the information in the DS title

While the above analysis of responses to the title in the RLS indicates clearcut transfer effects related to the link between comprehension and production, the performance of Finns and Swedes with other titles in *Modern Times* also provides evidence of transfer but with complications. The somewhat different results are evident in an apparently greater difficulty of the Dream Scene title 'I'll do it! We'll get a home even if I have to work for it!' Table 5.7 shows that far fewer individuals in each group used the information of this title. The main source of difficulty is probably the large number of words in the title, a factor that would likely affect the Swedes as well as the Finns. Indirect support for this interpretation comes from work on repetition and dictation that indicates that length is a factor (Natalicio, 1979: 174–175). More direct support comes from the fact no one at all reproduced the exact words of the title even though a small but equal number of Finns (two) and Swedes (two) managed to reproduce the words of the RLS title, which is much shorter. For the Dream Scene the result is the same even when the count of reproductions was limited to how many students correctly reproduced just the second sentence in the title (i.e. 'We'll get a home even if I have to work for it!'). That is, no one provided a verbatim reproduction of this sentence.

Despite the difficulty of the DS title, Swedish influence seems to have helped, as did years of study of English. Swedes with four years of English (S9) used title information the most, whereas Finns with only two years of English and no Swedish (F5) used it the least. It also seems that years of study and Swedish influence are largely independent factors, since Finns with six years of English study (F9A) used the title more than any other group of Finns yet the second highest group was F9B, which had only two years of English study but six years of Swedish. The importance of Swedish influence is also suggested by the S7 group, which had only two years of English yet used the information almost

Table 5.7 Information from title in the DS used or not used, by number of Finns and Swedes

	F5	F7	F9A	F9B	S7	S9
Used	5	14	19	17	9	21
Not used	30	21	16	18	26	14

Table 5.8 Use of the subordinating conjunction *if* by Finns and Swedes

F5	F7	F9A	F9B	S7	S9
1	1	8	4	7	13

twice as often as the F5 group. As in the case of the RLS, the simple non-use of information in the title of the DS cannot be equated with non-comprehension. Even so, the difference in use of the two titles is striking and suggests that the DS title was much harder to process.

When Swedish influence aided in the comprehension of the DS title, as the results for S7, S9 and F9B suggest, the facilitating effects were probably more global than local: that is, no single structural similarity between Swedish and English will likely explain the entire facilitating effect. Nevertheless, there are some specific differences in the performance of Finns and Swedes in reproducing the title information that are due to differences in Finnish and Swedish. Among those learners who did use information from the title, there is a remarkable difference in the presence of the subordinating conjunction *if* for Finns and Swedes, with the former tending to use it less, as seen in Table 5.8, a pattern that proves to be statistically significant ($\chi^2 = 19.1$, *df* 5, *p* <.005).

While Table 5.8 indicates that Swedish confers an advantage in processing *if*, the analysis is necessarily complicated for a number of reasons. One is that in a few cases a different subordinating conjunction besides *if* appears, as in *They dream little while about own house. Chaplin promise that he will get* [a house] *for them altought* [sic] *he must go to work* (F9A 23). These cases are rare, however, and straightforward to interpret (and they are counted as instances of using the information in the title). More challenging are the several instances involving the word *even*, which accompanies *if* in the title and which counts as an adverb in the target language. However, in several cases only *even* is present: e.g. *After that dreaming Charlie deside* [sic] *that he get home* [for] *them, even he have work for it* (F9B 33). Another possibility, but one consistent with the target language, is for *if* to appear but without the *even*, as in *Chaplin says – We can have a home – if I have work for it* (F5 14). The three possible outcomes involving *even* and *if* pattern differently in the writing of the Finns and Swedes, as seen in Table 5.9. The chi-square test of the distribution in

Table 5.9 Use of *even if*, *even* (and no *if*) and *if* (and no *even*) in the DS title

	Finns	Swedes
even if	11	17
even	9	0
if	3	3

the table indicates a non-random response pattern despite the nearly equal number of Finns and Swedes supplying one of the three choices ($\chi^2=10.0$, $df\,2$, $p <.01$),

No Swede used *even* without *if*, in contrast to nine Finns. The omission of *if* by several Finns suggests that they did not understand its meaning or its syntactic status as a subordinating conjunction. Perhaps some other test would indicate that these learners have at least a passive understanding of what *if* means, but it cannot be said that the conjunction is part of their productive interlanguage vocabulary. Neither partial nor complete incomprehension is necessarily attributable to Finnish influence – not knowing vocabulary is simply not knowing. However, the comparative success of the Swedes evident in avoiding the omission of *if* suggests positive transfer from Swedish, but it is transfer where crosslinguistic lexical similarity seems to play an important role. The adverb has a clear cognate in Swedish *även*: e.g. *även om han måste arbeta för det* (even if he must work for it, SX 12). The transparent similarity of the adverbs no doubt makes identifying the English *if* with the Swedish *om* easier and also makes it unlikely that *even* will be considered as anything other than an adverb.

One plausible analysis of the cases of *even* without *if* in Table 5.9 is that the Finns using it thus have erroneously classified *even* as a subordinating conjunction. Re-classifications of words are not unusual in interlanguage, and indeed speakers of fairly similar languages such as English and Spanish may misjudge the grammatical class of a target language word (Odlin & Natalicio, 1982). How much of a role Finnish influence may play in this hypothesized re-classification remains an open question but there is a candidate word in Finnish, *vaikka*, which seems a likely source. *Vaikka* has different translations in different contexts, but one common correspondence is with English *even if*, as in:

Teen	*sen*	*vaikka*	*minun*	*pitäisi*	*mennä*	*yliopistoon*
I-do	it	even-if	I	must	go	to-university[3]

I will do it even if I have to go to the university

Thus *vaikka* can function as a special kind of conjunction, one which functions in clauses that König (1988) terms 'concessive conditionals'. König's analysis details important semantic similarities between ordinary conditionals (typically marked with *if*) and concessives (typically marked with *although*), and his analysis can help in explaining why a learner might use a concessive in recounting the DS as was the case with *altought he must go to work*. In any event, *vaikka* codes a concessive notion (which in English is coded by *even*) and a conditional one (coded in English by *if*). Indeed, many native speakers of Finnish writing in Finnish translated *even if* as *vaikka*, as in this example:

Silloin	*Chaplin*	*lupaa,*	*että*	*hän*	*hankkii*	*heille*	*kodin*
Then	Chaplin	promises	that	he	gets	them	home

vaikka	*hänen*	*pitäisi*	*tehdä*	*töitä*	*sen eteen* (FY 36)
even-if	he		must	do	work it

Then Chaplin promises that he (will) get them a home, even if he has to work for it.

The titles of *Modern Times* were not translated into Finnish, and so the use of *vaikka* in such cases offers an insight into what many Finns (the native speakers in the groups in the research of Jarvis) regard as a valid interlingual identification – and translation – between English and Finnish.

Since *vaikka* codes both a concessive and conditional notion, any Finn not so familiar with the English vocabulary item *if* might conclude that the other form, *even*, would serve as an adequate translation of both the conditional and the concessive element. Such an interpretation is erroneous in terms of the target language norms, of course, but such transfer-induced reinterpretations are evident in the case of other grammatical morphemes, such as those used in the English perfect (Odlin & Alonso-Váquez, 2006). By this analysis, then, the *even* in *even he have work for it* is an interlanguage conjunction despite its status as an adverb in the target language.

Summary of Findings on Transfer

The main empirical findings of this study involve the different patterns of reproduction of the same target language input, with the different patterns reflecting differences between Finnish and Swedish. These patterns include:

- Greater use by Swedes than by Finns of cleft sentences in English to reproduce information from the RLS (and cleft sentences are frequent in the Swedish accounts of this scene).
- Few cases of errors involving articles in the RLS among the Swedes in contrast to frequent errors among the Finns, especially in the inappropriate use of indefinite articles and zero articles. This finding is consistent with the obligatory use of articles in Swedish and the absence of articles in Finnish.
- Greater use of the subordinating conjunction *if* from the DS title by Swedes, whose native language has the closely corresponding conjunction *om* and also has a close phrasal parallel to *even if: även om*.
- Frequent use of *even* as what seems to be a conjunction among the Finns (a pattern probably implicated with the Finnish conjunction *vaikka*).

- A superior performance by Finns with six years of Swedish and only two years of English (the F9B group) in comparison with a group with two years of English but no study of Swedish (the F5 group), in terms of using title information in the RLS and DS titles and also in article use, with such results suggesting L2 → L3 transfer effects.

In general, the similarities between Swedish and English proved helpful in processing target language input and avoiding errors in production. For Finns, the dearth of crosslinguistic similarities seems to have impeded processing and to have occasioned more errors. The evidence thus indicates that the degree of crosslinguistic similarity affects the link between comprehension and production. Put more concisely, the reconstructing of input does not seem immune to transfer.

Implications of Transfer in Comprehension and Production

The empirical findings presented thus offer evidence of crosslinguistic influence on how second language learners use target language input to produce sentences. As with earlier research on dictation and repetition testing, the results in this investigation do not support any claim that reproducing the titles of the Chaplin film involved just mimicry. Indeed, it could be argued that the use of information by Finns and Swedes owes even less to mimicry than might affect performances on repetition or dictation tests. As noted above, there were very few exact reproductions of the wording of the RLS title and none at all of the DS title.

The scarcity of verbatim reproductions points not only to the constructive nature of comprehension processes; it also raises very complex issues of memory, especially issues related to comprehension and acquisition. Although the importance of constructive processes in memory is not in doubt, the exact nature of the processes is unclear, including how they contribute to further acquisition of a second language or to stabilization or what some consider fossilization (cf. Han, 2010; Han & Odlin, 2006; Long, 2003). It is beyond the scope of this chapter to address all the issues in detail, much less offer a detailed model. Nevertheless, the following discussion may help to identify factors that will warrant close study in any future attempts to build or test a model of the role of transfer in the constructive processes of memory, comprehension, production and acquisition.

Central to any specific model should be the broader concerns raised by Slobin in what he and others have called Thinking-for-Speaking (e.g. Cadierno, 2008; Slobin, 1996, 2000). As Slobin puts it, the focus of such concerns is on:

> ...the fact that one cannot verbalize experience without taking a *perspective*, and further, that the language being used favors particular perspectives. The world does not present itself as 'events' to be encoded

in language. Rather, in the process of speaking or writing, experiences are filtered through language into verbalized events. (Slobin, 2000: 107; emphasis in the original)

Slobin argues, furthermore, that the filtering of experience is a language-specific process. Although the label Thinking-for-Speaking suggests that production, not comprehension, is the sole focus of this approach, Slobin asserts:

...we can go at least one step beyond on-line production to examine the *memory* that remains after receiving and processing a verbalized event... Thus while the speaker thinks for speaking, the listener listens for understanding and, ultimately, for remembering. (Slobin, 2000: 126; emphasis in the original)

Following this logic, Slobin proceeds to discuss Listening for Remembering and Reading for Remembering. Unlike in some earlier work (e.g. Slobin, 1996), he does not directly address transfer or other issues of SLA, although he does consider translation. In any case, the picture of memory that Slobin sketches requires attention to concerns specific to transfer in comprehension and memory.

A natural point of departure for considering memory and transfer is the oft-made distinction between long-term memory (LTM) and short-term memory (STM). Different tasks obviously make different demands on LTM and STM, and so while reconstruction is a common thread in dictation, repetition, and reporting titles in the Chaplin film, the differences of the tasks likely mean different relations between different memory capacities (cf. Robinson, 2001). In dictation and repetition, much of the performance depends on STM capacities, but in the narrative task, the demands for recall exceed normal STM capacities. As noted above, the two film segments viewed were 5 minutes and 3 minutes long, and the recall of the words of the RLS and DS titles would be affected not only by the extended intervals of the film segments (and possibly distracting events in them) but also by the intervals given to students to write their narratives (30 and 14 minutes for the writing tasks). In view of just the time factor in the writing tasks, the relation between STM and LTM would probably have to be quite different from the relations in tasks such as dictation and repetition.

While the STM/LTM dichotomy is a helpful point of departure, alternatives to the classic distinction are at least worth keeping in mind. Not all psychologists accept the distinction, and perhaps the more flexible concept of 'working memory' can compensate for the limitations of STM capacity (e.g. Harrington & Sawyer, 1992; Jarvis *et al.*, 2013). By such an analysis, perhaps a learner's retention of the title information remains in the working memory for a longer period than what a conventional model of STM might predict. Furthermore, it may prove best to see the narrative recall tasks as involving a continuum of capacities whereby LTM is not a monolith. Chafe (1973, 1994) views LTM as divisible into 'shallow' (less permanent) and 'deep' (more permanent) capacities. This distinction seems attractive since any acceptable model will have to distinguish the relatively permanent storage of the native language as well as the more stable parts of the interlanguage (IL) from the more 'permeable' (to use a term favored by Selinker, 1992) parts of the IL. Yet it also seems likely that many of the skills needed to reproduce the information in the film titles interact with shallow capacities which produce several possible IL variants. For instance, the highly diverse patterns of NP reference among the Finns seen in Table 5.5 contrast with the more uniform (and accurate) patterns of the Swedes in Table 5.6. In the latter group, the similarity of the L1 and English seems to limit any experimenting with NP structure in the IL. However, the Finns, who find little reliable help from their L1 on how English articles work, employ a wider range of patterns including NPs marked for indefinite articles and zero NPs, patterns that in other contexts would be appropriate recall though not in the case of the RLS title.

Still another alternative to the classic STM/LTM distinction holds that they are not altogether separate even while the former uses activated knowledge and focused attention (e.g. Cowan, 1995: 133–134). Such activation could survive long enough to report recent information such as that in the titles of film scenes. This approach is also compatible with Robinson's emphasis on the role of *rehearsal* in SLA (Robinson, 2003: 655–656). That is, by reproducing input, learners can create new structures that become memory traces in their interlanguage. It is important to note, accordingly, that the whole issue of memory in interlanguage is complicated by the fact that in any task such as the retelling of parts of the Chaplin film the IL of any learners may undergo certain changes because of the task itself. Perhaps, for example, the Finns who seem to believe that *even* is a conjunction had never hypothesized the possibility before. In this case the hypothesis turns out to be false, of course, but it might become a more or less permanent (and perhaps fossilized) part of the interlanguage. Alternatively, some learners might, after trying out their initial hypothesis, decide to consult a bilingual dictionary and thereby arrive at a pedagogically more desirable outcome: i.e. the discovery that *even if*, not *even*, is a better translation of *vaikka*.

New interlanguage structures can and do draw on native-language lexical and grammatical structures as well as on structures in a second language in cases of L3 acquisition (and the performance of the F9B group indeed suggests L2 Swedish influence on L3 English). In either L2 or L3 acquisition, the result may be positive transfer as in the cleft sentences and definite articles of Swedes or negative transfer as in the use of zero articles or *even* by Finns.

Taken altogether, the diverging patterns of Finns and Swedes in this study are compatible with the notion of a language-specific dimension in the reconstruction of L2 input. Although the approach known as Thinking-for-Speaking might seem to focus exclusively on production, it is, as Slobin (2000) has argued, an approach that also has major implications for comprehension and so for the link between comprehension and production. The link is even more complex than the findings in this chapter might suggest. With regard to cleft sentences, for example, issues involving translation are relevant and will be addressed in the following two chapters.

Notes

(1) In the second italicized example, the word *men* is probably not a misspelled attempt to use English *man* but rather an inappropriate use of the Swedish conjunction *men* (= but). Ringbom (1987) offers many examples of Swedish words that L1-Finnish learners use, apparently believing that they are also English words.

(2) Unlike the results for Table 5.3, those for Tables 5.5 and 5.6 involve a wider range of choices, and any inferential statistics would thus be less straightforward. Even so, the figures in the tables are consistent with the results of inferential tests done on zero articles in the same corpus (Odlin, 2012).

(3) Some Finnish grammatical details in this and the following examples have been deliberately ignored in the English glosses for the sake of simplicity, as in the translation of *yliopistoon*, which is not a prepositional phrase but rather an inflected noun.

6 Focus Constructions and Language Transfer

Introduction

As with several other terms in linguistics, the word *focus* means different things to different analysts. For example, it sometimes serves as a synonym for *topic* or *topicalization* (e.g. Keesing, 1991), while at other times it indicates something quite different (e.g. Celce-Murcia *et al.*, 1995). Along with the problem of diverse categories, there is also the problem of comparing focus constructions in different languages (e.g. Comrie, 1981). Attempting to review all the different possible meanings or to develop an entire theory of focus, topic, and related notions, is beyond the scope of this chapter, but a definition of *focus* is nevertheless essential. One given by Carston provides a useful point of departure: 'focus is the syntactic constituent which dominates all the information that contributes directly to relevance' (Carston, 1996: 311).

The last word in Carston's definition is no accident, as her approach is grounded in Relevance Theory (e.g. Wilson & Sperber, 1993). Later in her article Carston illustrates how a particular focus construction known as an *it*-cleft sentence plays a special role in contributing to relevance. She contrasts a simple sentence *A ROTTWEILER bit me* with an *it*-cleft: *It was a Rottweiler that bit me.* According to Carston, the special syntactic structure of the latter sentence 'constrains the sort of context in which it can be appropriately used' (Carston, 1996: 312). The structure leads hearers 'to treat as a background assumption that something bit the speaker and to derive cognitive effects from the information that the entity responsible was a Rottweiler' (1996: 312). The implied meaning (which is certainly one of the cognitive effects) could vary depending on the context, where the sentence might serve, as Carston observes, to forestall a hearer's interpretation that the dog that bit the speaker was a neighbor's Alsatian. Alternatively, the cleft might serve a speaker's aim to persuade the listener of the great danger of Rottweilers. Whatever the context, the *it*-cleft can function as a bridge between the information in the focused constituent and backgrounded information that might be either implicit or explicit in the communicative situation.

The metaphor of a bridge has in fact a fairly long history in discussions of the relation between grammar and meaning, as seen in a study by Haviland and Clark (1974) and in one by Prince (1978), who illustrates the bridge with, among other examples, a *wh*-cleft sentence found in a popular magazine:

> Nikki Crane, 19, does not want to be a movie star. *What she hopes to do is be a star on the horse-show circuit.* (Prince, 1978: 887; emphasis added)

According to Prince:

> ...one cannot know from the first sentence that N.C. wants to do something. When one hears the cleft, however, one simply constructs an inferential bridge—N.C. wants to do something—which is quite compatible with our knowledge of the world and of 19-year-olds. (Prince, 1978: 887)

Although the bridge metaphor helps to understand what focus constructions do, there exist important differences in the types of inferential bridges built with different grammatical structures. Much of Prince's classic article attempts to sort out differences in meaning between *it*-clefts and *wh*-clefts (the latter sometimes called *pseudo-clefts*). With regard to the former type of structure, she identifies subtypes that function quite differently, as will be discussed further on. In subsequent work Prince has attempted to distinguish the differences in other focus constructions as well (e.g. Prince, 1998). Similar efforts have been pursued by others (e.g. Birner & Ward, 1998) for English, but also with comparable work on other languages (e.g. Doherty, 1999, 2001).

Carston formulated her definition of focus broadly enough to accommodate not only specialized structures such as cleft sentences but also simple sentences, which often have a prominent stress on the final constituent as in her example *John invited LUCY* (Carston, 1996: 310). However, the more specialized structures will be the concern of this chapter. Although learning focal stress in simple sentences might itself pose problems for second language learners, there is a much greater challenge posed by *wh*-clefts, *it*-clefts, and other cases that Carston terms 'syntactically marked structures'. Since this chapter will concentrate on such cases, the use of *focus* in the chapter will serve as shorthand for Carston's three-word phrase 'syntactically marked structures'. The main theoretical issue that will be pursued with regard to these structures is crosslinguistic influence. The discussion will show that understanding transfer in this area requires a more detailed understanding of complex problems related to form, meaning, and crosslinguistic correspondences. These problems shape much of the learning environment that teachers must take into account if they wish to develop effective pedagogies.

Before the questions of transfer and pedagogy are addressed, it is necessary to consider variations both within and across languages in forms and meanings. After that survey the discussion will turn to cognitive effects and then to translation equivalence, a problem that both linguists and learners face. The analysis of transfer will review evidence of crosslinguistic influence on focus constructions but also indications of possible limits on such influence. Finally, some implications of the preceding analysis will be considered.

Variation in Forms

A typological survey of forms in focus constructions is now appropriate, after which there will be a complementary survey of meanings. This survey cannot do full justice to the wide range seen crosslinguistically, but it will nevertheless prove useful for the discussion of transfer later in the chapter. In this section the look at other languages will require translations, and the principle for deciding what counts as a focus construction in another language will be if the English translation shows what Carston calls a 'marked syntactic pattern'. This procedure has some theoretical perils (especially since English might somehow seem to be a descriptive norm). However, some of the perils will be examined in the later discussion of translation equivalence (see also Chapter 7). While the following discussion concentrates on diverse morphosyntactic forms, readers should remind themselves of the importance of phonological means of signaling focus or emphasis, such as extra-heavy stress on a word or syllable or, to the contrary, a lowered voice. Of course, such sound signals (or typographical marks such as a word spelled only with capital letters) often interact with morphosyntactic patterns.

The 'marked' syntax that Carston alludes to seems to imply grammatical complexity or at least a departure from the canonical Subject-Verb-Object (SVO) order of simple sentences in English (see also Chapter 4). Syntactic complexity makes cleft sentences quite different: in *it*-clefts there is a formulaic use of *it*, some form of the verb *be* (most often *is* or *was*), then a constituent in the focus position (usually stressed in speech), all of which is seen in *It was a Rottweiler*, and with a relative clause (*that bit me*) completing the cleft. Although the relative does not serve the usual function of such clauses (modification of a noun), it does have formal characteristics of such clauses, including the possible use of a relative pronoun. *Wh*-clefts likewise have syntactically complex patterns, and in addition allow different possible word orders: e.g. *A Rottweiler is what bit me* and *What bit me was a Rottweiler*.

Word-order variation proves important for other focusing structures as well. Various constituents can occur before SV patterns:

The gardeners pulled up every weed. *The flowers* they left undisturbed. (Fronted noun phrase)

The gardeners worked extra hours. *For their trouble*, they were given an extra day off. (Fronted prepositional phrase)

The gardeners promised to finish before the party began, and *finish* they did. (Fronted verb phrase)

The party was a success, but *quiet* it was not. (Fronted adjective phrase)

Birner and Ward (1998: 4–5) list similar examples of 'preposing', to use their term, and another pattern that they term 'postposing': e.g. *They were enormous, those pipes* (p. 6). Apart from the different word order, another difference of the last example from the preceding ones is that the postposed NP makes the same reference that the sentence-initial pronoun does. In preposing there can also be pairs of focused NPs along with pronouns following the verb, as in an example from Prince (1986: 217): *My copy of Antila, I don't know who has it*. Prince and many others see in such cases a 'topicalization' pattern distinct from the preposing patterns already described. Along with preposing and postposing another rearrangement is possible, one which Birner calls *inversion*, e.g.:

Labor savings are achieved because the crew is put to better use than cleaning belts manually: *also eliminated is the expense of buying secondary chemicals*. (Birner, 1994: 233)

Birner defines inversion as the placement of the subject after the verb (*the expense of...* in the example), along with other rearrangements before the verb.

Other languages, especially several in the Celtic, Germanic and Romance branches of Indo–European, show many similarities to English in the grammar of focus constructions. Thus several languages have cleft structures, as in the following italicized example from Swedish (written by a native speaker) which can be translated as an *it*-cleft, the example coming from a database developed by Jarvis (1998) as discussed in Chapter 5. The writer describes a scene in the Charlie Chaplin film *Modern Times*:

Charlie säger då att *det var han som tog brödet*

The literal translation is:

Charlie says then that *it was he who took bread-the*

In the discourse context of the film, Chaplin is trying to divert suspicion about the theft from a starving woman to himself.

Spanish also has structures quite similar to English clefts, as in the following example:

> ... lo que es absoluatamente claro es que en un mundo globalizado las lenguas de relación internacional van a ser muy pocas. (Gabilondo, 2002: 6)

Literal translation:

> ...what is absolutely clear is that in a world globalized, the languages of relation international go to be very few.

The *lo que* form is quite common in Spanish and is often translatable as *what*. As the literal translation indicates, very few changes would be needed to produce an acceptable English version.

While many languages rely heavily on clefting, others such as Russian intensively exploit another formal resource: word-order permutations. In Russian, preposing, postposing, and inversion can all signal focus constructions (Thompson, 1978):

Kolya kupil mašinu.	Kolya bought the car.
Kolya mašinu kupil.	Kolya BOUGHT the car.
Kupil Kolya mašinu.	Kolya did buy the car.
Kupil mašinu Kolya.	KOLYA bought the car.
Mašinu Kolya kupil.	The car, Kolya bought it.
Mašinu kupil Kolya.	The car, it was Kolya who bought it.

Both similarities and differences between Russian and English are evident in these examples. Like English, Russian is often analyzed as a language whose basic word order is Subject (*Kolya*) – Verb (*kupil*) – Object (*mašinu*). Moreover, *Mašinu Kolya kupil* and its English translation show similar preposing. Even so, the VOS and OVS sentences show that postposing and inversion are much more available as options in Russian than in English, which relies more on word stress and clefting. For most linguists, the great flexibility of Russian word order is attributable to its complex inflectional system in nouns, whereas the much sparer system of English leads to a heavier reliance on word order to mark grammatical functions such as subject and object. Thompson, moreover, contends that languages with rigid word order, like English, also tend to rely much more on clefting to signal focus.

Apart from word-order permutations and clefting, another common formal pattern is the focusing particle. Sankoff (1993: 117) emphasizes that in many languages of New Guinea and parts nearby '...focus... is mainly handled through a variety of markers occurring with the focused element remaining *in situ*, rather than through movement or clefting'. One of the cases she cites to support this claim comes from a dissertation on the Austronesian language Manam by Lichtenberk (1980: 482):

ási   ne-ng   ngau-ló-ʔa   i-anaʔúʔ-aʔ-i
bushknife   poss.-2sg.   1sg.-from-foc   3sg.-steal-trans-3sg.

It was from me that he stole your knife.

(In Lichtenberg's actual thesis, the IPA symbol for the velar nasal appears, but the citation above employs the <ng> digraph to indicate the phoneme.) The focus particle *-ʔa* does not involve subordination or a change of word order but it does serve the same function that the cleft in the translation does.

In some cases focus particles can have other functions as well. For instance, Keesing (1991) illustrates how the Kwaio language of the Solomons Islands has a morpheme that can serve as a focus marker in some sentences but as a marker of perfective aspect in others:

ŋgai ne-e aga-si-a
him TOP-he see-TRS-it
'He's the one who saw it.' (1991: 331)
e ʻakwa noʼo
she run away PERF
She has run away. (1991: 330)

In the first example, the *ne-e* is an allomorph of *no-o*, serving as a focus marker, where Keesing uses the abbreviation *TOP* (topicalizer) in the example but the term *focus* in his discussion. The other example shows that the allomorph *no-o* can also function as a marker of perfective aspect, as Keesing's translation with the English present perfect indicates.

Other languages show still other options. Tamil, for instance, combines word-order shifts in tandem with focusing particles (Asher, 1985: 89). Moreover, each of the three patterns discussed at some length – clefting, particles, and word-order permutations – can take fairly diverse forms. Finally, the question of just what does or does not count as a formal device indicating focus should be mentioned. For instance, certain constructions with the pronoun *one* are often considered a special type of focus construction, as in the translation of the Kwaio sentence as *He's the one who saw it*. The *one* pattern will indeed count as a focus construction in this chapter, as will another syntactic pattern often termed *raising*. Yet how many other such structures there may be is a difficult issue – and one related to problems to be discussed in the following sections.

Variation in Meanings

Prince (1978) noted a problem in earlier investigations (e.g. Akmajian, 1970) in ignoring meaning differences signaled by different types of focus constructions. In one way it does make sense to regard as equivalent *It was a Rottweiler that bit me* and *The one that bit me was a Rottweiler* (and Akmajian does compare *it*-clefts and *one* sentences in his analysis). On the other hand, Akmajian (1970: 149) went further, claiming that such sentences 'are synonymous, share the same presuppositions, answer the same questions, and in general are used interchangeably'. Like many other linguists, Akmajian used truth conditions as the main test of meaning equivalence: if the proposition in the sentence, *It was a Rottweiler that bit me* is true, the proposition in the *one* sentence must also be true. Prince has not disputed the value of truth-conditional analyses to help understand meaning, but her 1978 article makes clear that focus constructions are not interchangeable in all cases.

The lack of complete interchangeability sometimes involves syntactic factors. Prince (1978: 885) cites a *wh*-cleft recorded in conversation, *What you are saying is that the President was involved*, and she contrasts it with the ungrammaticality of the same proposition reformulated as an *it*-cleft: **It is that the President is involved that you are saying*; a nominal *that* clause (*that the President is involved*) can serve as the focus in a *wh*-cleft but not in an *it*-cleft. Along with syntactic constraints, there are strong statistical tendencies in actual discourse. For example, in Prince's study, the focus position of *it*-clefts (e.g. *a Rottweiler* in *It was a Rottweiler that bit me*) tended to be short, whereas the focus position in *wh*-clefts tended to be long (e.g. *be a star on the horse-show circuit* in *What she hopes to do is be a star on the horse-show circuit*).

The statistical differences between *wh*-clefts and *it*-clefts correlate in turn with differences in how they are used in everyday discourse. Prince's survey found that the *wh*-clause in *wh*-clefts normally codes information that speakers or writers assume to be in the consciousness of their audience or readily accessible, as in the case of metalinguistic comments such as: *What I mean is...*, or *What happened is...*; e.g. *What happened is that the agent asked if he could see the office* (Prince, 1978: 893). The speaker recorded saying this could assume that his audience shared his assumption that something had happened (see also Kim, 1995).

The uses of *it*-clefts are especially heterogeneous. Prince found many where a shared presupposition was evident in the subordinate clause, as in *So I learned to sew books. They're really good books. It's just the covers <u>that are rotten</u>* (1978: 896). In this case, the shared presupposition seems to be that something is damaged. In another type of *it*-cleft the subordinate clause has information that no speaker or writer can assume will be known to the audience: e.g. *It was just about 50 years ago <u>that Henry Ford gave us the weekend</u>* (1978: 898), where the cleft introduces a story about how the industrialist's new labor policies changed the working week in the United States.

As Prince notes, *it*-clefts show an interesting relation to discourse hedges (e.g. *perhaps, it seems that,* and *more or less*). Where hedges weaken a statement, *it*-clefts can strengthen one 'by presenting it as already known fact' (Prince, 1978: 900) even if a fact not known to the audience. Prince seems to have *it*-clefts of the second type primarily in mind in comparing hedges and clefts (although her position on this is not entirely clear). However, either type of *it*-cleft as well as *wh*-clefts and other focus constructions can likewise be viewed as cases where speakers and writers take a forceful stance: if hedges seem tentative, focus constructions convey some certainty. In this sense, such constructions communicate affective as well as propositional meanings.

There is a real, albeit only hazily understood, relation between affective meanings and mental states such as certainty and caution, even though these states may seem less 'emotional' than states such as joy and anger. In view of this relation, it is not surprising that in studies of modality and evidentiality (the basis one has for making an assertion), researchers sometimes also discuss the affective stances of speakers (e.g. Escobar, 1997). Focus constructions have likewise prompted some analysts to consider emotional meanings (cf. Kim, 1995: 265–268; Kruisinga, 1953: 74–75; Stein, 1995; see also Chapter 3). A study by Irvine (1990) is particularly instructive. She found that the use of focus constructions in Wolof varied by social class: aristocrats, who are expected to show great restraint, use relatively few focus constructions, whereas griots, the traditional poets and genealogists, frequently use them.

From the work of Prince and others, it is clear that different focus constructions are often not interchangeable but are instead specially tailored for different contexts. Many of the precise differences of meaning remain problematic, involving, as they do, complex questions such as the nature of presupposition and definiteness. One question, however, is especially relevant to the issue of meaning transfer: whether there are language-specific meanings in focus constructions.

Work on Yiddish and language contact between Yiddish and English indicates that different languages can and do have focus constructions with language-specific meanings (Prince, 1981, 1986, 1988). Yiddish-speaking immigrants to the United States developed a type of preposing that linguists frequently term Yiddish Movement, as seen in an example from Prince (1981: 260):

Q: How's your son?

A: Don't ask! A sportscar he wants!

Prince discusses the meaning difference as a difference between salience and plausibility. For Yiddish speakers or Yiddish/English bilinguals, any type of focus fronting is possible as long as the presupposed meaning is plausible. Prince (1981: 260) contrasts the previous dialogue with a less plausible one:

Q: How's your son?

A: Don't ask! A sportscar he stole!

The first use of movement is felicitous since 'it can be assumed to be general shared knowledge, but not necessarily salient/given that a son or at least this son wants things' (1981: 260). In contrast, the second case of fronting would only be felicitous with a shared assumption 'that a son or at least this son, steals things' (1981: 260).

For Prince, Birner and Ward, and for many other linguists (e.g. Weinreich, 1953a), the source of Yiddish Movement is Yiddish syntax, which is illustrated in the following example from Prince (1986: 217):

Q: vos hot zi geshonken ayer zun?
    What has she given your son?

A: a hemd hot zi geshonken mayn zun!
    A shirt has she given my son
    A shmatavate hemd!
    A lousy shirt

Q: What did she give your son!

A: A shirt she gave my son! A lousy shirt!

Prince provides a discourse context where the person answering the question was expecting that her son would receive more than a shirt as a gift. For Birner and Ward (1998), the transfer from Yiddish also involves an extension from mere salience to plausibility, but they also speculate that for bilinguals, '…Yiddish Movement and other focus preposings are not distinct types of focus preposing, but rather a single construction that is less constrained than Standard English focus preposing' (1998: 92–93). For monolingual speakers of English outside of the New York area, Yiddish Movement usually does seem distinct, although not so much for New Yorkers who are not Jewish but have been influenced by the Yiddish/English contact situation (Feinstein, 1980).

Cognitive Effects

As noted in the introduction to this chapter, Carston (1996) maintains that focus constructions enable listeners to 'derive cognitive effects' from the information organized in a particular syntactic pattern. Along with like-minded advocates of Relevance Theory as well as others (e.g. Levinson, 1997), Carston stresses that the semantic structure of a proposition will often not be sufficient information for listeners to understand a specific meaning in its context. Accordingly, speakers may use particular structures to guide their audience, choosing focus patterns and other constructions. In this view, syntax serves the interrelated aims of semantic coding and pragmatic enrichment of meaning (e.g. Givón, 1984b, 1990). Devices such as clefting and word-order permutations are thus implicated both in a speaker's (or writer's) construction of meaning and in an audience's reconstruction of that meaning. This point is illustrated in Chapter 5 in the analysis of how different groups of writers use or do not use *it*-cleft sentences under the same discourse conditions.

While such reconstructive activity is the cognitive effect that Carston foregrounds in her analyses, it is not the only possible one. Psycholinguistic evidence points to concomitants that will be discussed in this section. Before that discussion, however, it is necessary to contemplate the problem of the psychological reality of meaning categories often invoked in analyses of focus devices. As noted in the introduction to this chapter, terms such as *focus* and *topicalization* are often used interchangeably, and the variable use certainly has its critics, such as Tomlin (1994: 150): 'most linguistic functions, particularly pragmatic functions like *old information* or *topic* or *focus* lack either theoretically satisfying definitions or reliable means of identification'. Tomlin (1997: 165) goes much further in a discussion of the semantics and pragmatics of the passive voice:

> ...the function of the syntactic subject in English is solely to code or index what has been called conventionally the clause-level theme or topic.

Furthermore:

> ...the pragmatic notion of clause-level theme or topic has no standing as a theoretical category but can be fully understood and reduced to the referent in a conceptual representation attentionally detected at the moment an utterance is formulated; that is, the functional category of topic or theme does not exist but reflects the linguist's naïve view and understanding of one cognitive basis of utterance formulation. (Tomlin, 1997: 165)

While extreme and expressly reductionist, Tomlin's claim does have some empirical support from investigations of the passive where speakers' choices of syntactic subject could be manipulated experimentally (see also Tomlin, 1995).

In effect, Tomlin holds that the linguistic representation of the passive requires only a characteristic syntactic formula (more or less NP + BE auxiliary + main verb in perfective form), and that a non-linguistic behavior, attention, is what triggers the use of the syntactic formula. Although his approach might be considered one sort of 'cognitive linguistics', Tomlin's position is nevertheless a curious throwback to the behaviorist model of meaning sketched by Bloomfield (1933) in his influential textbook, where he sought to reduce meaning to observable behavior (see Chapter 2 of this volume). Most seriously, perhaps, Tomlin's approach seems to offer no way to account for grammatical patterns quite different from the passive. In the case of *it*-clefts and *wh*-clefts, for example, something other than a sentence subject is often in focus yet it commands attention. Defenders of Tomlin's position might argue that experimental manipulation will eventually identify the precise conditions involving the particular type of attention given when a particular structure such as an *it*-cleft is used. However, such a defense will not help with cases where the focus position is marked lexically, as in the Manam particle -*ʔa* given earlier. The English translation of the example as a cleft sentence suggests that Manam speakers would be directing their attention in a way similar to that of English users of the cleft. By Tomlin's logic, -*ʔa* must not be a morpheme even though it appears to be so. If such a focusing particle has no meaning, by Tomlin's logic, the same would presumably hold for the so-called topic and subject particles of Japanese and Korean and many other cases as well.

Despite Tomlin's skepticism, it does seem necessary for linguists to continue to assume that focus constructions and other grammatical devices have real meanings, however difficult they may be to specify precisely. Although Tomlin's strongest claims seem dubious, empirical research such as that which he advocates certainly matters in any attempt to understand the cognitive effects of focus constructions. In fact, there is growing evidence of such effects on readers (e.g. Birch *et al.*, 2000; Klin *et al.*, 2004). Birch *et al.* found a difference among readers given texts with *it*-clefts in comparison with those who read texts without such structures; the former group outperformed the latter on tasks involving recall and recognition memory. In experiments using different versions of stories prepared with and without *wh*-clefts, Klin *et al.* obtained similar results, which they see as support for an inference that 'linguistic cues function as mental processing instructions, informing readers about the importance of concepts' (Klin *et al.*, 2004: 519). Klin *et al.* allude to a similar analysis of Givón (1992), and it is also remarkably like Carston's.

While Carston emphasized the effects on listeners and Tomlin the effects on speakers, it seems clear that any thorough explanation of the cognitive impact of focus constructions will have to account for the needs of both speakers and listeners as well of writers and readers (and there are textual studies showing a different patterning of such structures in speech and writing, e.g. Biber *et al.*, 1999). Along with the evidence on memory and attention, there is the fact that focusing devices change over time, and such change seems likely to involve new pragmatic or semantic mappings by speakers or writers who feel that the available resources do not fully express what they wish to say. It is beyond the scope of this chapter to consider any particular mappings, but the history of *it*-clefts shows that structures that were rare in the Old English period grew common by the end of the Middle English period (c. 1500), with new expressive patterns thus arising (Ball, 1994). The diachronic pattern here no doubt has implications for SLA, since learners whose competence continues to develop may find their available interlanguage resources insufficient, and so may look for new ways to express focus.

A quest for new ways may sometimes call upon the resources of the native language, as evidence on transfer of forms and meanings from the L1 will show later in this chapter. One question that the available evidence cannot answer is whether language-specific focus patterns ever reflect different patterns of cognizing. If such patterns involve L1 influence, they can be called conceptual transfer. Since focus constructions interact with attention and memory, perhaps recall and memory sometimes reflect language-specific factors. This possibility is discussed by Odlin (2008).

Translation and Crosslinguistic Comparability

One probable linguistic universal is that all languages have focus constructions of one kind or another. However, variations in forms and meanings make it hard to construct good typologies or to make fully accurate contrastive predictions, and such difficulty is often evident in translation problems (see also Chapters 3 and 7).

Translators naturally try to construct new texts, often aligned closely in meanings and forms with those of the original text (Frawley, 1984). In similar (usually historically related) languages, the challenge will often be less than in the case of dissimilar languages from very different cultures. Yet even languages as similar as German and English show significant points of contrast in their focus systems so that translators cannot invariably rely on formal similarities. Doherty (1999, 2001) stresses that although both languages have cleft constructions, these structures are not always formally or pragmatically equivalent. In a discussion of English-to-German translation, she illustrates one type of problem with the English sentence: *It is here that Freud's is a theory or a prototheory peopled with actors*, where the German translation does not have clefting (Doherty, 1999: 300).

> Gerade hier ist die Freudsche Theorie eine Theorie oder Prototheorie mit Akteuren.

[Literally: Just here is the Freudian theory a theory or prototheory with actors.]

To establish a pragmatic equivalent, the translation employs an intensifying adverb (*gerade*) along with *hier*, with the adverbial phrase appearing in preverbal position and the subject in postverbal position (*die Freudsche Theorie*).

As for German-to-English translation, a cleft in the English version sometimes reflects a cleft in the original, as in the following example (Doherty, 2001: 287–288; emphases added):

Grenouille found his heart pounding, and he knew that *it was not the exertion of running that set his heart pounding* but rather his excited helplessness in the presence of the scent.

Grenouille spürte, wie sein Herz pochte, und er wusste, dass *es nicht die Anstrengung des Laufens war, die es pochen machte*, sondern seine erregte Hilflosigkeit vor der Gegenwart dieses Geruchs.

[Literally: Grenouille perceived how his heart pounded and he knew, that *it not the exertion of the running was, that it to pound made*, rather his excited helplessness before the presence of this scent.]

However, in other instances, the cleft in the translation reflects something quite different in the original (Doherty, 2001: 287–288; emphases added):

He suspected that *it was not he who followed the scent*, but the scent that had captured him and was drawing him irresistibly to it.

...denn er ahnte, dass *nicht er dem Duft folgte*, sondern dass der Duft ihn gefangengenommen hatte und nun unwiderstehlich zu sich zog.

[Literally: ...then he suspected, that *not he the scent followed*, rather that the scent him captured had and now irresistibly to (it)self drew.]

In this case the translator found an *it*-cleft to be pragmatically similar enough even though the original has no cleft but instead has a focus construction that starts with a negator, *nicht*, followed then by the subject pronoun (*er*), then by the object NP (*dem Duft*), and ends with the verb (*folgte*).

What these cases show, therefore, is that although cleft sentences belong to the repertory of focus constructions in both German and in English, the former language also employs intensifiers and word-order shifts to evoke pragmatic meanings like those that English evokes through clefting. Yet even though clefting shows a high functional load in English, there are other crosslinguistic contrasts where English behaves somewhat like German. The following example comes from a native speaker of Irish beginning a story about the fairies, and the English translation is by a native speaker of Irish and English (Ó Catháin, 1985: 23):

Is é an dream a cuirfeadh amach as na Flaithis iad...

Is it the crowd that put out the Heaven them

Translation by Ó Catháin: They are really the crowd that was put out of heaven...

Ó Catháin's translation renders the object pronoun of the original (*iad*) as a subject pronoun (*they*), probably because a literal translation of the verb (*cuirfeadh*) is not viable in the specific context. Some descriptions of Irish mislabel forms such as *cuirfeadh* 'passive', but more accurate descriptors are 'autonomous' and 'impersonal', the latter preferred by Ó Siadhail (1989: 180), who would translate *cuirfeadh* with the aid of an impersonal pronoun, thus *one put*. In any case, Ó Catháin had few viable options, and a passive translation at least preserves the truth conditions of the original. The Irish sentence shows the characteristic pattern of clefting (Ó Siadhail, 1989: 236): it begins with a formulaic *Is é*, followed by the phrase in focus (*an dream*, 'the crowd'), and then by the pronoun (*a*) which begins the relative clause having the predicate *cuirfeadh amach...iad* ('put them out...'), where the Irish *iad* in this clause is technically a resumptive pronoun (i.e. repeating the reference made by the pronoun *a*). In contrast, the English translation does not employ a cleft. To preserve what he could of the pragmatic force of the cleft, however, Ó Catháin used *really*. No such word appears in the Irish version, but the English adverb clearly serves to suggest what the cleft in Irish indicates, and this use thus resembles what the German *gerade* helped to achieve in the translation of an English cleft.

The preceding example suggests that clefting in Irish allows for a wider pragmatic range than clefting in English does. The Irish cleft expresses an affective meaning not possible to state in English except through a formally different pattern, i.e. an intensifier. As noted earlier, focus devices can signal affect in various languages. Moreover, there are affective constructions that are even harder to translate. One such instance appears in a Spanish flamenco song where a jilted woman rails at her one-time lover saying (Morente, 2002):

Quien no te quiere a tí soy yo.

[Literally: Who not you loves to you am I]

Although this example appears in a song, the type of focus construction here is common in everyday language as well. Whitley (2002: 279) notes two variants that can intensify the sentence: *Miss Chile lo va a ganar* (Miss Chile it goes to win, i.e. 'Miss Chile is going to win it').

Quien lo va a ganar es Miss Chile.

And:

Es Miss Chile quien lo va a ganar.

In all these examples, the pronoun *quien* (who) can be replaced by *la que* (she who); the two emphatic sentences might thus be translated: *The one who is going to win is Miss Chile* and *Miss Chile is the one who is going to win*, or, in the case of the latter, *It's Miss Chile who is going to win*. In the flamenco song, however, a translation aligned closely with the focus construction sounds bizarre: *I am she who does not love you*, and *I am the one who does not love you* is not much of an improvement. Several native speakers of Spanish whom I have consulted agree that the focus construction in the flamenco line is very emotionally charged, and it seems that in some cases close translations of syntactically expressed affect become virtually impossible.

Such translation difficulties obviously pose serious problems for contrastive analysts interested in assessing the similarity of focus constructions across languages. The examples used in this section all involve Indo–European languages with somewhat similar typologies, and even so, the crosslinguistic correspondences are only partial either in form or meaning. With languages showing greater typological distance, the contrastive problem is even greater.

Whatever the difficulties, linguists will no doubt continue to try to improve on their understanding of the correspondences of form and meaning in focus constructions. Along with clefts and other special constructions, intensifiers certainly warrant close study (e.g. Siemund, 2000), since they can have pragmatic functions similar to clefts; and yet intensifiers also have a life of their own including structures such as reflexive pronouns, which do not seem to overlap as much with clefting as adverbs do. One useful approach may well be what Kamio (1991, 1997) calls 'territory of information', which attempts to characterize a wide range of grammatical structures including clefts in terms of different subjective stances a speaker or writer might take (see also Finegan, 1995).

If the wide range of stances challenges translators and comparative linguists, it clearly poses even greater problems for second language learners. The next two sections consider just how the native language may reduce or increase such challenges.

Evidence of Transfer

Several kinds of evidence show that the transfer of focus constructions occurs in many language-contact situations involving SLA. This section will consider first some of the evidence of formal L1 influences, then influences of L1 meaning, and then some quantitative evidence.

One kind of formal influence is sometimes evident when the word order of one language differs from another. Such influence may involve basic word order (see Chapter 4); however, word-order permutations are a common formal device to express pragmatic meanings, as examples in preceding sections show. Thus, it is sometimes possible to identify language-specific focus patterns in interlanguage productions. The discussion of translation involving German and English cited cases where German word-order permutations correspond to cleft sentences in English – even though German also has clefts in the toolbox. Not surprisingly, such formal differences occasionally lead to interlanguage English patterns that reflect the flexibility of German word order.

The following example comes from a postgraduate student (here given the name of Robert) at an American university and very close to finishing his English requirements:

> *That this book caters to students shows the glossary and the exercises at the end of each chapter which is helpful for every exam preparation.*

The assignment that Robert had was to write critiques of textbooks in his field. The nominal clause at the beginning is the direct object of *shows*, and the subject is the coordinate NP that stretches to the end of the sentence. It seems likely that Robert relied on his L1 to formulate this very heavy subject NP, which in turn contributed to his use of OVS word order, a possibility exploited much more in German than in English. Another factor may well have been a wish to preserve the presentation order of old information before new information, the latter being expressed by the heavy subject. In any case, Robert produced other instances of a special word order and in fact told his instructor that it was something that other teachers had also pointed out in his writing. Further on in this section other examples of word-order transfer indicate that Robert's use of pragmatic word order from his L1 is not at all unusual.

Aside from word-order permutations, another formal pattern susceptible to transfer is an L1 morpheme used in focus constructions that appear in the second language. For instance, Tok Pisin uses a focusing particle *yet* which is, according to Sankoff (1993), the result of the influence of a similar particle *iat* in the Austronesian language Tolai. Like the morpheme *-ʔa* in Manam discussed earlier, *iat* follows the focused constituent, but the Tolai form is phonetically similar to the English *yet*. One Tok Pisin sentence with *yet* is translated by Sankoff with the *one* construction (1993: 131):

Tok 'Orait yu yet kilim pikinini bilong mi'

Say Alright 2sg foc kill child poss 1sg

(She) said, 'Alright, you're the one who killed my child'

Interestingly, other sentences with *yet* that Sankoff cites are translated with reflexive pronouns, which shows that meanings of intensifiers, reflexives, and clefts all overlap in certain ways even though there are also differences as noted earlier.

Another case of crosslinguistic influence involving a focusing particle comes from the South American creole Saramaccan (Smith, 1996). In this instance the particle is *we*, as in the following example (1996: 118):

De we ko ta fan ku Masa Jesosi de

They foc come prog speak with Master Jesus there

It was THEM who came to talk with Lord Jesus there.

Although *we* might seem to have English *we* as its source, such an explication seems highly improbable in the context of the sentence. Moreover, Smith identifies a very similar use of *we* as a focusing particle in the Niger–Congo language Fon, which he views as the source for this construction. Still another case of a focusing particle due to crosslinguistic influence appears in Melanesian Pidgin (Keesing, 1991), and it will be discussed further on.

Although contact languages such as Tok Pisin and Saramaccan offer some of the clearest examples, the importation of L1 morphemes in L2 focus constructions is not restricted to pidgins and creoles. A study by Odlin and Jarvis (2004) cites the following use of the Swedish relative pronoun *som*:

He [Chaplin] say it were he som take the bred.

The context here was the Charlie Chaplin film that is described in detail in Chapter 5, and the interlanguage structure reflects the influence of cleft sentence patterns in Swedish such as *Charlie säger då att det var han som tog brödet* (Charlie says then that it was he who took the bread). English does, of course, use *some* as a pronoun, but not as a relative. Not surprisingly, though, some native speakers of Swedish misjudge the grammatical fit between the cognates *some* and *som* to be closer than is really the case. It is worth noting that students whose native language is Finnish sometimes over-rely on Swedish when they use English, but the only erroneous clefts with *som* found by Odlin and Jarvis came from native speakers of Swedish.

While focus particles and similar morphemes such as *som* provide clear indicators of transfer, there is another type of formal evidence as well. Special syntactic characteristics of clefting in Irish and Scottish Gaelic appear in the contact varieties of English in traditionally Celtic regions. One example of a cleft sentence in Irish was presented earlier; another example is closer to English cleft patterns (Ó Siadhail, 1989: 236):

(Is é) an fear a bhí ag péinteáil cathaoir inné

Is him the man who was at-painting chair yesterday

It is the man who was painting a chair yesterday.

For all the similarities, however, important differences also exist. Along with the initial VS word order, there is another detail of this sentence that differs from the usual English clefting pattern: the possibility of deleting the words *Is é*. That is, a normal clefting pattern in Irish is also *An fear a bhí ag péinteáil cathaoir inné*. Scottish Gaelic likewise allows for this deletion option, and so does Welsh. The longstanding contact between the Celtic languages and English led to the rise of some new patterns of clefting in English. In Ireland and Scotland there are attested cases of a cleft pattern where *It is* or *It's* would be deleted, as in the following example (Odlin, 1997: 38) from a bilingual speaker (H) interviewed in one of the Hebrides Islands by an ethnographer (E):

H.: And they're [cattle] eating in the *machaire* [plain]. [E. Yes] in the wintertime when there there's no grass. [E. Yes, yes] But mind up there, down on the west end there, you could cut it like corn. [E. mm] But not now. No. [E. No] *The cattle that's eating it*. E: Did the factor object?

In the discourse context here, H. might have chosen to say *It's the cattle that's eating it* to explain the barren condition of the turf, but instead he felt free to use the same option available in Gaelic cleft sentences. Odlin (1997) terms such structures 'truncated clefts'.

There is other evidence of formal characteristics of the L1 influencing the form of L2 focus constructions (e.g. Filppula, 1986), but L1 meanings also influence L2 constructions, and such cases offer especially interesting challenges for SLA research. As discussed earlier, Prince and others see Yiddish Movement differing from other types of preposing where the plausibility of information more than its salience accounts for why sentences like *A sportscar he wants* are felicitous in contrast to ones such as *A sportscar he stole* in particular discourse contexts.

Along with plausibility and salience, affect is another dimension in the communicative profile of focus constructions. One example already discussed is the Irish story involving the fairies, *Is é an dream a cuirfeadh amach as na Flaithis iad...*, which was translated with an intensifier into English: *They are really the crowd that was put out of heaven...* . For bilingual speakers of English and Irish (or Scottish Gaelic), the contact varieties of English developed a special kind of cleft that likewise expresses an affective meaning. Even after the period of widespread bilingualism in these Celtic regions ended, monolinguals using such constructions could still be found in certain regions in the 20th century. The following example comes from such an area in County Roscommon: *It's me that was afraid o' him*, which Henry (1957: 196) translates as, *I assure you that I was very much afraid of him*. Like Ó Catháin's translation of the Irish, Henry's paraphrase of the English vernacular uses adverbial intensifiers *very much* but also a verb that has an intensifying function (*assure*). Henry attributes the special meaning in such clefts to Irish influence.

Focus particles sometimes have more than one meaning, and there is at least one case in the literature where the polysemy shows up in L2. The Kwaio allomorphs *no-o/ ne-e* can signal either focus or perfective aspect (examples of which were given earlier). Keesing identifies *nao* as the morpheme in Melanesian Pidgin that recodes those Kwaio meanings and gives a number of examples, including this focus construction (Keesing, 1991: 331):

hem nao i save
him he know
'He's the one who knows'

One of the examples of the perfective *nao* given by Keesing is in *hem i-ranawe nao*, which he translates as: *She has run away* (1991: 330). The transfer here involves, in Keesing's judgement, the phonetic similarity of Kwaio *no-o* and English *now*, even where the grammatical functions served by *nao* go far beyond the meanings of the adverb *now*.

Along with transfer involving forms and meanings, there is another kind of evidence of crosslinguistic influence: from studies of quantitative variation. Filppula (1986) pioneered such a methodology for investigations of substrate influence by looking at the frequency of cleft sentences in interviews he conducted with speakers of English in different parts of Ireland and also with speakers of British English. He found that the incidence of *it*-clefts varied strikingly: while the Dublin sample showed 1.3 clefts per thousand words, the sample from two western counties (Clare and Kerry) showed 2.8, more than twice as many. Filppula's explanation invokes the differing histories of these regions, where Dublin was long the center of English speakers (both settlers from England and Irish residents who adopted English) whereas Clare and Kerry shifted relatively recently from Irish to English, mainly in the 19th century. Further support for this interpretation comes from data from County Wicklow, a traditionally rural and mountainous area but closer to Dublin than to Clare or Kerry: the frequency of *it*-clefts was in between those for Dublin and the western counties: 1.8. Moreover, the British English sample showed a much smaller figure: 0.7 clefts (about half the Dublin figure). As with other linguists who have studied clefts in the English of Ireland, Filppula attributes the high frequency of these focus constructions to Irish influence, since the latter language uses clefting even more than English does.

In a subsequent investigation of English in Wales, Paulasto (2006) has employed a methodology similar to Filppula's and obtained comparable results for *focus fronting*, a structure more or less equivalent to what Birner and Ward term *preposing*. As noted earlier, Welsh has a pattern of truncated clefting very much like that found in Irish and Scottish Gaelic (Thorne, 1993: 371). However, the type of substrate influence that Paulasto examined did not have a relative pronoun *that*. It is not clear whether Welsh English ever had truncated clefts such as *The cattle that's eating it*, but Paulasto's evidence abounds with cases of fronting that indicate the influence of the Welsh truncation pattern. In some the preposing results in the appearance of a prepositional phrase before the rest of the clause: e.g. *I was a tomboy, <u>with the lads</u> I used to go you know*. Older bilinguals showed a distinct preference for fronting, especially in comparison with speakers of English in England. Quantitative studies such as those of Filppula and Paulasto thus corroborate other evidence of transfer.

One possible criticism of the methodology of these studies merits attention. Since Filppula and Paulasto obtained their data on focus constructions from conversations on everyday topics, there was inevitably only a limited attempt to standardize the discourse context. Thus, a conversation about a certain topic might prove more conducive to the use of focus constructions than might another topic (though of course it is only speculative to posit such a difference in the effect of topics without actual evidence). Yet whatever the possible merits of such a critique, findings from the *Modern Times* research discussed in Chapter 5 show that crosslinguistic influence on focus constructions is demonstrable even when the discourse context is uniform for all participants. Part of the discussion in the next section will highlight the evidence.

Ultimate Attainment

While the evidence involving form, meaning, and quantitative variation points to the reality of crosslinguistic influence in focus constructions, there remain challenges in understanding just how such influence operates. One problem is the rarity sometimes seen in the production of certain focus constructions among other grammatical patterns. Researchers have long noted the problem, as the following observation by Schachter (1988) shows:

Even more striking is the non-occurrence in proficient second-language-speaker-production of a number of the so-called movement transformations, particularly raising, clefts, pseudoclefts, topicalizing rules, adverb movement rules... Frequency counts of the occurrence of these constructions in conversational English are difficult to find, but my strong impression is that many of them occur quite frequently in my speech and that of other native speakers, indicating that their non-occurrence in the speech of non-natives is remarkable and difficult to explain. What is clearly the case is that communicative fluency can be attained without complete grammatical mastery of the language. (Schachter, 1988: 224)

As the last sentence in the passage suggests, a prime concern of Schachter is the question of how possible it is for adult learners to acquire grammatical patterns such as cleft sentences even when 'communicative fluency' does not require such complete attainment. She regards the ultimate attainment of the target language by adult L2 learners as quite different from the ultimate attainment by children of their mother tongue in a monolingual setting.

Schachter's conclusion about fluency without full mastery seems to be language-neutral: i.e. it apparently assumes that the conclusion holds true of all L1 groups in all circumstances. This assumption does not make Schachter skeptical about the importance of transfer: in the same article she judges it as another trait of adult L2 acquisition that distinguishes it from child language acquisition. Even so, she does not consider in any detail the possible interaction between transfer and ultimate attainment, in contrast to, for example, Selinker and Lakshmanan (1993). While Schachter's language-neutral assumption can be questioned (and will be further on this section), her analysis offers more than mere speculation, as she cites a detailed study (Schachter & Hart, 1979) that showed the infrequency of certain syntactic structures in a group of advanced ESL students whose writing was studied along with the writing of less advanced groups.

Schachter and Hart did not specifically investigate clefting or similar focus patterns. Still, a corpus-based study by Callies (2008) on raising, one of the patterns that Schachter refers to, proves consistent with her surmise that such structures are rare in interlanguage production. That study will be considered at the end of this section. With regard to clefts, Schachter's contention does not seem to have led to much investigation. However, one study (Odlin, 1992) did find support for her contention. In a sample of 125 essays that served as exit examinations of ESL students (generally showing advanced L2 proficiency), very few essays had any clefts at all – only about 10% of the total sample. Even so, some details argue for caution in interpreting the results. The student writers had many different native languages, in several cases with only one individual having that language. Moreover, the topics varied, so that the same concern raised about the Celtic English studies mentioned above could be relevant for the exit exam sample. Finally, there were no parallel essays written in the native languages, and thus it is hard, if not impossible, to determine which L1 grammatical structures might influence a writer's choice to use a cleft or some other focus pattern. Even so, it does seem significant that, despite the sample having more than two dozen L1 Chinese ESL writers, not a single student used even one cleft sentence.

One possible explanation for the complete absence of clefts in the Chinese ESL exams is how the student writers perceived the crosslinguistic distance. That is, a writer might refrain from drawing on a Chinese focus construction to help construct an English cleft pattern if differences between the languages seemed either too great or even too small – the latter possibility is well known from work by Kellerman (1977) on the intuitions of some Dutch students who judged parallels between Dutch and English idioms as too good to be true, which will be considered further in Chapter 7 (see also Odlin, 2016).

As already observed, there were no parallel texts in the native languages of the student writers, and thus it remains uncertain what, if any, Chinese focus constructions might be relevant to the sample. As for judgements of crosslinguistic distance, it would be necessary to employ methods such as those of Kellerman and other researchers who have studied the problem. However, the findings on cleft sentences in Chapter 5 offer insights relevant to Schachter's surmise. In one well-defined discourse context, the Rich Lady Scene (RLS) of the film *Modern Times*, native speakers of Swedish frequently opted for a cleft pattern in Swedish to identify who stole some bread, whereas only one native speaker of Finnish produced a cleft sentence in Finnish in the same context. Most crucially, the strong preference for cleft patterns in Swedish is reflected in the frequency of clefts in Swedish speakers' English accounts of the RLS. It should be recalled that the native-speaker groups were not composed of the same individuals as the groups writing in English. Nevertheless, many more Swedes than Finns used cleft sentences to identify who took the bread in their native language and in English.

The Swedes' use of clefts in English therefore calls into question Schachter's apparent assumption that the L1 will have no role in how frequent or infrequent a particular structure may be in the interlanguage used for communicative purposes. Even if Swedes do not often produce any of the other patterns mentioned by Schachter, their fondness for clefts makes them different from the L1 groups that Schachter had in mind.

It also seems likely that the Swedes' predisposition to clefts is shared by at least a few other L1 groups. The evidence from Irish and Hebridean English considered above points to two similarities with the Swedish case: (1) great formal similarity between clefting in the L1 Celtic languages and English; and (2) a high frequency of the patterns in Celtic and English discourse.

Although the Swedish and the Celtic data challenge Schachter's assumption about language neutrality, this evidence strengthens her contention that crosslinguistic influence is a key factor distinguishing adult SLA from children's acquisition of a first language. Much of the transfer from Swedish to English is positive, even though certain cases of negative transfer occur (e.g. the use of *some* or *som* as a relative pronoun).

The success of many Swedes in using clefts points to a wider inference: namely, that the ultimate attainment of individuals depends somewhat on the particular native language they speak – in addition, of course, to factors such as the opportunities they have to achieve high L2 proficiency, the motivation that they have to do so, etc.

With regard to the Finns, the infrequent use of cleft sentences in the English accounts of the RLS should *not* be viewed as evidence supporting Schacther's surmise. The use of a cleft in the RLS to identify who took the bread is not obligatory. In the control group, consisting of 66 native speakers of English, only 2 used a cleft in the RLS. Any native speaker of English presumably does have the syntactic knowledge needed to use clefts, whatever the actual usage statistics, and the existence of such knowledge also seems possible among the Finns. Although hardly any Finn took advantage of the similarity, the cleft pattern in *se oli se nainen joka sen leivän varasti* (see Chapter 5) could serve as a template for positive transfer. Yet this pattern was rare among native speakers of Finnish, and so it may be that most Finns writing in English did not consider any crosslinguistic similarity. In any case, what the *Modern Times* statistics strongly suggest is that high frequency in L1 Swedish as well as high formal similarity will often lead to positive transfer.

Although the Swedes' use of clefts suggests that ultimate attainment is sometimes affected by L1-specific patterns, a study by Callies (2008) finds underproduction of one of the patterns mentioned by Schachter – raising – in essays written by advanced learners of English. This corpus-based research does not cite Schachter's surmise but is consistent with it, in that native speakers of Polish and German seem to have often avoided using raising structures or lack knowledge of the discourse functions of those structures.

English has a wide range of raising patterns, as seen in two subtypes in the sentences *Mosquitoes are tough to fight*, and *Alice heard Gene come back*. In the first example, the notional object of *fight* (*mosquitoes*) is, in a transformational analysis, raised to the subject position in the preceding clause, and in the second, the notional subject of *come back* (*Gene*) is raised to direct object position in the preceding clause. Linguists interested in the discourse functions of syntactic structures (e.g. Givón, 1990) have often analyzed raising as a kind of focusing device wherein the raised element becomes more topical, and Callies adopts a similar position. He also considers the likelihood of comprehension problems for L2 learners. Although some German and Polish students do attempt to use such constructions, pragmatic anomalies in their use as well as underproduction strongly suggest that the specific discourse meanings of raising patterns in English remain elusive for many. In such cases, there are comprehension problems implicated in what Schachter deemed communicative fluency without grammatical mastery.

Conclusion

This chapter has reviewed a wide range of work on focus constructions and has given special attention to the problem of transfer in relation to those structures. The key findings are these:

- While there exists considerable typological variation in focus constructions, three major formal types are clefting, word-order shifts, and focus particles. All three are involved in specific cases of crosslinguistic influence.
- Relevance Theory allows for insights about pragmatic commonalities in focus constructions. Even so, the meanings of these constructions vary both within and between languages, and L1-specific meanings sometimes appear in bilinguals' use of the L2 (e.g. those in Yiddish Movement).
- Studies of monolingual performance indicate that focus constructions can have special cognitive effects involving attention and memory. Accordingly, certain effects seem likely to appear in language-contact situations also.
- Crosslinguistic similarity is an important factor encouraging the use of focus constructions in L2 even while transfer in such cases sometimes results in errors. However, the frequency of particular focus structures in L1 discourse also strongly affects transfer, as seen in structures in the English in the Celtic lands and in the English of many Swedish speakers.
- The comparability of focus constructions across languages is a major problem for translators – and also for linguists and language learners. In some cases, learners may be skeptical about the equivalence of such structures in two languages, and they may therefore be reluctant to use them – and such reluctance may hinder ultimate attainment of the target language. On the other hand, some learners do attempt to use radically different structures of the L1 in the L2, as the case of Robert shows.

Space does not allow for discussion of other concerns such as work on Universal Grammar and other formal analyses (e.g. Culicover & McNally, 1998; Hertel, 2003). But another issue of interest is the possible effects of transfer involving, for example, L2 → L3 influence. The figures in Table 5.3 do not, however, provide much evidence, since the group of Finns who had several years of L2 Swedish (F9B) did not show as strong a group tendency to use cleft sentences as did a comparable group of L1 Swedish speakers. Even so, there is clearly a need for further study of any possible effects involving multilingualism.

The conclusions drawn by Callies, whose study of raising was considered at the end of the preceding section, may have implications for other focus constructions and for other SLA situations. For example, L1 speakers of English may underproduce or misunderstand some similarities or differences between cleft sentences and word-order shifts in their native language and in (partially) corresponding patterns in L2 German since the correspondences are sometimes quite subtle, as the translation research of Doherty suggests. Indeed, work in translation studies sometimes offers insights on the link between comprehension and production, and the next chapter will consider processing issues that arise in translation and language transfer.

7 Translation and Language Transfer

Despite considerable research on transfer in SLA, inquiries about the relation between translation and transfer seem to be rare. However, an early pioneer, Hugo Schuchardt, sensed the importance of the relation, and one of his terms for transfer (*übertragen*) sometimes denotes translation (see also Chapter 2). Indeed, a considerable part of his analysis of language contact and bilingualism among speakers of L2 German and Italian discusses problems of translation correspondences. Few students of language contact, however, appear to have followed or broadened the trail that Schuchardt marked out.

Translation has received some attention in earlier chapters, as in the discussion of focus constructions in German and English (Chapter 6). Even so, the more general relation between translation and transfer warrants a chapter of its own. Deciding how to contemplate the relation requires some difficult choices regarding what to include or exclude. Translation studies have attracted researchers from linguistics, literary studies, computer science and philosophy, as well as from other disciplines. A remarkable variety of studies indeed shows intriguing overlaps with work in SLA, and particularly with work on transfer. Accordingly, this chapter will highlight three concerns:

- crosslinguistic equivalence;
- individual variation;
- cognitive processing.

Before each of these topics is addressed, however, some other concerns require attention.

At first glance, defining translation seems a straightforward matter. The following definition from a commonly used English dictionary sums up much of the commonsense notion of what it means to translate: 'To express in another language, systematically retaining the original sense' (*American Heritage Dictionary*, s.v. *translate*). A definition of *traducir*, the closest equivalent in Spanish to *translate*, offers a similar characterization: '*Expresar en un idioma una cosa dicha o escrita originalmente en otro*'

(To express in one language something spoken or written in another, *Diccionario de uso del español*, s.v. *traducir*). Both the Spanish and the English definitions are the primary senses offered in the dictionary entries, yet both also specify other senses that *translate* and *traducir* can have. In a detailed discussion of the linguistics of translation, Jakobson (1959) considers the complications in greater detail while offering a threefold classification: (1) *intralingual translation*, or 'rewording'; (2) *interlingual translation*, or 'translation proper'; and (3) *intersemiotic translation*, or 'transmutation'. Intralingual translation includes cases such as paraphrases and definitions in monolingual dictionaries, as all the rewording done is in the same language. The words, sentences, or other units in the intralingual translation constitute alternative choices in the same language. The 'proper' in the second kind suggests that interlingual translation represents the prototypical sense of the word, and indeed the topic of much of this chapter. As for intersemiotic translation, the transmutation that Jakobson invokes is where one kind of medium, e.g. a ballet, is employed to recreate something represented in another medium such as the language in a drama (e.g. Shakespeare's *Romeo and Juliet*).

While the focus of this chapter is on interlingual translation, the importance of the other types merits a little discussion. The paraphrases, definitions, and other manifestations of intralingual translation can constitute learning challenges for speakers of other languages, especially if they do not have experience in, for example, writing summaries or abstracts. The challenge of such writing tasks does not seem to be often considered as involving a translation problem, but its relevance to 'translation proper' is undeniable. Likewise, the relevance of intersemiotic translation to 'translation proper' seems clear. Speech typically involves some paralinguistic signals as well, and, as the Chinese–American linguist Ren Chen Chao noted, the problem of translation is thereby made more complicated:

> The translation of live speech in practical situations is linguistically interesting precisely because it involves extra-linguistic or marginal factors, such as voice quality, intonation, gesture, etc. If the same desired effect is to be attained, sometimes a word or sentence in one language may have to be 'translated' by a gesture... (Chao, 1968: 149)

Research by Gullberg (2008, 2011), Brown (2007) and others has focused on language-specific gestures, and these pose special problems for interpreters, as translators of spoken language are often called (e.g. Nolan, 2005). Furthermore, some kinds of intersemiotic translation may have to accompany translation of spoken language yet involve one non-verbal sign being transmuted into another kind of sign during the interpretation. Chao gives an example of speaking Chinese to an audience in Japan where the interpreter noted the speaker's pauses, which were simply silent intervals in Chao's address, with a paralinguistic signal apparently known to Japanese audiences whereby the interpreter audibly inhaled air.

Crosslinguistic Equivalence

The English definition of *translate* and the Spanish of *traducir* indicate, as suggested above, prototypical notions of how people understand the words. Even so, the definitions do not really indicate everything that an ordinary understanding of the words may entail. For example, both definitions characterize translation as expression, and they do not say anything about comprehension of an expression in another language. Clearly, one criterion for any successful translation is a good understanding of what is spoken or written in both languages involved in the translation, and of course such understanding is also a criterion for successful second language acquisition.

Dictionary definitions of translation seem able to offer only a suggestion of what everyday notions of translation involve. Such notions themselves may underestimate the complexity of the process, as Lyons observes:

> The naive monolingual speaker of English (or any other language) might be tempted to think that the meanings of lexemes (their sense and denotation) are independent of the language that he happens to speak and that translation from one language to another is simply a matter of finding the lexemes which have the same meaning in the other language, selecting the grammatically appropriate forms and putting them together in the right order... But this is not the case, as anyone who has any practical experience of translation is well aware. (Lyons, 1977: 235)

The naïve assumptions about crosslinguistic equivalence noted by Lyons manifest themselves in various ways, but perhaps most tellingly in the uncritical belief of many language learners in the utter reliability of translation software such as Google Translate (Ducar & Schocket, 2018). It proves quite easy to demonstrate how perilous such a belief is, as the following examples show. The source text is a passage from the *Modern Times* narratives (see Chapter 5), part of a film synopsis written by a native speaker of Finnish in middle school:

> Tyttö on yksin ja hänellä on nälkä. Hän katselee ruokakaupan ikkunaa, huomaa vieressä olevan leipomon auton ja varastaa siitä leivän. Eräs nainen kuitenkin näkee tapahtuman ja kutsuu leipurin paikalle. Tyttö törmää Chapliniin, joka poliisin saavuttua väittää varastaneensa leivän. Nainen kuitenkin sanoo, että sen varasti tyttö, ei Chaplin.

The following is my own translation of the passage:

> A girl is alone, and she is hungry. She looks at a grocery shop window, notices a bakery truck nearby and steals bread from it. A certain woman, however, sees what happens and calls the baker to the scene. The girl crashes into Chaplin, who claims to a policeman arrived on the

scene to have stolen the bread himself. The woman, however, says that the girl stole it, not Chaplin.

On four different occasions (spaced apart by 2-year intervals), Google Translate produced the following English versions of the passage:

2015

The girl is alone, and he is hungry. He looks at the grocery store window, notice the bakery next door and steal a car from the bread. However, a woman sees the event and invites you to a baker's site. Girl runs into Chaplin, who claims the police arrived to the theft of bread. However, the woman says that it stole the girl, not Chaplin.

2017

The girl is alone and she is hungry. He looks at the Food Shop window, notices the car next to the bakery and steals it from the bread. However, a woman sees the event and invites the baker to the place. The girl crashes to Chaplin, who, after police arrives, claims to have stolen the bread. The woman, however, says she is stolen by a girl, not Chaplin.

2019

The girl is alone and she's hungry. He looks at the Grocery Store window, notices the car next to the bakery and steals bread from it. However, one woman sees the event and invites the baker to the scene. The girl collides with Chaplin, who, after the police, claims to have stolen the bread. However, she says she was stolen by a girl, not Chaplin.

2021

The girl is alone and hungry. He looks out the window of the Grocery Store, notices the car of the bakery next door, and steals bread from it. However, one woman sees the event and calls the baker to the scene. The girl collides with Chaplin, who, upon arrival at the police, claims to have stolen bread. However, the woman says it was stolen by a girl, not Chaplin.

The four versions show the dynamic character of Google Translate processing, and they reflect the efforts of Google to improve the process, efforts that have gotten attention both in academic and wider communities (e.g. Ducar & Schocket, 2018; Shahani, 2016). In general the results in the four versions show clear signs of improvement but also of major unsolved problems as well as occasional backsliding. (The last of these terms seems apt in light of the use of the word for a category of behavior of aspiring bilinguals that Selinker (1972) termed *backsliding*.)

The differences between the 2015 and the 2021 versions often indicate progress. In the most recent version, comic errors such as the 2015 *steal a car from the bread* are less frequent. The 2021 version also uses *calls* instead of *invites*, a far better choice in the specific context of the scene. The latest version also shows no zero articles before countable nouns, and, in this sense, the Google Translate program outperforms many Finnish learners of English who struggle with articles (see Chapter 5). One remarkable departure from overly simple interlingual identification is where the 2021 version employs the passive *was stolen* to translate the active voice *varasti* (stole), thereby evoking the word order of the original. Because of this use of the passive, the SVO order of the English manages to reflect the Finnish OVS order, which signals a contrastive focus (i.e. contrasting two possible suspects in the theft of the bread), with the focus stated at the end of the sentence in both the Finnish and English versions.

Despite the improvements, however, the 2021 version also shows Google Translate still unable to cope with the ambiguity of the Finnish pronoun *hän*, which can denote either females or males. The pronoun chosen in the second sentence in each version is *he* instead of *she* despite the context of the passage requiring *she*. (Some Finnish learners produced very similar errors, although such cases were not especially common.)

Another major challenge for Google Translate has been the ambiguity of the Finnish word *auton*, which can denote either a car or a truck, and the difficulties entailed by this ambiguity appear in all four translations; the linguistic context provided by *leipomon* (denoting a bakery) makes *truck* a better translation of *auton* than does *car*.

The progress seen from 2015 to 2021 might seem irreversible, but close inspection of all the Google Translate versions shows some backsliding. For example, one specific difference between the 2015 and 2017 translations involves the contrast between the 2015 *Girl runs into Chaplin* and the 2017 *The girl crashes to Chaplin*. Although the 2017 version does have an article that was absent in the 2015 version, the predicate *crashes to Chaplin* constitutes a regression in quality compared with the 2015 *runs into Chaplin*. The choice of *to* instead of *into* is consistent with the analysis of Jarvis and Odlin (2000), who found that the English prepositional choices of Finns were often influenced by the case system of Finnish.

The changes seen in the 2019 and 2021 versions show the 2017 backslide to be no more than a transient flaw; even so, the 2021 version contains similar problems, as with *upon arrival at the police*, where nothing in the preceding context suggests that Chaplin has gone to the police whereas the 2017 version asserts (correctly) that a single police officer has arrived at the scene where the other characters are.

Both successes and failures in the Google Translate versions probably arise from statistical decisions about correspondences in bilingual corpora (i.e. databases) of Finnish and English texts of many kinds. With regard to the Finnish *hän*, for instance, the Google Translate processing routines seem to be trained on English corpora where *he* may appear more often than *she* in the texts. However, such statistical inferences fail to take into account the central role of topic continuity (e.g. Givón, 1990; Jarvis, 2002); thus *she* is obviously the correct translation of *hän* when the antecedent in the first sentence is *tyttö* (girl). Future versions of Google Translate may attempt to take topic continuity into greater account by devising more refined statistical methods (or, algorithms). However, analysts familiar with similar statistical approaches (Williams *et al.*, 2016: 143) have noted that pronominal anaphora (i.e. pronoun reference) remains an unsolved problem – and one inextricably linked to the demands of topic continuity. A question therefore arises as to whether statistical modeling – however good – can overcome this longstanding challenge.

Overreliance on statistical tendencies may also explain the backsliding of cases such as *crash to*, and, if so, any progress in translation quality may be at the mercy of the size of huge yet misleading corpora. Cases such as *crashes to* do indicate 'product' similarities in the interlingual identifications made by humans and by computers. However, the processes involved in such identifications are hardly the same, and it would be mistaken indeed to view Google Translate as a good predictor, at least in the early years of this decade, of all the equivalences (whether accurate or inaccurate) established by human learners.

Even such cases of similar translation products show only a partial overlap. Sometimes the Google Translate program seems more capable, as in its steadily improving ability to supply appropriate articles, as with *tyttö* (a/the girl). Yet human learners draw on more complex decision-making processes, leading both to plausible and less plausible correspondences in their efforts at comprehension and production.

If Google Translate is any guide, machine translation still appears incapable of modeling several equivalences with Finnish *auto* in the context already discussed. While writing in English, some L1 Finnish speakers did use the erroneous *car* seen in all Google Translate versions, but several individuals discovered alternatives: other words chosen include *truck*, *van*, *lorry*, and *bil*; the last of these being a Swedish word that can denote either a car or a truck (like Finnish *auto*). In this instance, *bil* indicates L2 Swedish → L3 English transfer. No Finn, it might be noted, chose English *auto*, which suggests that learners were unaware of this Finnish/English correspondence.

Although few if any researchers might object to considering *bil* a case of transfer in the current context, some might dispute any claim that the other word choices likewise reflect crosslinguistic influence. A skeptic might argue, for example, that the choice of *truck* does not necessarily imply that a Finn recalling the film scene actually brought to mind the Finnish word *auto*; it could be enough simply to recall the film scene and remember the English form *truck* without any mediation of Finnish *auto*. This conceivable objection may hold true for some of the Finnish learners; nevertheless, considerable evidence does suggest that many students had L1 forms in mind that were identified with English forms. For example, *bakery's car*, *bakery's van*, and *bakerys lorry* [*sic*] all appear in the learner corpus (i.e. the English accounts written by Finns and Swedes). In these cases, the writers seem intent on translating the genitive form *leipomon* (bakery's). (The final *–n* in *leipomon* indicates the genitive case although the same consonant ending *auton* indicates the accusative case.) Interestingly, the 2021 Google Translate version also translates the genitive construction but with a prepositional phrase: *of the bakery*. While it may be misguided to claim that every Finnish learner first recalled forms from the L1 and then translated them, examples such as *bakery's car* suggest that translation often takes place after an L1 expression has been formulated. The relation between L1 formulation and subsequent translation will be considered at greater length in the third section of this chapter.

The persistence of difficulties in the Google Translate versions of the Finnish passage illustrates longstanding problems. One pioneer in machine translation, Yeshua Bar-Hillel (1915–75), recognized the usefulness of computers, but he also came to sense insurmountable limits to how good translation programs could ever be (Bar-Hillel, 1960; Hutchins, 2000). In theory such programs might produce translations that would require no subsequent editing by human beings, in which case the strides in technology beyond those in Bar-Hillel's time would be enormous. By the mid-20th century, technology had made it possible for computers to translate certain types of texts (e.g. weather reports). Yet Bar-Hillel grew more skeptical about the feasibility of computational solutions for all conceivable problems of translation.

The theoretical goal of creating software that would require no human editing seems essentially the same from the time of Bar-Hillel to the current era of software such as Google Translate. By the same token, the theoretical goal of fully autonomous capabilities still seems, as Bar-Hillel put it, 'chimerical'. One example that he used to illustrate a key challenge was the English homonym *pen*, which in some contexts denotes a writing implement and in other contexts an enclosed space such as a baby's playpen. If a fully autonomous program were to use Spanish *corral* in the latter context and *pluma* in the former, both would be correct interlingual identifications (although it should be noted that these Spanish examples are mine, not Bar- Hillel's). The translation program would have to cope with the vast extra-linguistic knowledge that forms a part of everyday human experience, such as the fact that boxes normally do not fit inside writing pens but often do fit inside play pens.

What Bar-Hillel has argued is that humans typically resolve linguistic ambiguity by drawing on encyclopedic knowledge to decide on the best interpretation of a word (or phrase or larger unit) in a particular context. Thus, fully autonomous software presupposes artificial intelligence that successfully models any and all aspects of human understanding relevant to flawless interlingual identifications. The encyclopedic knowledge underlying such equivalences includes, no doubt, elusive pragmatic principles such as those that led translators of English and German to equate very different syntactic patterns in focus constructions (Chapter 6). Achieving the artificial intelligence required to formulate similarly good translations may come only after many years if ever at all.

The limited success of machine translation in the Finnish example brings to mind the successes and limitations of spellchecking programs. In both cases, the successes argue cogently against naysayers who might wish to ban current technology from language instruction. Even so, the persisting problems in machine translation show that any naïve faith in technology should be met with a skeptical eye. Language instructors will fare best by acknowledging that machine translation can prove valuable – as long as a capable human remains available to iron out any problem, as also in the case of spellchecking problems. In effect, the greater the successes of machine translation, the greater the illusion is that users can utterly rely on its interlingual equivalences. Well-informed teachers need to warn their students that what may seem highly intelligent systems remain far more limited than learners' own capacities, even if the latter require help from teachers in developing (see Chapter 8).

The successes of machine translation seem due mainly to ever-improving algorithms, as where the active voice *varasti* (stole) was satisfactorily equated with the passive voice *was stolen* in a particular context in the 2021 Google Translate product seen above. Even so, this statistical approach has yet to prove adequate for solving the problem of topic continuity, as seen in the persistent error of supplying *he* when *she* is needed. This lack of progress may reflect inherent limitations of the research environment in which the algorithms are developed. In a recent survey of different statistical approaches, Williams *et al.* (2016) acknowledge that 'For the most part researchers and practitioners do not worry about the linguistic and philosophical question of what it means to talk about language and cognition as probabilistic processes' (2016: xiii). The statistical models developed are primarily tools, and the practical value of particular tools controls the focus of research. This tool-making environment may not be conducive to efforts at modeling cognitive processes such as those underlying topic continuity, especially attention and memory.

Nevertheless, a radically revised approach to machine translation in recent years may lead to modelling at least some dimensions of cognitive processes. Most significant are efforts of machine translation specialists (including Google teams) to employ neural network modeling for translation problems (Ducar & Schocket, 2018; Koehn, 2020). Indeed, neural network models of translation might be integrated into the neural models that some SLA researchers (e.g. Ellis, 2008) have proposed. In any case, discussion in this chapter should now return to what human users of language do when translating.

There has not been, to my knowledge, a systematic study of translators as language learners, but research in translation studies does offer valuable insights. Mary Howitt (1799–1888), a writer of the Victorian era, has been studied in some detail regarding her translations from Danish to English of the tales of Hans Christian Andersen (Malmkjaer, 2001, 2005). Malmkjaer's analysis focuses on two facets of the translations: (1) cases where Howitt seems to have willfully altered the Andersen stories to suit the perceived needs of an audience of Victorian children; and (2) cases of apparently unintentional changes of meaning in Andersen's stories. It is the second type that offers insights most relevant to the interests of SLA researchers.

A native speaker of English, Howitt did not study Danish until middle age, and then most of her experience with the language seems to have come from living and working in the university town of Heidelberg, Germany, where she also studied German. Malmkjaer gives examples of translations indicating that Howitt was apparently misled by false-friends or by other deceptive similarities, as in the following cases (Malmkjaer, 2005: 68–69). First appears the Danish expression, then a word-by-word gloss of the expression, and finally Howitt's translation.

Sometider,   om   Natten
Sometimes   at   night-the
Howitt: 'in the summer season at night'

In the above example the formal similarity between Danish *some* and English *summer* seems to have misled Howitt, even though the English *some* offered the chance for positive transfer. In the next example (Malmkjaer, 2001: 153), a partial formal similarity between a Danish verb and English *stood* occasioned the erroneous translation:

Muldvarpen   stØdte   til   den
Mole-the   knocked   to   it
Howitt: 'the mole stood beside it'

Howitt also mistook some single lexical items for phrases, as when she translated *Sommerfugelne* ('the butterflies') as a longer phrase, 'the summer birds' (Malmkjaer, 2001: 152). Not all of Howitt's misjudgements involved L1/L2 relations (Malmkjaer, 2005: 68):

over   Iseen
across   ice-the
Howitt: 'over the iron'

In this instance, the influence of L3 German *Eisen* ('iron') apparently overrode the positive transfer that would have resulted from an interlingual identification between Danish *ise* and English *ice*.

Misinterpretation of texts as in the case of Howitt does not constitute the only hazard for a translator in her position. Castagnoli (2016) studied the productions of native speakers of Italian who translated L2 English texts into their native language. The translators in this case were students enrolled in a professional translation program. The structures that Castagnoli focused on were various devices to link clauses, especially conjunctions and conjunctive adverbs. In comparison with a group of professional translators, the trainees showed greater 'adherence' (as Castagnoli puts it) to English patterns in their Italian renditions. For example, there was a tendency to use more sentence-initial adverbs, a tendency that Castagnoli sees as more pronounced in English than in Italian. She equates such 'adherence' with interference although, crucially, her study involves L2 → L1 transfer (see Chapter 1). To counter such interference, she developed classroom materials from corpora of translations so that students might compare the merits of different translations. Such pedagogical solutions resemble ones employed to help L2 learners become more aware of crosslinguistic similarities and differences (see Chapter 8).

Individual Variation

Translators normally have options in just how to represent the meanings of one language in the words of another. Malmkjaer (2005: 65) offers several examples of translations of a single sentence of Hans Christian Andersen: *See, det war en rigtig Historie!* Among them are the following renditions:

- And this, mind you, is a real story.
- Look you, this is a true story.
- There now, that was a real story!
- There's a fine story for you!
- How about that for a real story!
- Now that was a real story!

Only a few characteristics of the original Danish invariably appear in these translations, such as the rendering of *en* as an indefinite article *a*. Other grammatical morphemes, such as the past tense *war* ('was'), do not always have their prototypical meanings reflected in each translation, as with the use of present tense *is* in three of the translations (including one contracted form). Danish *see*, which is cognate with English *see*, proves to be even more variable in the translations; such variability probably reflects the fact that in the Danish original, the use of *see* has a discourse function that lends itself to different interpretations, including *there now*, *now*, and *how about*.

Literary translations often show wide variation, as with the alternative versions of the Andersen sentence. Classical authors such as Homer have challenged translators for centuries, and there may be no limit to possible renderings of poems, plays or novels. The reasons for such variation reflect, among other things, different assumptions and theories about translation itself. According to Schulte and Biguenet (1992), Western theories of translation did not frequently emphasize the importance of fidelity to the source language in the text of the original work before the 18th century. Even after the rise of that emphasis, the ancient art of re-creating a source text by translating it has remained strong, as in the famous 19th-century English translation by Edward FitzGerald of the medieval *Rubaiyat* of the Persian poet, Omar Khayyam (with interesting samples of both FitzGerald's and a literal version provided by Kennedy & Gioia, 2013: 953–954).

Yet even when a translator shows little interest in creating a new work, so to speak, the ideal of a definitive translation can prove elusive, partly because of linguistic ambiguities in the source text. Tabakowska (1993) compares two different English versions of a passage in Polish in a novel by Stanisław Łeim and finds several cases of where the translators diverged considerably in how they construed the novelist's description of a Swiss hotel. (The study also considered two translations of the same passage into French, but space does not permit a discussion of the results, which were similar in some ways to the English translations.) The divergences often involve subtle grammatical points, as in the following cases (1993: 791), where E1 stands for one of the translations and E2 the other:

E1: the Swiss chocolate smokes in delicate porcelain cups.

E2: the Swiss chocolate is steaming in the delicate china.

The Polish original is as follows:

z	cienkiej	porcelany	dymi	szwajcarska czekolada
from	delicate	porcelain	smokes	Swiss chocolate

Although different in several ways, E1 and E2 do share some traits, including basic word order since both versions show the canonical English SV pattern whereas in the Polish clause the subject (*szwajcarska czekolada*) follows the verb (*dymi*). Some vocabulary is also the same in both versions, such as *delicate* and *chocolate*. Even so, the divergences between E1 and E2 are striking. E1 uses a different verb and verb tense, the present simple, in *smokes*, while E2 uses the present progressive *is steaming*. What contains the Swiss chocolate is also represented differently: E2 expresses it as *the delicate china*, whereas E1 expresses it as *delicate porcelain cups*, with no article at the beginning of the noun phrase.

Tabakowska describes the translators who produced E1 and E2 as 'bilingual native speakers of English' (1993: 788). She also considers E1 and E2 as accurate translations of the Polish original, so any divergences are not misreadings. Nevertheless, the examples seen here as well as others in the same paper show that E1 and E2 differ in consistent ways. The use by E2 of a definite article in *the delicate china* and the present progressive in *is steaming* illustrate what Tabakowska calls an 'instantaneous' construal of the Polish original, whereas the simple present *smokes* and the absence of an article in *delicate porcelain* illustrate a 'recurrent' construal by E1 of the Polish original. Tabakowska likens the instantaneous/recurrent contrast to the difference between describing a picture while one is looking at it and describing a picture for a museum catalog. The definite article and the present progressive contribute to making the scene more vivid in E2 while the absence of an article and the use of the present simple make the E1 version more schematic. Readers of the two descriptions may see the use of a definite article as the first word in each translation as confounding the instantaneous/recurrent analysis. For Tabakowska, however, such uses of articles help suggest that the Swiss setting is highly accessible to the fictional speaker whose voice is represented in the passage.

Throughout this summary of Tabakowska's analysis, the words *construed* and *construal* have appeared, since her analysis draws heavily on the theory of cognitive grammar of Langacker (1987) in which the notion of construal figures prominently. Space does not permit a detailed look at this approach to construal, and indeed the approach has evolved over the years (e.g. Langacker, 2008) to give the theory of cognitive grammar wider scope. However, underlying both early and later versions of the theory is the assumption that speakers may construe situations in different ways and may thus choose different perspectives and concomitant grammatical structures to realize their construals. Translation poses interesting challenges for cognitive grammar, since any production of the translator requires trying to understand the construal of the author of the source text. For this reason, Tabakowska characterizes the translator's interpretation of the original author's construal as a 'reconstrual' (1993: 796).

The individual variation evident in the products of E1 and E2 shows to Tabakowska the 'inherently subjective character' of the process of reconstrual of a source text (1993: 796). Although the structures in that text normally reduce the range of accurate interpretations, the subjective experience of reconstructing meanings can lead to differing translations, as in the recurring/instantaneous interpretations of E1 and E2. In this subjectivity Tabakowska sees implications for L2 pedagogy: 'What the teacher considers an error is frequently only an interpretational difference which merely reflects the possibility of alternative views of reality' (1993: 785). The same subjectivity rules out, in her judgement, textbook rule formulations of translation equivalence.

The study of Castagnoli (discussed in the preceding section) likewise considers the challenges of ambiguity for translators although, in this instance, the ambiguities do not arise from crosslinguistic differences in the determiner systems but rather from differences involving conjunctions and conjunctive adverbs. Castagnoli notes cases where translator trainees provided more explicit cohesive devices in their Italian versions of English texts. In effect, the trainees often seemed to try to minimize L2 → L1 transfer by offering their own interpretations of the meaning relations between successive clauses in the English source texts.

Individual variation in interpreting not only shows the importance of human judgement but also what is often called linguistic indeterminacy. This issue has also interested philosophers, as will be discussed briefly at the end of this chapter. Indeterminacy also poses a problem for SLA researchers when they provide interpretations in, for example, standard English for interlanguage utterances. For instance, it is virtually impossible to decide if the first noun phrase in the following sentence should be interpreted as indefinite or definite: *Girl take bread* (F5 04). Written by a native speaker of Finnish, the sentence is the first in this individual's narration of the *Modern Times* film (details on F5 and other groups as well as on procedures appear in Chapter 5). SLA and translation studies of article use by Finns show caution in interpreting NPs in Finnish and in learner English (Chesterman, 1991; Jarvis, 2002), and a similar caution is advisable in general. Zero marking in noun phrases having either indefinite or definite reference is common in Finnish, and the potential ambiguity of an NP with no determiner makes for uncertainty as to whether *a girl* or *the girl* would be the most accurate translation of the above sentence. Either translation would be consistent with native-speaker usage and, indeed, native speakers of English in the same corpus collected by Jarvis use both indefinite and definite article – and even if they had all used the same article, native-speaker behavior would be insufficient for understanding interlanguage productions (Bley-Vroman, 1983). With semantic uncertainty, then, the best procedure for an SLA researcher will be to offer alternative versions: e.g. *a/the girl*, for the standard English translation.

Not all cases of interlanguage cause interpretive difficulty, however. Some individual variation manifests itself in the different morphosyntactic options that learners choose for translating something from the native language to their version of the target language. The following cases from the *Modern Times* corpus illustrate some of the possible variation found in the writing of native speakers of Finnish:

A policeman came *behind of they*. (F9A 14)

Suddenly girl sow [saw] *their behind* is police and their run away. (F5 62)

The discourse context in these descriptions is the same but the syntactic structures locating Charlie Chaplin and Paulette Goddard in relation to the policeman are different (Odlin, 2012). The first uses a prepositional phrase, albeit with a *they* instead of *them* and with a superfluous *of* (that is, unnecessary according to the norms of the target language). However, the superfluous *of* seems to hint why *their* is used in the second example and why a somewhat similar sentence describing another event in the film also uses a possessive construction:

> *In their back* was a litle [*sic*] house where came man and a women out of doors. (F9B 20)

Even though each learner's pattern is distinct, all of them reflect a common structure in Finnish using a postposition to govern the case of the preceding noun or pronoun, which is frequently marked as a genitive (i.e. possessive), as in this example:

Poliisi   tulee   heidän   taakse (FX 02)
Police (sg) comes   they-GEN   behind
'The policeman comes behind them'.

The word *taakse* is not the only form used by Finns writing about the same scenes, but the other forms likewise trigger the genitive case. As for the three interlanguage sentences above, they are clearly attempts of inexpert translators who have sought to preserve some trace of an L1 grammatical pattern that has no justification (by the norms of the target language). It might seem tempting to regard all variation as differences in subjective assessments, as 'reconstruals' like those that Tabakowska studied. However, some of the variation clearly involves differences in the interlanguage grammatical classifications of bilinguals who are much less advanced than those studied by Tabakowska or Castagnoli.

The examples considered so far show individual variation both in what translators comprehend and in what they produce. SLA research proves valuable in showing still another kind of variation, namely, in the judgements of bilinguals about what qualifies as a good translation. As noted in Chapter 3, Kellerman (1977) considered the problem of the close equivalence of some idioms in Dutch and English. For example, he found that several Dutch students doubted whether certain English idioms such as *dyed-in-the-wool*, which has a close parallel in Dutch, were bona fide expressions in the target language. In other words, some translation parallels between Dutch and English seemed too good to be true to these learners. Kellerman, it will be recalled, put too much emphasis on the notion of a 'constraint' on transfer, with counter-evidence for his claim coming from Irish English and other language-contact situations. Furthermore, despite Kellerman's focus on learner skepticism, his graphs and figures (e.g. 1977: 119) show a great deal of individual variation. Thus, although some learners had serious doubts about the transferability of Dutch idioms, other learners had few if any doubts.

Why individuals may vary in their comprehension, their production, or their judgements of translations is a topic well worth investigating, but the answers to such questions may be complex. In any case, individual variation is a key challenge for anyone seeking to understand translation processes.

Translation and Cognitive Processing in Acquisition

Individual differences and problems in interlingual identifications show, as already seen, some of the overlap between transfer and translation. In this section, two further dimensions of the overlap will be considered: first, the implications of translation for one particular model of speech production (a model that claims to account for the role of transfer); and second, a review of certain processing factors involved in interlingual identifications.

One prominent model of production in SLA is what Pienemann (1998) and colleagues call Processability Theory (PT). This approach focuses on certain grammatical properties, and it posits an acquisition sequence of five stages: (1) words; (2) category procedure; (3) phrasal procedure; (4) S-procedure; and (5) subordinate clause procedure (Pienemann *et al.*, 2005: 141). The first PT stage shows a use of L2 word forms that have meanings but not, according to PT, any syntactic categorization. The next stage, category procedure, reflects the onset of using affixes such as the English plural *-s*, whereas the third stage involves phrase formation, including noun phrases and prepositional phrases. The fourth stage involves intra-clausal relations of constituents such as between subjects and verbs, and the final stage reflects inter-clausal relations. All the preceding stages are tantamount to 'processing prerequisites' (Pienemann *et al.*, 2005: 143), and in this sense the sequence is strictly implicational:

> ....according to PT, both the construction of the L2 from 'square one' and developmental constraints on L1 transfer follow from the hierarchical nature of the learning task... In this scenario, there is no other logical point of departure for this L2 construction process than the beginning of the processability hierarchy because the hierarchy at this point is stripped off [*sic*] all language-specific lexical features and syntactic routines. (Pienemann *et al.*, 2005: 143)

The PT sequence posits a chronology, as seen in the hypothesis 'that the distinctive syntactic features of subordinate clauses will be acquired *after* inter-phrasal exchange of information' [i.e. after the fourth stage] (Pienemann, 1998: 68; emphasis added). A related assumption holds that 'the learner will construct the formulator of the L2 from scratch' (Pienemann *et al.*, 2005: 143), where 'formulator' designates an ensemble of language-specific morphosyntactic routines required in the production of speech or writing, the construct of the formulator being central to a highly influential model of speech production proposed by Levelt (1989).

The relation of translation to transfer calls into question some assumptions of Processability Theory and evidence on that point will be considered shortly. However, it will first help to examine a few details of Levelt's notion of the formulator and Pienemann's use of that notion in PT. The formulator stands between what Levelt calls the 'conceptualizer' and the 'articulator', two systems whose functions are self-evident in their names. The formulator 'translates conceptual structure into linguistic structure' (Levelt, 1989: 11), and, by the same token, what the formulator produces 'becomes the input to the next processing component: the Articulator' (1989: 12). The formulator is thus posited as a psychologically real grammatical component involving semantics, morphosyntax, phonology and even phonetics.

Levelt's model also incorporates a lexicon, and it acknowledges the interrelation between production and comprehension although his discussion of the latter is, by his own admission, minimal – even so, another part of the model, a monitor to track production, leads him to discuss the role of comprehension a little. Objections to Levelt's model might arise over locating phonological and phonetic processing in the formulator instead of in the articulator, but one advantage of Levelt's approach is that it provides a way to account for 'internal speech', to use his term (1989: 13). Unarticulated formulations are probably what most people have in mind when they discuss 'thinking in English' or in any other language, and the formulations can provide the input for messages to be written rather than spoken.

Proponents of Processability Theory use Levelt's model in their own approach, and they consider it applicable to the analysis of writing as well as speaking in a new language, as seen in a study by Håkansson et al. (2002). This investigation focused on L3 German word order by L1 speakers of Swedish. The results indicate that Swedish learners did not make much use of the crosslinguistic similarity between their native language and German in the word-order pattern known as V2, and Håkansson et al. deem there to be little positive transfer, with this conclusion supporting their hypothesized hierarchy. They also disavow any major influence from L2 English that might explain the L3 patterns seen in their data.

The conclusions of Håkansson et al. about transfer have proved controversial. Bohnacker (2005), for example, obtained quite different results in her investigation of L2 German word order as her participants had Swedish as their L1 but no L2 English. Pienemann and Håkansson (2007) have offered a rebuttal of Bohnacker's analysis, but still other research by Bohnacker and Rosén (2008) suggests that L1 Swedish influence may exist in ways contrary to PT predictions. Moreover, work on the English of L1 Finnish speakers indicates patterns of individual variation not compatible with the PT hierarchy in relation to transfer (Odlin, 2013).

Along with the empirical challenges it has faced, the PT approach to transfer suffers from an unwarranted assumption involving translation. In its 'developmentally moderated' approach to crosslinguistic influence (to use a phrase of Pienemann and Håkansson), the only formulator available for L2 speakers or writers is the one built 'from scratch', a formulator that will restrict L1 influence to just those stages where, by the criteria of PT, the 'developmental prerequisites' have been met. Yet this assumption about one – and only one – formulator fails to take into account another option that learners at any stage of L2 proficiency have: namely, to use the L1 formulator and then to translate either a part or the entirety of that formulation into the L2.

Different kinds of evidence point to some use of translation among language learners. Not surprisingly, the evidence indicates very different degrees of success in the translations. One case of highly successful translation involves Prince Albert, the German-born consort of Queen Victoria of England. Albert, a passionate opponent of the international slave trade, undertook to deliver a short address on the issue in London in 1840. A biographer provides the following account:

> He wrote his own brief address—only about two hundred words—in German, then translated it with Victoria's help. Nervously he memorized it, trying out on Victoria his ringing phrases about the slave trade… Then, on 1 June 1840, he spoke before five or six thousand people (in his estimate) in Exeter Hall in the Strand… On his conclusion, he reported to Victoria, there was 'great applause'. To attempt the address at all was an act of courage for a twenty-year-old to whom English was a foreign tongue. (Weintraub, 1997: 105)

The prince was no beginner in English, it should be added. Before his marriage to Victoria, the couple apparently wrote to each other in both English and German (Weintraub, 1997: 4). For Albert to write in L2 English and Victoria in L2 German there would obviously be good opportunities for practice. As for the advantages of composing in their native languages, the couple could rely on their L1s to achieve the greatest possible precision in their internal speech. From the evidence that Albert's biographer gives (Weintraub, 1997: 4), the prince showed a clear awareness of this advantage of L1 formulation. Of course, when Albert chose that option to prepare for his London speech, he could count on attentive help with his translation into what was, quite literally, the Queen's English.

Clearly, the L2 re-creation of an L1 formulation can offer considerable precision, as long as the L1 version is translated well, notwithstanding fears of the speaker (or writer) that something has been lost in translation. However, examples of inexpert translation are not hard to find, such as *Their behind is police*, considered in the preceding section. Another remarkable example from the same corpus comes also from a learner whose native language was Finnish:

> And policeman come to streets and he see a man who (jolla) is a bread. (F9B 19)

The discourse context allows for the following paraphrase:

> 'And a [*or*, the] policeman came along the street and saw a man with a loaf of bread.'

The learner's sentence comes from a short account of the first events in the *Modern Times* episode described in Chapter 5, events referred to as the Rich Lady Scene. In this context, the fourth sentence asserts, though with ill-formed syntax, the fact that the police officer sees Charlie Chaplin holding the bread. Chaplin's possession of the stolen item can be signaled by a Finnish relative pronoun *jolla*, which takes an inflection known as the adessive case. There is no commonly used verb in Finnish corresponding to English *have*. Instead, the adessive case is used with a noun or pronoun along with some form of the Finnish verb that is more or less the translation equivalent of the English copular verb *be*. Thus, to say in Finnish *I have money*, the normal translation would be *Minulla on rahaa* (At-me is money), where the *-lla* marks the adessive case form often translated as *at*, and where *on* corresponds to *is* and *rahaa* to *money*.

The very great structural difference between Finnish and English in the expression of possession in such instances is undoubtedly reflected in: the *man who (jolla) is a bread*. The learner's putting *jolla* in parentheses suggests uncertainty about whether *who* is the best way to translate the adessive form and also suggests that the Finnish formulation translated into English was probably *mies, jolla on leipää* (man at-whom is bread).

Between the extremes of highly expert and utterly inexpert translation, there are many possible intermediate degrees of success for L2 users. For example, in the sentence *In their back was a lit[t]le house* the possessive *their* suggests influence of the Finnish genitive pattern discussed in the preceding section, but the sentence pattern comes closer to the English norm for prepositional phrases and does not show the postpositional structure of: *Their behind is police*.

The gradations of quality in translations strongly argue that the translation processes are complex and subject to much individual variation. As to the capacities required for successful translators and interpreters, there are at least three evident in existing research: processing experience, metalinguistic awareness and focus on meaning.

Although it seems prudent to regard these as three independent factors, they often occur together in the studies to be discussed. Tymczyńska (2012) sees processing experience as a more important factor than formal similarity in explaining judgements about whether selected pairs of words are translation equivalents, the pairs coming from L1 Polish, L2 English and L3 German (with different lists involving different language pairs). Compared with a group of conference interpreters, a group of trilingual philology students did not make as many accurate judgements, nor did a group of interpreter trainees. Tymczyńska also predicted that the professional interpreters would be faster in making their judgements, but the results indicate a rather mixed picture in this regard. What matters more, according to Tymczyńska, is the efficient organization of processing resources. From their years of professional experience, the interpreters managed far better to stay focused on the meaning relations between words in three different languages.

The focus on meaning that Tymczyńska sees as especially characteristic of highly experienced interpreters is a skill that can start to develop early and go hand in hand with increasing metalinguistic awareness. Among monolingual children, some parts of this awareness begin in preschool years and constitute a prerequisite for (among other things) reading readiness (Hakes, 1980). In work on young bilinguals, Malakoff (1992) found the translation abilities of the Canadian children she studied to be quite sound in many cases, and their sensitivity to meaning was impressive, even if not as developed as among the adult multilinguals studied by Tymczyńska. The young bilinguals were able to avoid pitfalls such as false cognates, e.g. English *blessed* and French *blessé* (which means 'wounded'). For Malakoff, translation is a 'natural' metalinguistic ability (see also Malakoff & Hakuta, 1991).

Experience, metalinguistic awareness, and focus on meaning all affect the translation process. But there remains the question of how common translation is in the everyday behavior of language learners in either comprehension or production. Some research has sought to address the question. For example, O'Malley *et al.* (1985) consider a wide range of learning strategies in SLA, including translation. In interviews with a group of 70 beginning and intermediate ESL students about the strategies they used, the responses indicated that translation was especially frequent among the beginners and somewhat less so among the intermediates. Compared with other strategies such as using imagery and taking notes, translating was one of the more preferred options that learners pursued. O'Malley *et al.* note that the participants were mainly L1 Spanish speakers but with some L1 Vietnamese speakers as well. The authors do not, however, provide details on variation between the L1 groups or between individuals in their reliance on translation. Even so, the evidence suggests that translation has a prominent place in the toolbox of options available to learners.

The results of one study do not necessarily settle the question of how frequent translation is in SLA, of course. Apart from the details not reported by O'Malley *et al.*, there are other unconsidered problems, such as whether self-reports on a process as complex as translation are highly reliable. Even if they are, there is also the question of whether the translation process is equally common in written and oral production. Still other questions arise with regard to the role that translation may or may not play in listening versus reading comprehension.

Despite many uncertainties, some tentative generalizations seem possible from the cases considered in this section. One is that the role of translation must be part of any plausible theory of second language production; by ignoring the fact that some bilinguals rely on translation, Processability Theory fails to account for some of the variation in L2 production data or to consider factors such as experience and metalinguistic awareness that affect translation quality. Another viable generalization is that translation processes overlap with concerns such as crosslinguistic influence. Clearly the scope of SLA research should be widened.

Conclusion

This chapter has considered the overlap of translation with transfer with much attention being given to problems involving crosslinguistic equivalence, individual variation and cognitive processing. Specific findings include these:

- Some of the difficulties in making an interlingual identification are evident both in shortcomings of translation software and in similar errors of second language learners.
- Although the products of faulty equivalences are comparable in SLA and in machine translation, the processes differ radically, with second language learners usually more able to use world knowledge and contextual information to make more reliable interlingual identifications.
- Professional translators sometimes experience problems no different from those encountered by language learners. When the source language is non-native to the translator, transfer-induced miscomprehension may occur, and when the target into which the translation is made is not native, the risk of transfer-induced production may be high.
- Individuals often vary in how they translate a source text, with such variation being due (partly) to subjective factors in the translation process, including how translators understand something ambiguous in the source. Second language teachers should keep in mind the possibility of source-language ambiguities when they judge student translations, and SLA researchers should be cautious in their interpretations of interlanguage speech or writing.

- Some individual differences do not entail ambiguity but do appear in the grammatical options that learners decide on in transferring something from the native language to their own version of the target language.
- The model of L2 speech production known as Processability Theory (PT) assumes that learners must construct their L2 formulator from scratch and that unless learners have fulfilled the developmental prerequisites of a particular stage, their L2 formulations will be limited in the kinds of structures they can produce and in the kinds of structures they can transfer from L1 to L2. However, the putative developmental constraints do not take into account an alternative mode of production: to use the L1 formulator to construct a message and then to translate it into the target language.
- When language learners do resort to L1 formulations that are then translated, the results often vary in their accuracy. Among the factors affecting variation in successful translation are the experience of the individual in translating, metalinguistic awareness and focus on meaning.

The examples in this chapter do not exhaust the topic of how translation intersects with transfer. Indeed, in the final chapter translation proves relevant to questions of language-specific processing and to effective pedagogies for bilingual and multilingual classrooms.

8 Conclusion

Summaries appear at the beginning of Parts 1 and 2 for each of the chapters, and so no repetition of the findings seems necessary here. Instead, the discussion will follow various threads running through those chapters that have implications for research and teaching.

Research Implications

Part 1, it will be recalled, focused on predictions about transfer, while Part 2 focused on language-specific processing. Although these are separate topics, they are interdependent. Indeed, understanding the implications of language-specific processing will affect how researchers think about predictions. For example, Chapter 3 detailed some empirical results of processing research that underlie new predictions, as in the findings of Jarvis (2002) about topic continuity and positive transfer of articles. Nevertheless, it remains unclear what the exact limits are to the scope of such predictions. The same chapter considered the problem of affect, especially with regard to focus constructions, and Chapter 6 provided a closer look at such cases, including possible processing implications. Although every human language, it seems safe to claim, has focusing constructions, the cross-linguistic comparability in form and function remains problematic – and likewise problematic are challenges in understanding or producing such constructions. Not surprisingly, translation is highly relevant to such questions of comparability and processing, and Chapter 6 uses evidence involving the (non)translatability of focus patterns, while Chapter 7 considers still wider overlaps in regard to comprehension, production and translation.

Not all language professionals agree with the premises of this book, that language-specific processing exists and that predictions of transfer are useful. Chapters 2 and 3 have considered some of the skepticism about predictions but also much of the evidence justifying them. As for language-specific processing, the term might seem synonymous with linguistic relativity, i.e. language-specific influences on cognition. However, it seems best to see relativity as just a special case of such processing. The following results were discussed at length in the volume yet none of them should be regarded as evidence for relativity:

- L1 → L2 transfer of basic word order and likewise L2 → L1 transfer (Chapter 4).
- Greater use of *it*-cleft sentences by native speakers of Swedish (in comparison with speakers of Finnish) in written accounts of the film *Modern Times* (Chapter 5).
- Use of focus constructions to express emotions in L2 similar to modes of expression in L1 (Chapters 3 and 6).
- Use of target-language words with classifications found in L1 but not in the L2, as in the use by some Finns of *even* as a conjunction and *behind* as a postposition (Chapters 5 and 7).
- A misunderstanding by the translator Mary Howitt of L3 Danish *Iseen* (the ice) from her knowledge of L2 German *Eisen* (iron) (Chapter 7).

These cases, as well as others, do suggest that transfer often results from interlingual identifications that guide comprehension or production in distinct ways that depend very much on what the native language of the learner is, or on what the L2 or L3 may be in cases of trilingual or multilingual acquisition. As for cases of actual relativity, this subset of language-specific processing does seem to exist, but this subset (often termed *conceptual transfer*) has gotten less attention in this book, although I have discussed it elsewhere (e.g. Odlin, 2005).

The suspicion that some linguists and psychologists have shown about linguistic relativity often arises from a widely shared assumption about the existence of language-neutral cognition, as Pinker (1994) succinctly expresses it: 'People do not think in English, Chinese, or Apache; they think in a language of thought. This language of thought probably looks a bit like all of those languages' (1994: 81). Space does not allow any extended discussion of Pinker's assertion; nevertheless, there is no reason to believe that *all* cognition is language-independent even though much of it may be. Furthermore, the likelihood seems high that some language-specific processing (including much of what is called transfer) does not require seeing relativity as involved.

Not surprisingly, relativistic thinkers have shown an interest in topics such as transfer and translation. With regard to transfer, the philosopher Wilhelm von Humboldt considered the language-specific conceptual world of the L1 as inevitably transferring, at least to some extent, in a learner's attempts to acquire the new conceptual viewpoint found in the target language (Chapter 1). The 20th-century philosopher Willard Van Orman Quine, also saw transfer, which he termed 'projection' (1961: 70), as indispensable for language learning, but the interlingual identifications inherent in such projections were subject to some degree of uncertainty about the extent of actual crosslinguistic equivalence.

In an earlier discussion focused on translation, Quine (1959: 172) stressed that the 'indeterminacy' of crosslinguistic identifications greatly complicates the question of what constitutes a good translation, especially in cases involving two highly divergent languages. Another philosopher strongly interested in translation was the 19th-century thinker Arthur Schopenhauer (1992[1891]). Like von Humboldt, he considered every language to have its own conceptual profile or, as he put it, *Begriffssphäre* (concept sphere). Schopenhauer was arguably even more skeptical than Quine about the adequacy of translations, but his views on the value of crosslinguistic awareness and on the value of multilingualism in promoting such awareness seem ahead of their time and, indeed, resemble assumptions found in work on translation and pedagogy to be discussed in the next section.

Before turning to that pedagogical research, however, it seems appropriate to consider, albeit briefly, how future SLA research could incorporate points about predictions and processing raised here. As considered before, all linguistic relativity can be viewed as a subset of language-specific processing even while, by the same logic, not all language-specific processing should be considered as relativity. Even so, the stress that thinkers such as von Humboldt, Schopenhauer, and Quine placed on crosslinguistic differences may have implications not only for relativity but for processing more widely. The implications suggest questions, such as how intractable processing difficulties are when highly divergent languages come in contact, how the acquisition of new processing routines affects efforts to learn a third or a fourth language, how such new processing affects the processing of one's native language, and how such routines affect the ultimate attainment of any new language.

One area where the preceding questions might be studied is grammatical gender. A well known difference between English and French is that *the sun* translates as a masculine *le soleil*, whereas *the moon* translates as the feminine *la lune*. Thus celestial objects that have no gender undergo an arbitrary classification in French (and in other Romance languages) as either feminine or masculine. Objections to the word *arbitrary* in the previous sentence might invoke Freudian notions of subliminal sexual assumptions to argue that the classification is natural, but an obvious problem with such an argument is that, in some other languages, the gender classification of the same celestial objects is the opposite of the Romance pattern: German, for example, classifies *Sonne* (sun) as feminine and *Mond* (moon) as masculine. The arbitrariness of such classifications seems clear even though some research on semantic transfer makes a case for the classifications having real effects on bilingual judgements (Jarvis & Pavlenko, 2008). The most interesting implications of grammatical gender may, however, involve the function of the systems, regardless of how individual words may be classified.

Linguists have differed on the problem of the systemic functions of gender. Some analysts (e.g. Jespersen, 1922) have been skeptical about any processing implications of gender, yet others (e.g. Corbett, 1999) have regarded it as an aid to reference tracking in discourse. One difficulty in resolving the issue arises from the fact that not all languages have grammatical gender: French, German, Swedish, Dutch and Arabic do, whereas English, Persian, Finnish and Japanese do not. If there is any cognitive particularity involved in using grammatical gender to track ongoing reference in spoken or written discourse, SLA research might offer valuable perspectives on the problem. For example, studies of transfer and gender might help ascertain whether language-specific processing figures in performance.

One relevant study (Sabourin *et al.*, 2006) focused on the acquisition of grammatical gender in Dutch, finding considerable positive transfer among speakers of German, a language quite similar to Dutch. However, results in the same study also indicate that even speakers of French, Spanish, and Italian outperformed speakers of English even though the L1 German group did best of all. The Romance languages do have grammatical gender, as the examples from French given above show, but French, Spanish, and Italian show many systemic differences from Dutch and German. Even so, the results of the study strongly suggest that the processing routines acquired with a grammatical gender system are somewhat transferable. This inference has further support from a study by Alhaware (2009) of the acquisition of Arabic gender by speakers of French and English. French speakers outperformed English speakers in the acquisition of Arabic gender.

The results of both studies thus suggest possible language-specific processing advantages related to gender systems. Accordingly, the results invite predictions for future research, such as these:

> Speakers of Persian as a group will have greater difficulty with the gram-
> matical gender markings of French than will speakers of Pashto as a group.

The form of such predictions was discussed in Chapter 3, and other predictions about gender appear elsewhere (Odlin, 2014).

As noted above, Persian has no grammatical gender, and so acquiring gender in French may constitute as much of a problem for this group as for, say, a group of English speakers. However, Pashto, an Iranian language closely related to Persian (and very distantly to English) does have grammatical gender, so that there may in fact be a processing advantage for speakers of this group.

Without a doubt, many questions remain involving predictions and processing. For example, if speakers of Persian or English do surmount most, or even all, of the challenges of gender in a language such as French, there is the question of whether such new processing abilities confer an advantage in acquiring the gender system of yet another language, e.g. Dutch. Also uncertain is what cognitive changes, if any, successful acquisition of a new gender system may promote in general domains such as attention and memory. If such advantages prove to be real, there would be, of course, further evidence for conceptual transfer. As intriguing as such surmises are, the practical issues related to transfer in the classroom now require attention.

Implications for Teaching

Three concerns intersecting with transfer have especially clear implications for language teaching: predictions, translations, and metalinguistic awareness. The first of these can be addressed quite briefly, partly because of the discussion in the preceding section as well as in preceding chapters. Thus, teachers and curriculum planners might be able to make informal but credible predictions involving speakers of a language previously unheard at a school, as might happen, for instance, when a new immigrant group becomes part of a community. If the target language has articles but the new language does not, the new learners may perform like the Finns learning English (who have been considered at various points in this book).

With regard to translation, various examples in Chapter 7 and elsewhere indicate attempts of some learners to translate from their L1 to aid in comprehension or production. There are, furthermore, recent examples of the value of translation tests to help establish cases of language transfer, as in a study by Li and Yang (2016) of Chinese learners confronting topic continuity in English and a study by Chang and Zhang (2016) of L1 English learners seeming to engage in translation in attempting to use causative verbs in L2 Chinese.

While such research can remind teachers of the relevance of translation to SLA, there is also empirical work showing the value of translation as a teaching tool. For example, Laufer and Girsai (2008) compared two groups of learners, one given translation tasks as part of their EFL instruction and the other group given only the same reading passage that the former group had. The tasks of the experimental group involved both L2 English → L1 Hebrew and L1 Hebrew → L2 English translation. The teacher encouraged group participation in various ways and devoted time to collocations as well as to individual words. The experimental and control groups later took vocabulary tests that required L2 → L1 and L1 → L2 translation. The results show that the experimental group did far better, with the differences in scores being statistically significant,

The superior performance of the experimental group on collocations is consistent with an earlier study by Kupferberg and Olshtain (1996) which used L2 English → L1 Hebrew translation as part of an instructional procedure to raise learners' awareness of differences between the L1 and L2 in compound nouns. In English, the head noun follows the modifying noun, so that in *wall paper*, the head noun is *paper*, whereas in *paper wall*, the head noun is *wall*. In Hebrew, the word-order pattern is just the opposite, so that the head noun comes first and is followed by the modifying noun. The two languages differ in other ways as well, but a translation exercise given to the experimental (but not to a control) group was intended to help learners focus on crosslinguistic contrasts. In fact, the experimental group did outperform the control group, which had no such translation practice (as determined by tests of receptive and productive skills).

The studies by Laufer and Girsai and by Kupferberg and Olshtain make clear that part of the instruction that the experimental groups received included activities of teachers to foreground contrasts in form and meaning in the two languages; the approach was thus tantamount to a practical exercise in contrastive analysis. In still another study, using somewhat similar teaching methods, Kupferberg (1999) provides evidence that learners are likely to produce the English past perfect tense in particular discourse contexts when they have had L2 English → L1 Hebrew translation practice together with instruction on the contrasts between verb tenses in Hebrew and English.

The aim of such contrastive instruction in the above studies was to increase learners' knowledge of L2 words, collocations, and grammatical patterns. The translation process itself was less of a concern than the use of translation as a learning tool. Even so, pedagogical problems in translating texts have also gotten some attention in a very different classroom setting. As discussed in Chapter 7, Castaglioni (2016) noted problems of L2 English → L1 Italian transfer among native speakers of Italian in a course to refine their translation skills. To reduce L2 English interference on translations into students' L1 Italian, Castaglioni developed classroom materials from corpora of translations so that students could compare the merits of various translations. If similar materials do not exist now in many other settings, such corpora could be created. For example, translation texts might be collected from learners of a particular language, with a source text being provided to them. Activities might include comparisons of attempts by different learners, whether successful or not, to recreate the original text in their own interlanguage version. Such attempts could also allow for useful contrastive discussions not only of concerns such as differences in vocabulary and grammar, but also stylistic and other pragmatic differences.

The demonstrated value of translation in teaching does not imply that all other techniques lack value. Indeed, with regard to compounding, a recent commentary by Tyler and Ortega (2018) offers useful suggestions to instructors of L2 German about ways to help learners overcome difficult areas of compounding identified in a corpus study by Zeldes (2018). Tyler and Ortega recommend corrective feedback focusing on particular types of errors along with visual devices such as highlighting compound structures in an actual texts, and explanatory materials that use theories and schematic conventions of cognitive linguistics to enhance learners' awareness of the putative cognitive bases for compounding. The insights offered by Tyler and Ortega show that the instructor's toolbox offers more than one option for solving any particular problem, but the empirical work on translation reviewed in this section certainly points to still another possible tool – this fact seems especially relevant since Zeldes found some evidence of transfer (see below).

Crosslinguistic contrasts in form sometimes indicate meaning differences where translators have to cope with ambiguity. The discussion of a study by Tabakowska in Chapter 7 noted that the absence of articles in Polish may lead to different but equally valid translations into English or French, where one translation might use an article while another translation uses no article. Tabakowska herself stresses the need for teachers to be aware of such possibilities and to eschew any rigid policy of accepting one and only one translation as correct in all cases. Tabakowska's point about possible ambiguities can be extended to the recasts or paraphrases of speech or writing produced by learners. In many cases, a paraphrase might prove useful to model a target-like form, but teachers may sometimes need to check to see what individual speakers or writers have in mind before attempting a recast.

Occasionally it is a crosslinguistic similarity in form that leads to difficulty, as in the false friends that resulted in the mistranslations of Mary Howitt (Chapter 7). The dangers of negative transfer in such cases have long been known and contrastive instruction should continue to alert learners to the risk of comprehension as well as production errors.

Although technology can help with translation practices in the classroom and outside, pitfalls have become increasingly obvious, especially the overreliance of some learners on highly imperfect software. The poor translations from Finnish to English in Chapter 7 could probably be replicated in other settings, such as from Korean to English or Arabic to German. In any case, instructors might directly or indirectly point to the continuing advantage that human learners have over machines in making better interlingual identifications even in moderately complex contexts such as the events in the *Modern Times* story.

Metalinguistic awareness, the final topic addressed in this section, inevitably overlaps with concerns about translation. As discussed in Chapter 7, bilinguals studied in Canadian research showed impressive sensitivity to language, with the awareness contributing to their efforts at translation. While Malakoff focused on putatively natural metalinguistic abilities that emerged as those younger learners became bilingual, work with older learners in Israel has indicated that overt teaching can help develop greater metalinguistic awareness and better comprehension and production. Laufer and Girsai interpret the classroom translation tasks as ways to foster greater cognitive involvement because L2 → L1 and L1 → L2 translation together require active searches for meaning and for forms; the evaluation of translation alternatives emerging from such searches depends on increased attention to form–meaning relations in comprehension and production. Greater focus on such relations seems inextricably linked to greater metalinguistic awareness.

Laufer and Girsai make a persuasive case for the potential of translation to foster cognitive involvement. Even so, other classroom practices also seem promising, such as a grammaticality judgement task used by Kupferberg and Olshtain. While the researchers employed interlingual translation to raise awareness of differences between Hebrew and English in compounding, they used grammaticality judgements for teaching about reduced relative clauses as in:

The old woman *knitting a sweater* is my grandmother.
The policeman *who standing at the corner* lives in Tel Aviv.

The first example shows a normal reduced relative pattern (with italics added), whereas the second shows an ungrammatical pattern. It is possible to reconstruct full-form relative clauses for each sentence:

The old woman who is knitting a sweater is my grandmother.
The policeman who is standing at the corner lives in Tel Aviv.

Students given the grammaticality judgement task had to evaluate specific sentences, of course, and this evaluation must evoke comparisons between alternative reduced or full patterns, some alternatives being acceptable and others not. The reduced versions are in effect paraphrases (if often extremely close ones) of the full forms. The 'rewording' that Jakobson deemed to be one kind of translation (Chapter 7) thus seems highly relevant to the grammaticality judgement task.

Greater cognitive involvement thus seems possible through a careful use of grammaticality judgement tasks in addition to 'translation proper' as Jakobson put it. In tandem with these methods Kupferberg and colleagues introduced overt comparisons of similarities and differences in grammatical patterns. Kupferberg (1999) and Kupferberg and Olshtain (1996) describe how teachers provided explicit contrastive information about the past perfect, about compounding, and about reduced relative clauses to students in the experimental groups. The interpretation of the results in both investigations credits the minutes spent on the succinct contrasts that were drawn with helping learners sharpen their focus although, it should be stressed, the contrastive descriptions formed only part of a larger set of classroom activities to raise awareness.

The studies from Israel thus make a strong case for using a variety of consciousness-raising activities including overt contrastive descriptions. Even so, questions such as the following seem inevitable: (1) How much detail should there be in any contrastive description? (2) How much variation in metalinguistic awareness among learners may there be in any particular classroom setting? (3) Do some structures warrant more contrastive attention than others? These and other questions suggest areas for further investigation, but some observations now seem possible in the light of findings from available research.

One conclusion supported by evidence is that even learners with considerable education do not always recognize crosslinguistic similarities that they could take advantage of, and, in such cases, teachers will do well to help them perceive the similarities. Otwinowska-Kasztelnic (2010) investigated cognate recognition in L2 and L3 contexts among Polish university students. Although there might not seem to be any problem in recognizing the similarity of Polish *optymistyczny*, German *optimistisch*, and English *optimistic* as cognate forms, Otwinowska-Kasztelnic found that when the students had not received explicit training in cognate recognition, they did not perform as well on a reading test as students who had received such training.

The degree of similarity between languages should count as one factor in deciding how much attention to give to similarities or differences. The study by Zeldes (2018) mentioned above found that speakers of some languages tended to use compounding in L2 German much more than did speakers of other languages. Speakers of two other Germanic languages, Danish and Norwegian, showed especially high usage rates in sharp contrast with speakers of Romance languages, which use compounding less. Yet while these results suggest strong positive transfer, they are complicated by the fact that speakers of another Germanic language, Dutch, did not perform as successfully as the Scandinavian groups. Zeldes attributes the difference in use of compounds to a somewhat lower level of L2 proficiency among the Dutch students (as determined by a C-test). Perhaps the lower degree of proficiency also involved a lower degree of metalinguistic awareness.

Whatever the exact relations between crosslinguistic similarity, target language proficiency, and metalinguistic awareness, there is also evidence that multilinguals have increased capacities for analyzing language. For example, Otwinowska-Kasztelnic (2011) compared bilingual and multilingual groups at a Polish university in their ability to recognize cognate vocabulary. In general, the multilingual group showed the greatest success, although it is noteworthy that the high-proficiency subgroup of bilinguals also showed considerable awareness. (See also discussions by De Angelis, 2007 and Jessner, 2006.) From her results, Otwinowska-Kasztelnic argues not only for raising learners' awareness but also for increasing the awareness of teachers to enable them to help their pupils sharpen their metalinguistic skills. The merits of this approach will be considered in more detail later in this chapter.

While it may be relatively easy to raise awareness of crosslinguistic similarities in vocabulary, other areas of structure may raise questions about how accessible particular structures are and how much detail is desirable either in classroom activities or in materials designed for use outside class. Some evidence suggests that bilinguals can identify certain types of errors as probable cases of transfer involving their own native language. Odlin (1996) found that Spanish speakers consider cases such as: *The car is the transportation system most popular* (as opposed to *the most popular transportation system*) as a characteristic transfer error of a Spanish speaker; while Korean bilinguals similarly judged cases such as: *She fell in love with a different country man* (as opposed to *a man from a different country*) as a characteristic transfer error of a Korean speaker. The examples are consistent with word-order differences in Spanish and Korean and, in the examples given to the bilingual judges, there was additional context to make the sentences and correct versions of them as clear as possible. In most cases, the two groups of bilingual judges did not mistake examples from the other group as likely transfer errors for speakers of their own languages. This finding about word order is consistent with the analysis in Chapter 4, which argued that basic word order is often accessible to crosslinguistic awareness, and this analysis can help explain why examples of basic word-order transfer, although real, do not appear more often in the professional literature.

The degree of detail appropriate for any particular classroom will, of course, depend on several factors, including the age of the learners, the extent of previous formal education, the aims of the course (e.g. more emphasis on comprehension than on production), and the preparation of teachers for the instruction to be given. Some valuable insights about linguistic detail appear in a study by Flege and Hammond (1982) to ascertain the sensitivity of English-speaking learners of Spanish to phonetic characteristics of the target language. The technique employed was to give learners a task where they would mimic the English pronunciation of Spanish native speakers who showed L1 influence on their L2 speech. Highly accurate mimicry would include, for instance, using no aspiration after the voiceless word-initial stop /t/ in items such as *tape, toad* and *tube*, since L1 varieties of English typically have *aspirated* pronunciations of /t/ instead. Flege and Hammond indeed found the native speakers of English often using an unaspirated instead of an aspirated /t/. The anatomical and terminological details of phonetics (such as the term *voiced onset timing*) were not part of the information given to participants, who simply had to attempt mimicking a Spanish-accented variety of English. (Flege and Hammond report that the participants had already had exposure to this variety of English.) The activity that participants engaged in merely encouraged them to use their earlier-gained awareness of audible differences in transfer-affected speech.

Flege and Hammond do not offer any opinion as to whether such an activity might help L1 English speakers also become more accurate in pronouncing Spanish, but the results at least suggest that detailed phonetic instruction may not be necessary in some contexts. The results also provide an interesting counterpoint to the beliefs of Whorf about how to reduce the L1 English influence on pronunciation of L2 French. Writing of a hypothetical (and generic male) learner, Whorf states:

> If, however, he is so fortunate as to have his elementary French taught by a theoretic linguist, he first has the patterns of the English formula explained in such a way that they become semiconscious, with the result that they lose their binding power over him which custom has given them, though they remain automatic as far as English is concerned. Then he acquires the French patterns without inner opposition, and the time for attaining command of the language is cut to a fraction.... (1956[1941]: 224–225)

This passage comes from an article that Whorf wrote for the alumni magazine of Massachusetts Institute of Technology, thus an audience of non-specialists in linguistics but graduates of an elite university. The kind of linguist–instructor that Whorf had in mind would clearly have been someone able to make accessible the anatomical details and terminology required for a detailed comparison of the phonetic and phonological differences between French and English (e.g. unaspirated word-initial / t/ in the former but not the latter). The kind of instruction and instructor that Whorf extols should not be considered as fanciful – indeed, linguists of all kinds often teach foreign language courses. However, such instruction is neither available nor desirable in all settings. It seems probable that the imitation techniques used by Flege and Hammond would be accessible to many more learners who would not have the backgrounds that Whorf likely had in mind when addressing an audience of MIT graduates.

Whorf's reference to the 'binding power' of the native language clearly refers to transfer, but it also suggests that his thinking conflated the ideas of linguistic relativity and language-specific processing. Such a conflation would force a conclusion that English-influenced pronunciation of French counts as conceptual transfer, even though the claim is dubious (phonetic forms are forms, after all, not concepts). As argued already, it seems best to consider conceptual transfer as only a subset of transfer phenomena. Despite this caveat, however, Whorf's optimism warrants some reflection. Clearly, he did not view transfer as highly deterministic or insurmountable. Although he and von Humboldt were both aware of transfer, their judgements about its force differed, with Whorf more confident, believing in the potential of instruction to overcome negative transfer whereas von Humboldt showed no such optimism.

Whether or not mimicry involves an awareness that can lead to improved pronunciation, the other studies of crosslinguistic awareness reviewed in this chapter show that teachers and curriculum designers can usefully explore diverse ways to raise consciousness.

The case thus made for raising learner awareness constitutes yet another argument that helping guide attention contributes to effective teaching. As such, the analysis is consistent with others, e.g. the suggestions of Tyler and Ortega (2018), and form part of a long tradition of trying to ground classroom practices on empirical research. Thus, the current chapter as well as evidence from other chapters in this volume should remind readers that the consciousness to be raised includes learner judgements of similarities and differences between languages. It remains uncertain whether the results of further work will tend to confirm more the optimism of Whorf or the pessimism of von Humboldt, but surely such investigations will benefit both practical and theoretical language study.

References

Abdullah, K. and Jackson, H. (1998) Idioms and the language learner: Contrasting English and Syrian Arabic. *Languages in Contrast* 1, 83–107.

Ahlqvist, A. (1871) *Det vestfinska språkets kulturord*. Helsinki: Frenckell.

Ahlqvist, A. (1875) *Die Kulturwörter der westfinnischen Sprachen*. Helsinki: Warsenius.

Akmajian, A. (1970) On deriving cleft sentences from pseudocleft sentences. *Linguistic Inquiry* 1: 149–168.

Algeo, J. (1960) Korean Bamboo English. *American Speech* 35, 117–123.

Alhawary, M. (2009) Speech processing prerequisites or language transfer? Evidence from English and French L2 learners of Arabic. *Foreign Language Annals* 42, 367–390.

Andersen, R. (1984) The One-to-One principle of interlanguage construction. *Language Learning* 34, 77–95.

Asher, R. (1985) *Tamil*. Amsterdam: North Holland.

Ball, C. (1994) The origins of the informative–presupposition *it*–cleft. *Journal of Pragmatics* 22, 603–628.

Bar-Hillel, Y. (1960) The present status of automatic translation of languages. *Advances in Computers* 1, 91–163.

Bialystok, E. (1979) Explicit and implicit judgements of grammaticality. *Language Learning* 29, 81–103.

Biber, D., Johansson, S., Leech, G., Conrad, S. and Finegan, E. (1999) *Longman Grammar of Spoken and Written English*. London: Longman.

Bickerton, D. and Givón, T. (1976) Pidginization and syntactic change: From SXV and VSX to SVX. In S. Seever, C. Walkerer and S. Mufwene (eds) *Papers from the Parasession on Diachronic Syntax* (pp. 9–39). Chicago, IL: Chicago Linguistic Society.

Birch, S., Albrecht, J. and Myers, J. (2000) Syntactic focusing structures influence discourse processing. *Discourse Processes* 30, 285–304.

Birdsong, D. (1999) Introduction: Whys and why nots for the Critical Period Hypothesis in second language acquisition. In D. Birdsong (ed.) *Second Language Acquisition and the Critical Period Hypothesis* (pp. 1–22). Mahwah, NJ: Lawrence Erlbaum.

Birner, B. (1994) Information status and word order: An analysis of English inversion. *Language* 70, 233–259.

Birner, B. and Ward, G. (1998) *Information Status and Noncanonical Word Order in English*. Amsterdam: Benjamins.

Bley-Vroman, R. (1983) The comparative fallacy in interlanguage studies: The case of systematicity. *Language Learning* 33, 1–17.

Bloomfield, L. (1933) *Language*. New York, NY: Holt, Rinehart & Winston.

Bock, J.K. and Warren, R. (1985) Conceptual accessibility and syntactic structure in sentence formation. *Cognition* 21, 47-67.

Blumenthal, A. (1985) Psychology and linguistics. In S. Koch and D. Leary (eds) *A Century of Psychology as Science* (pp. 804–824). New York, NY: McGraw-Hill.

Bohnacker, U. (2005) Nonnative acquisition of verb second: On the empirical underpinnings of universal L2 claims. In M. den Dikken and C. Tortora (eds.) *The Function of Function Words and Functional Categories* (pp. 41–77). Amsterdam: Benjamins.

Bohnacker, U. and Rosén, C. (2008) The clause-initial position in L2 German declaratives: Transfer of information structure. *Studies in Second Language Acquisition* 30, 511–538.

Brown, A. (2007) Cross-linguistic influence in first and second languages: Convergence in speech and gesture. Unpublished PhD dissertation, Boston University.

Cadierno, T. (2008) Learning to talk about motion in a foreign language. In P. Robinson and N. Ellis (eds) *Handbook of Cognitive Linguistics and Second Language Acquisition* (pp. 239–275). New York, NY: Routledge.

Callies, M. (2008) Easy to understand and difficult to use: Raising constructions and information packaging in the advanced learner variety. In G. Gilquin, S. Papp and S. Diez-Bedmar (eds) *Linking up Contrastive and Learner Corpus Research* (pp. 201–226). Amsterdam: Rodolphi.

Caramazza, A., Miozzo, M., Costa, A., Schiller, N. and Alario, F. (2001) A crosslinguistic investigation of determiner production. In E. Dupoux (ed.) *Language, Brain, and Cognitive Development* (pp. 209–226). Cambridge, MA: MIT Press.

Carroll, J. (1968) Contrastive linguistics and interference theory. In J. Alatis (ed.) *Report of the Nineteenth Annual Meeting on Linguistics and Language Study* (pp. 113–122). Georgetown University Monograph Series on Language and Linguistics. Washington, DC: Georgetown University Press.

Carston, R. (1996) Syntax and pragmatics. In K. Brown and J. Miller (eds) *The Concise Encyclopedia of Syntactic Theories* (pp. 306–313). New York, NY: Pergamon.

Castagnoli, S. (2016) Investigating trainee translators' contrastive pragmalinguistic competence: A corpus-based analysis of interclausal linkage in learner translations. *Interpreter and Translator Trainer* 10, 343–363.

Celce-Murcia, M., Larsen-Freeman, D. and Williams, H. (1999) *The Grammar Book: An ESL/EFL Teacher's Course* (2nd edn). Boston, MA: Heinle & Heinle.

Cenoz, J., Hufeisen, B. and Jessner, U. (eds) (2001) *Cross-linguistic Influence in Third Language Acquisition: Psycholinguistic Perspectives*. Clevedon: Multilingual Matters.

Chafe, W. (1973) Language and memory. *Language* 49, 261–281.

Chafe, W. (1994) *Discourse, Consciousness, and Time*. Chicago, IL: University of Chicago Press.

Chang, H. and Zhang, L. (2016) The role of L1 in the acquisition of Chinese causative constructions by English-speaking learners. In L. Yu and T. Odlin (eds) *New Perspectives on Transfer in Second Language Learning* (pp. 145–167). Bristol: Multilingual Matters.

Chao, R. (1968) *Language and Symbolic Systems*. Cambridge: Cambridge University Press.

Chesterman, A. (1991) *On Definiteness: A Study with Special Reference to English and Finnish*. Cambridge: Cambridge University Press.

Chomsky, N. (1959) Review of Skinner (1957). *Language* 35, 26–58.

Comrie, B. (1981) *Language Universals and Linguistic Typology*. Chicago, IL: University of Chicago Press.

Conrad, A. and Fishman, J. (1977) English as a world language: The evidence. In J. Fishman, R. Cooper and A. Conrad (eds) *The Spread of English* (pp. 3–76). Rowley, MA: Newbury House.

Corbett, G. (1999) Agreement. In J. Miller (ed.) *Concise Encyclopedia of Grammatical Categories* (pp. 12–18). Amsterdam: Elsevier.

Corder, S. (1983) A role for the mother tongue. In S. Gass and L. Selinker (eds) *Language Transfer in Language Learning* (pp. 85–97). Rowley, MA: Newbury House.

Cowan, N. (1995) *Attention and Memory: An Integrated Framework*. Oxford: Oxford University Press.

Culicover, P. and McNally, L. (eds) (1998) *The Limits of Syntax*. San Diego, CA: Academic Press.

Dalgado, S.R. (1906) Dialecto Indo–Portugues do norte. *Revista Lusitana* 9, 142–166, 193–228.

Dawkins, R.M. (1916) *Modern Greek in Asia Minor*. Cambridge: Cambridge University Press.

De Angelis, G. (2007) *Third or Additional Language Acquisition*. Clevedon: Multilingual Matters.

De Angelis, G. and Dewaele, J.-M. (eds) (2011) *New Trends in Cross-linguistic Influence and Multilingualism Research*. Bristol: Multilingual Matters.

Dechert, H. (2006) On the ambiguity of the notion of 'transfer'. In J. Arabski (ed.) *Cross-linguistic Influence in the Second Language Lexicon* (pp. 3–11). Clevedon: Multilingual Matters.

Dixon, R.M.W. (1972) *The Dyirbal Language of Northern Queensland*. Cambridge: Cambridge University Press.

Doherty, M. (1999) Clefts in translation between English and German. *Target* 11, 289–315.

Doherty, M. (2001) Discourse theory and translation of clefts between English and German. In I. Kenesei and R. Harnish (eds) *Perspectives on Semantics, Pragmatics, and Discourse* (pp. 273–292). Amsterdam: Benjamins.

Domingue, N. (1971) Bhojpuri and Creole in Mauritius: A study of linguistic interference and its consequences in regard to synchronic variation and language change. Unpublished Ph.D. dissertation, University of Texas at Austin.

Ducar, C. and Schocket, D. (2018) Machine translation and the L2 classroom: Pedagogical solutions for making peace with Google Translate. *Foreign Language Annals* 51, 779–795.

Dulay, H., Burt, M. and Krashen, S. (1982) *Language Two*. New York, NY: Oxford University Press.

Dušková, L. (1984) Similarity: An aid or hindrance in foreign language learning? *Folia Linguistica* 18, 103–115.

Elliott, A.M. (1886) Speech mixture in French Canada, Indian and French. *Transactions and Proceedings of the Modern Language Association of America* 2, 158–186.

Ellis, N. (2008) Usage-based and form-based language acquisition. In P. Robinson and N. Ellis (eds) *Handbook of Cognitive Linguistics and Second Language Acquisition* (pp. 341–405). New York, NY: Routledge.

Ellis, N. and Robinson, P. (2008) An introduction to cognitive linguistics, second language acquisition, and language instruction. In P. Robinson and N. Ellis (eds) *Handbook of Cognitive Linguistics and Second Language Acquisition* (pp. 3–24). New York, NY: Routledge.

Ellis, R. (1985) *Understanding Second Language Acquisition*. Oxford: Oxford University Press.

Elston-Güttler, K. and Williams, J. (2008) L1 polysemy affects L2 meaning interpretation: Evidence for L1 concepts active during L2 reading. *Second Language Research* 24, 167–187.

Escobar, A. (1997) From time to modality in Spanish in contact with Quechua. *Hispanic Linguistics* 9, 64–99.

Feinstein, M. (1980) Ethnicity and topicalization in New York City English. *International Journal for the Sociology of Language* 26, 15–24.

Fender, M. (2003) English word recognition and word integration skills of native Arabic- and Japanese-speaking learners of English as a Second Language. *Applied Psycholinguistics* 24, 289–315.

Filppula, M. (1986) *Some Aspects of Hiberno–English in a Functional Sentence Perspective*. Joensuu, Finland: Joensuu Publications in the Humanities.

Filppula, M., Klemola, J. and Paulasto, H. (2008) *English and Celtic in Contact*. New York, NY: Routledge.

Finegan, E. (1995) Introduction. In D. Stein and S. Wright (eds) *Subjectivity and Subjectivisation: Linguistic Perspectives* (pp. 1–15). Cambridge: Cambridge University Press.

Firbas, J. (1992) *Functional Sentence Perspective in Written and Spoken Communication.* Cambridge: Cambridge University Press.

Fisiak, J., Lipinska-Grzegorek, M. and Zabrocki, T. (1978) *An Introductory English/Polish Contrastive Grammar.* Warsaw: Panstwowe Wydawnictwo Naukowe.

Flege, J. and Hammond, R. (1982) Mimicry of non-distinctive phonetic differences between language varieties. *Studies in Second Language Acquisition* 5, 1–17.

Foley, C. and Flynn, S. (2013) The role of the native language. In J. Herschensohn and M. Young-Scholten (eds) *The Cambridge Handbook of Second Language Acquisition* (pp. 97–113). Cambridge: Cambridge University Press.

Foss, D. and Hakes, D. (1978) *Psycholinguistics: An Introduction.* Englewood Cliffs, NJ: Prentice-Hall.

Frawley, W. (1984) Prolegomenon to a theory of translation. In W. Frawley (ed.) *Translation: Linguistic, Literary, and Philosophical Perspectives* (pp. 159–175). Newark, DE: University of Delaware Press.

Fries, C. (1945) *Teaching and Learning English as a Foreign Language.* Ann Arbor, MI: University of Michigan Press.

Gabilondo, I. (2002) La salud de la lengua esspañola: Entrevista con Victor García de la Concha [The state of the Spanish language: Interview with Victor García de la Concha]. *Puerta del Sol* 11, 4–9.

Gabryś-Barker, D. (ed.) (2012) *Cross-linguistic Influences in Multilingual Language Acquisition, Second Language Learning and Teaching.* Berlin: Springer.

Galambos, S. and Goldin-Meadow, S. (1983) Learning a second language and metalinguistic awareness. In A. Chukerman, M. Marks and J. Richardson (eds) *Papers from the Nineteenth Regional Meeting* (pp. 117–133). Chicago, IL: Chicago Linguistic Society.

Gass, S. (1979) Second language acquisition and language universals. In R. Dipietro, W. Frawley and A. Wedel (eds) *The First Delaware Symposium on Language Studies* (pp. 249–260). Newark, DE: University of Delaware Press.

Givón, T. (ed.) (1983) *Topic Continuity in Discourse.* Amsterdam: Benjamins.

Givón, T. (1984a) Universals of discourse structure and second language acquisition. In W. Rutherford (ed.) *Language Universals and Second Language Interaction* (pp. 110–139). Amsterdam: Benjamins.

Givón, T. (1984b) *Syntax. Volume 1.* Amsterdam: Benjamins.

Givón, T. (1990) *Syntax. Volume 2.* Amsterdam: Benjamins.

Givón, T. (1992) The grammar of referential coherence as mental processing instructions. *Linguistics* 30, 5–55.

Goodman, M. (1971) The strange case of Mbugu. In D. Hymes (ed.) *Pidginization and Creolization of Languages* (pp. 243–54). Cambridge: Cambridge University Press.

Grabe, W. (2002) Reading in a second language. In R. Kaplan (ed.) *Oxford Handbook of Applied Linguistics.* (pp. 49–59). New York, NY: Oxford University Press.

Graham, G. (2010) Behaviorism. In E. Zalta (ed.) *Stanford Encyclopedia of Philosophy.* Stanford, CA: Metaphysics Research Lab. [http://plato.stanford.edu/entries/behaviorism/]

Greenberg, J. (1966) Some universals of grammar with particular reference to the order of meaningful elements. In J. Greenberg (ed.) *Universals of Language* (pp. 73–113). Cambridge, MA: MIT Press.

Gullberg, M. (2008) Gestures and second language acquisition. In P. Robinson and N. Ellis (eds) *Handbook of Cognitive Linguistics and Second Language Acquisition* (pp. 276–305). New York, NY: Routledge.

Gullberg, M. (2011) Language-specific coding of placements in gestures. In J. Bohnemeyer and E. Pederson (eds) *Event Representation in Language and Cognition* (pp. 166–188). Cambridge: Cambridge University Press.

Guo, J.S. (1999) From information to emotion: The affective function of right dislocation in Mandarin Chinese. *Journal of Pragmatics* 31, 1103–1128.

Håkansson, G., Pienemann, M. and Sayehli, S. (2002) Transfer and typological proximity in the context of second language processing. *Second Language Research* 18, 250–273.

Hakes, D. (1981) *The Development of Metalinguistic Abilities in Children.* Berlin: Springer.

Hammarberg, B. (2009) *Processes in Third Language Acquisition.* Edinburgh: Edinburgh University Press.

Hammarberg, B. and Hammarberg, B. (2009) Re-setting the basis of articulation in the acquisition of new languages: A third language study. In B. Hammarberg (ed.) *Processes in Third Language Acquisition* (pp. 74–85). Edinburgh: Edinburgh University Press.

Han, Z. (2001) Fine-tuning corrective feedback. *Foreign Language Annals* 34, 582–599.

Han, Z. (2010) Grammatical inadequacy as a function of linguistic relativity: A longitudinal case study. In Z. Han and T. Cadierno (eds) *Linguistic Relativity in SLA: Thinking for Speaking* (pp. 154–182). Bristol: Multilingual Matters.

Han, Z. and Odlin, T. (2006) Introduction. In Z. Han and T. Odlin (eds) *Studies of Fossilization in Second Language Acquisition* (pp. 1–20). Clevedon: Multilingual Matters.

Harrington, M. and Sawyer, M. (1992) L2 working memory capacity and L2 reading skill. *Studies in Second Language Acquisition* 14, 25–38.

Haugen, E. (1953) *The Norwegian Language in America.* Philadelphia, PA: University of Pennsylvania Press.

Haviland, S. and Clark, H. (1974) What's new? Acquiring new information as a process in comprehension. *Journal of Verbal Learning and Verbal Behavior* 13, 512–538.

Hawkins, J. (1983) *Word Order Universals.* New York, NY: Academic Press.

Hearn, V. (1989) Interpretations of and attitudes toward emotional expression: A Polish–American comparison. Unpublished PhD dissertation. The Wright Institute, Berkeley, California.

Heeschen, V. (1978) The metalinguistic vocabulary of a speech community in the highlands of Irian Jaya (West New Guinea). In A. Sinclair, R. Jarvella and W. Levelt (eds) *The Child's Conception of Language* (pp. 155–187). Berlin: Springer.

Helms-Park, R. (2003) Transfer in SLA and creoles: The implications of causative serial verbs in the interlanguage of Vietnamese ESL learners. *Studies in Second Language Acquisition* 25, 211–244.

Henry, P.L. (1957) *An Anglo–Irish Dialect of North Roscommon: Phonology, Accidence, Syntax.* Dublin: Department of English, University College.

Hertel, T. (2003) Lexical and discourse factors in the L2 acquisition of Spanish word order. *Second Language Research* 19, 273–304.

Hoffman, E. (1988) *Lost in Translation: A Life in a New Language.* New York, NY: Dutton.

Hoijer, H. (1954) The Sapir–Whorf Hypothesis. In H. Hoijer (ed.) *Language and Culture* (pp. 92–105). Chicago. IL: University of Chicago Press.

Huebner, T. (1979) Order-of-acquisition versus dynamic paradigm: A comparison of method in interlanguage research. *TESOL Quarterly* 13, 21–28.

Huebner, T. (1983) *A Longitudinal Analysis of the Acquisition of English.* Ann Arbor, MI: Karoma.

Humboldt, W. von (1960[1836]) *Über die Verschiedenheit des menschlichen Sprachbaues und ihren Einfluss auf die geistige Entwickelung des Menschengeschlechts* [*On the Diversity of Human Language Construction and Its Influence on Human Mental Development*]. Bonn: Dümmler.

Hutchins, J. (2000) Yeshua Bar-Hillel: A philosopher's contribution to machine translation. In J. Hutchins (ed.) *Early Years in Machine Translation* (pp. 299–312). Amsterdam: Benjamins.

Irvine, J. (1990) Registering affect: Heteroglossia in the linguistic expression of emotion. In C. Lutz and L. Abu-Lughod (eds) *Language and the Politics of Emotion* (pp. 126–161). Cambridge: Cambridge University Press.

Isurin, L., Winford, D. and de Bot, K. (eds) (2009) *Multidisciplinary Approaches to Code-switching*. Amsterdam: Benjamins.

Izumi, S. (2003) Comprehension and production processes in second language learning. In search of the psycholinguistic rationale of the Output Hypothesis. *Applied Linguistics* 24, 168–196.

Jackson, J. (1974) Language identity of the Colombian Vaupés Indians. In R. Baumann and J. Sherzer (eds) *Explorations in the Ethnography of Speaking* (pp. 50–64). Cambridge: Cambridge University Press.

Jakobson, R. (1959) Linguistic aspects of translation. In R. Brower (ed.) *On Translation* (pp. 232–239). Cambridge, MA: Harvard University Press.

Jansen, B., Lallerman, J. and Muysken, P. (1981) The Alternation Hypothesis: Acquisition of Dutch word order by Turkish and Moroccan foreign workers. *Language Learning* 31, 315–336.

Jarvis, S. (1998) *Conceptual Transfer in the Interlanguage Lexicon*. Bloomington, IN: Indiana University Linguistics Club.

Jarvis, S. (2000) Methodological rigor in the study of transfer: Identifying L1 influence in the interlanguage lexicon. *Language Learning* 50, 245–309.

Jarvis, S. (2002) Topic continuity in L2 English article use. *Studies in Second Language Acquisition* 24, 387–418.

Jarvis, S. and Odlin, T. (2000) Morphological type, spatial reference, and language transfer. *Studies in Second Language Acquisition* 22, 535–556.

Jarvis, S. and Pavlenko, A. (2008) *Cross-linguistic Influence in Language and Cognition*. New York, NY: Routledge.

Jarvis, S., O'Malley, M., Jing, L., Zhang, J., Hill, J., Chan, C. and Sevostyanova, N. (2013) Cognitive foundations of crosslinguistic influence. In J. Schwieter (ed.) *Innovative Research and Practices in Second Language Acquisition and Bilingualism* (pp. 287–308). Amsterdam: Benjamins.

Jespersen, O. (1922) *Language: Its Nature, Development, and Origin*. London: Allen & Unwin.

Jessner, U. (2006) *Linguistic Awareness in Multilinguals: English as a Third Language*. Edinburgh: Edinburgh University Press.

Kamimoto, T., Shimura, A. and Kellerman, E. (1992) A second language classic reconsidered: The case of Schachter's avoidance. *Second Language Research* 8, 251–277.

Kamio, A. (1991) Cleft sentences and the territory of information. In C. Georgopoulos (ed.) *Interdisciplinary Approaches to Language. Essays in Honor of S.-Y. Kuroda* (pp. 353–371). Dordrecht: Kluwer Academic Publishers.

Kamio, A. (1997) *Territory of Information*. Amsterdam: Benjamins.

Keesing, R. (1991) Substrates, calquing, and grammaticalization in Melanesian Pidgin. In E. Traugott and B. Heine (eds) *Approaches to Grammaticalization. Volume I* (pp. 315–342). Amsterdam: Benjamins.

Kellerman, E. (1977) Towards a characterisation of the strategy of transfer in second language learning. *Interlanguage Studies Bulletin* 2, 58–145.

Kellerman, E. (1995) Crosslinguistic influence: Transfer to nowhere? In W. Grabe *et al.* (eds) *Annual Review of Applied Linguistics. Volume 15* (pp. 125–150). New York, NY: Cambridge University Press.

Kelly, L. (1969) *25 Centuries of Language Teaching*. Rowley, MA: Newbury House.

Kennedy, X. and Gioia, D. (2013) *Literature: An Introduction to Fiction, Poetry, Drama, and Writing*. New York, NY: Pearson.

Kim, K. (1995) *Wh*-clefts and left-dislocation in English conversation: Cases of topicalization. In P. Downing and M. Noonan (eds) *Word Order in Discourse* (pp. 199–246). Amsterdam: Benjamins.

Klee, C. and Ocampo, A. (1995) The expression of past reference in Spanish narratives of Spanish–Quechua bilingual speakers. In C. Silva-Corvalán (ed.) *Spanish in Four Continents* (pp. 52–70). Washington, DC: Georgetown University Press.

Klin, C., Weingartner, K., Guzman, A. and Levine, W. (2004) Readers' sensitivity to linguistic cues in narratives: How salience influences anaphor resolution. *Memory and Cognition* 32, 511–522.

Koehn, P. (2020) *Neural Machine Translation*. Cambridge: Cambridge University Press.

König, E. (1988) Concessive connectives and concessive sentences: Cross-linguistic regularities and pragmatic principles. In J. Hawkins (ed.) *Explaining Language Universals* (pp. 145–166). Oxford: Blackwell.

Kortmann, B. (1991) *Free Adjuncts and Absolutes in English*. London: Routledge.

Kortmann, B. and Szmrecsanyi, B. (2004) Global synopsis: Morphological and syntactic variation in English. In B. Kortmann, K. Burridge, R. Mesthrie, E. Schneider and C. Upton (eds) *Handbook of Varieties of English, Volume 2 (* pp. 1142–1202). Berlin: Mouton de Gruyter.

Kruisinga, E. (1953) *An English Grammar. Volume I: First Part*. Groningen: Noordhoff.

Kuno. S. (1973) *The Structure of the Japanese Language*. Cambridge, MA: MIT Press.

Kupferberg, I. (1999) Explicit L2. *Language Awareness* 8, 210–222.

Kupferberg, I. and Olshtain, E. (1996) Explicit L2 instruction facilitates the acquisition of difficult L2 forms. *Language Awareness* 5, 149–165.

Lado, R. (1957) *Linguistics across Cultures*. Ann Arbor, MI: University of Michigan Press.

Lakoff, G. and Johnson, M. (1980) *Metaphors We Live By*. Chicago, IL: University of Chicago Press.

Lakoff, G. and Johnson, M. (1999) *Philosophy in the Flesh: The Embodied Mind and its Challenge to Western Thought*. New York, NY: Basic Books.

Lane, R. and Nadel, L. (eds) (2000) *Cognitive Neuroscience of Emotion*. New York, NY: Oxford University Press.

Langacker, R. (1987) *Foundations of Cognitive Grammar*. Stanford, CA: Stanford University Press.

Langacker, R. (2008) Cognitive grammar as a basis for language acquisition. In P. Robinson and N. Ellis (eds) *Handbook of Cognitive Linguistics and Second Language Acquisition* (pp. 66–88). New York, NY: Routledge.

Larsen-Freeman, D. and Long, M. (1991) *An Introduction to Second Language Acquisition Research*. London: Longman.

Laufer, B. and Girsai, M. (2008) The use of native language for improving second language vocabulary: An exploratory study. In A. Stavans and I. Kupferberg (eds) *Studies in Language and Language Education* (pp. 261–275). Jerusalem: Hebrew Magnes University Press.

Lehrer, A. (1983) *Wine and Conversation*. Bloomington, IN: Indiana University Press.

Le Page, R.B. and Tabouret Keller, A. (1985) *Acts of Identity: Creole-based Approaches to Language and Ethnicity*. Cambridge: Cambridge University Press.

Leslau, W. (1945) The influence of Cushitic on the Semitic languages of Ethiopia. *Word* 1, 59–82.

Levelt, W. (1989) *Speaking: From Intention to Articulation*. Cambridge, MA: MIT Press.

Levelt, W. (2013) *A History of Psycholinguistics*. Oxford: Oxford University Press.

Levinson, S. (1997) From outer to inner space: Linguistic categories and non-linguistic thinking. In J. Nuyts and E. Pederson (eds) *Language and Linguistic Categorization* (pp. 13–45). Cambridge: Cambridge University Press.

Li, C. (1984) From verb-medial analytic language to verb-final synthetic language: A case of typological change. In C. Brugman *et al.* (eds) *Proceedings from the Tenth Annual Meeting of the Berkeley Linguistics Society* (pp. 307–323). Berkeley, CA: Berkeley Linguistics Society.

Li, S. and Yang, L. (2016) An investigation into topic-prominence in the interlanguage of Chinese EFL learners: In a discourse perspective. In L. Yu and T. Odlin (eds) *New Perspectives on Transfer in Second Language Learning* (pp. 111–123). Bristol: Multilingual Matters.

Lichtenberk, F. (1980) A grammar of Manam. Unpublished PhD dissertation, University of Hawaii.

Loftus, E. and Palmer, J. (1974) Reconstruction of automobile destruction: An example of the interaction between language and memory. *Journal of Verbal Learning and Verbal Behavior* 13, 585–589.

Long, M. (2003) Stabilization and fossilization in interlanguage development. In C. Doughty and M. Long (eds) *Handbook of Second Language Acquisition* (pp. 487–535). Oxford: Blackwell.

Lucy, J. (1992) *Grammatical Categories and Cognition*. Cambridge: Cambridge University Press.

Lucy, J. (2016) The implications of linguistic relativity for language learning. In R. Alonso Alonso (ed.) *Crosslinguistic Influence in Second Language Acquisition* (pp. 53–70). Bristol: Multilingual Matters.

Luján, M. Minaya, L. and Sankoff, D. (1984) The Universal Consistency Hypothesis and the prediction of word order acquisition stages in the speech of bilingual children. *Language* 60, 343–371.

Lyons, J. (1977) *Semantics* (2 vols). Cambridge: Cambridge University Press.

MacWhinney, B. (2008) A unified model. In P. Robinson and N. Ellis (eds) *Handbook of Cognitive Linguistics and Second Language Acquisition* (pp. 341–371). New York, NY: Routledge.

Malakoff, M. (1992) Translation ability: A natural bilingual and metalinguistic skill. In R. Harris (ed.) *Cognitive Processing in Bilinguals* (pp. 515–529). Amsterdam: North Holland.

Malakoff, M. and Hakuta, K. (1991) Translation skill and metalinguistic awareness in bilinguals. In E. Bialystok (ed.) *Language Processing in Bilingual Children* (pp. 141–166). Cambridge: Cambridge University Press.

Malmkjaer, K. (2001) Censorship or error: Mary Howitt and a problem in descriptive TS. In G. Hansen, K. Malmkjaer and D. Gile (eds) *Claims, Changes, and Challenges in Translation Studies* (pp. 141–155). Amsterdam: Benjamins.

Malmkjaer, K. (2005) *Linguistics and the Language of Translation*. Edinburgh: Edinburgh University Press.

Meillet, A. (1933) Sur le bilinguisme. *Journal de Psychologie* 30, 167–171.

Meisel, J. (1983) Transfer as a second language strategy. *Language and Communication* 3, 11–46.

Morente, E. (2002) Tangos de Pepico [Tangos of Pepico]. *Mi cante y una poema* [My song and a poem]. Virgin Records España.

Morgan, C. and King, R. (1971) *Introduction to Psychology*. New York, NY: McGraw-Hill.

Mufwene, S. (2010) SLA and the emergence of creoles. *Studies in Second Language Acquisition* 32, 1– 42.

Mühlhäusler, P. (1986) *Pidgin and Creole Languages*. Oxford: Blackwell.

Muysken, P. (1984) The Spanish that Quechua speakers learn: L2 learning as norm-governed behavior. In R. Andersen (ed.) *Second Languages* (pp. 192–219). Rowley, MA: Newbury House.

Nagara, S. (1972) *Japanese Pidgin English in Hawaii: A Bilingual Description*. Honolulu, HI: University of Hawaii Press.

Nash, R. (1979) Cognate transfer in Puerto Rican English. In R. Andersen (ed.) *The Acquisition and Use of Spanish and English as First and Second Languages* (pp. 33–42). Washington, DC: Teachers of English to Speakers of Other Languages.

Natalicio, D. (1979) Repetition and dictation in language testing. *Modern Language Journal* 63, 163–176.

Nolan, J. (2005) *Interpretation: Techniques and Exercises* (1st edn). Clevedon: Multilingual Matters.

Ó Catháin, S. (1985) *Uair An Chloig Cois Teallaigh* [An Hour by the Haerth]: *Told by Pádraig Eoghain Phádraig Mac an Luain / collected, translated and annotated by Séamas Ó Catháin*. Dublin: Comhairle Bhéaloideas Éireann, University College.

Odlin, T. (1986) On the nature and use of explicit knowledge. *International Review of Applied Linguistics* 24, 123–144.

Odlin, T. (1989) *Language Transfer: Cross-linguistic Influence in Language Learning*. Cambridge: Cambridge University Press.

Odlin, T. (1991) Irish English idioms and language transfer. *English World-Wide* 12, 175–193.

Odlin, T. (1992) Language transfer and cleft constructions. Paper presented at the Keck Symposium, Department of Linguistics, University of Oregon, March 1992.

Odlin, T. (1996) On the recognition of transfer errors. *Language Awareness* 5, 166–178.

Odlin, T. (1997) Bilingualism and substrate influence: A look at clefts and reflexives. In J. Kallen (ed.) *Focus on Ireland* (pp. 35–50). Amsterdam: Benjamins.

Odlin, T. (2003) Cross-linguistic influence. In C. Doughty and M. Long (eds) *Handbook of Second Language Acquisition* (pp. 436–486). Oxford: Blackwell.

Odlin, T. (2005) Cross-linguistic influence and conceptual transfer: What are the concepts? *Annual Review of Applied Linguistics* 25, 3–25.

Odlin, T. (2008) Conceptual transfer and meaning extensions. In P. Robinson and N. Ellis (eds) *Handbook of Cognitive Linguistics and Second Language Acquisition* (pp. 306–340). New York, NY: Routledge.

Odlin, T. (2012) Nothing will come of nothing. In B. Kortmann and B. Szmrecsanyi (eds) *Linguistic Complexity in Interlanguage Varieties, L2 Varieties, and Contact Languages* (pp. 62–89). Berlin: de Gruyter.

Odlin, T. (2013) Accelerator or inhibitor? On the role of substrate influence in interlanguage development. In D. Schreier and M. Hundt (eds) *English as a Contact Language* (pp. 298–313). Cambridge: Cambridge University Press.

Odlin, T. (2014) Rediscovering prediction. In Z. Han and E. Tarone (eds) *Interlanguage 40 Years Later* (pp. 27– 45). Amsterdam: Benjamins.

Odlin, T. (2016) A few more questions. In L. Yu and T. Odlin (eds) *New Perspectives on Transfer in Second Language Learning* (pp. 257–250). Bristol: Multilingual Matters.

Odlin, T. and Natalicio, D. (1982) Some characteristics of word classification in a second language. *Modern Language Journal* 66, 34–38.

Odlin, T. and Jarvis, S. (2004) Same source, different outcomes: A study of Swedish influence on the acquisition of English in Finland. *International Journal of Multilingualism* 1, 123–140.

Odlin, T. and Alonso-Vázquez, C. (2006) Meanings in search of the perfect form: A look at interlanguage verb phrases. *Rivista di Psicolinguistica Applicata* 6, 53–63.

Odlin, T. and Yu, L. (2016) Introduction. In L. Yu and T. Odlin (eds) *New Perspectives on Transfer in Second Language Learning* (pp. 1–16). Bristol: Multilingual Matters.

O'Malley, M., Chamot, A., Stewner-Manzanares, G., Kaupper, L. and Russo, R. (1985) Learning strategies used by beginning and intermediate ESL students. *Language Learning* 35, 21–46.

Orr, G. (1987) Aspects of the second language acquisition of Chichewa noun class morphology. Unpublished PhD dissertation. University of California, Los Angeles.

Ortony, A., Clore, G.L. and Collins, A. (1988) *The Cognitive Structure of Emotions*. Cambridge: Cambridge University Press.

Osgood, C. (1949) The similarity paradox in human learning: A resolution. *Psychological Review* 36, 132–143.

Osgood, C. and Sebeok, T. (eds) (1965) *Psycholinguistics: A Survey of Theory and Research Problems*. Bloomington, IN: Indiana University Press.

Ó Siadhail, M. (1989) *Modern Irish*. Cambridge: Cambridge University Press.

Otwinowska-Kasztelnic, A. (2010) Language awareness in using cognate vocabulary: The case of Polish advanced students of English in light of the theory of affordances. In J. Arabski and A. Wojtaszek (eds) *Neurolinguistic and Psycholinguistic Perspectives on SLA* (pp. 175–190). Bristol: Multilingual Matters.

Otwinowska-Kasztelnic, A. (2011) Awareness and affordances: Multilinguals versus bilinguals and their perception of cognates. In G. De Angelis and J.M. Dewaele (eds) *New Trends in Crosslinguistic Influence and Multilingualism Research* (pp. 1–18). Bristol: Multilingual Matters.

Paulasto, H. (2006) *Welsh English Syntax: Contact and Variation*. University of Joensuu Publications in the Humanities 43. Joensuu, Finland: Faculty of Humanities, University of Joensuu.

Pavlenko, A. (2003) 'I feel clumsy speaking Russian': L2 influence on L1 in narratives of Russian L2 users of English. In V. Cook (ed.) *Effects of the Second Language on the First* (pp. 32–61). Clevedon: Multilingual Matters.

Pavlenko, A. (2005) *Emotions and Multilingualism*. Cambridge: Cambridge University Press.

Pienemann, M. (1998) *Language Processing and Second-language Development: Processability Theory*. Amsterdam: Benjamins.

Pienemann, M. and Håkansson, G. (2007) Response article. Full transfer vs. developmentally moderated transfer: A reply to Bohnacker. *Second Language Research* 23, 485–493.

Pienemann, M., Di Biase, B., Kawaguchi, S. and Håkansson, G. (2005) Processing constraints on L1 transfer. In J.F. Kroll and A.M.B. de Groot (eds) *Handbook of Bilingualism: Psycholinguistic Approaches* (pp. 128–153). Oxford: Oxford University Press.

Pinker, S. (1994) *The Language Instinct: How the Mind Creates Language*. New York, NY: Morrow.

Porte, G. (2003) English from a distance: Code-mixing and blending in the L1 output of long-term resident overseas EFL teachers. In V. Cook (ed.) *Effects of the Second Language on the First* (pp. 103–119). Clevedon: Multilingual Matters.

Prince, E. (1978) A comparison of *it*-clefts and *wh*-clefts in discourse. *Language* 54, 883–908.

Prince, E. (1981) Topicalization, Focus-Movement, and Yiddish-Movement: A pragmatic differentiation. *Berkeley Linguistics Society* 7, 249–264.

Prince, E. (1986) On the syntactic marking of presupposed open propositions. In A. Farley *et al.* (eds) *Papers from the Parasession on Pragmatics and Grammatical Theory at the 22nd Regional Meeting of the Chicago Linguistic Society* (pp. 208–222). Chicago, IL: Chicago Linguistic Society.

Prince, E. (1988) On pragmatic change: The borrowing of discourse functions. *Journal of Pragmatics* 12, 505–518.

Prince, E. (1998) On the limits of syntax, with reference to left-dislocation and topicalization. In P. Culicover and L. McNally (eds) *The Limits of Syntax* (pp. 281–302). San Diego, CA: Academic Press.

Quine, W. (1959) Meaning and translation. In R. Brower (ed.) *On Translation* (pp. 148–172). Cambridge, MA: Harvard University Press.

Quine, W. (1961) *Word and Object*. Cambridge, MA: MIT Press.

Reddy, M. (1979) The conduit metaphor: A case of frame conflict in our language about language. In A. Ortony (ed.) *Metaphor and Thought* (pp. 284–324). Cambridge: Cambridge University Press.

Reed, D., Lado, R. and Shen, Y. (1948) The importance of the native language in foreign language learning. *Language Learning* 1, 17–23.

Ringbom, H. (1987) *The Role of the First Language in Foreign Language Learning*. Clevedon: Multilingual Matters.

Ringbom, H. (2007) *Cross-linguistic Similarity in Foreign Language Learning*. Clevedon: Multilingual Matters.

Robinson, P. (2001) Task complexity, task difficulty, and task production: Exploring interactions in a componential framework. *Applied Linguistics* 22, 27–57.

Robinson, P. (2003) Attention and memory during SLA. In C. Doughty and M. Long (eds) *Handbook of Second Language Acquisition* (pp. 631–678). Oxford: Blackwell.

Rocca, S. (2007) *Child Second Language Acquisition*. Amsterdam: Benjamins.

Rouchdy, A. (1980) Languages in contact: Arabic–Nubian. *Anthropological Linguistics* 22, 334–344.

Rutherford, W. (1983) Language typology and language transfer. In S. Gass and L. Selinker (eds) *Language Transfer in Language Learning* (pp. 358–370). Rowley, MA: Newbury House.

Rutherford, W. (1986) Grammatical theory and L2 acquisition: A brief overview. *Second Language Studies* 2, 1–15.

Sabban, A. (1982) *Gälisch–Englischer Sprachkontakt*. Heidelberg: Julius Groos.

Sabourin, L., Stowe, L. and de Haan, G. (2006) Transfer effects in learning a second language grammatical gender system. *Second Language Research* 22, 1–29.

Sankoff, G. (1993) Focus in Tok Pisin. In F. Byrne and D. Winford (eds) *Focus and Grammatical Relations in Creole Languages* (pp. 117–140). Amsterdam: Benjamins.

Sapir, E. (1921) *Language*. New York, NY: Harcourt, Brace, Jovanovich.

Sapir, E. (1929) The status of linguistics as a science. *Language* 5, 207–214.

Schachter, J. (1974) An error in error analysis. *Language Learning* 24, 205–214.

Schachter, J. (1988) Second language acquisition and its relation to Universal Grammar. *Applied Linguistics* 9, 215–235.

Schachter, J. and Hart, B. (1979) An analysis of learner production of English structures. *Georgetown University Papers in Languages and Linguistics* 15 (pp. 18–75). Washington, DC: Georgetown University Press.

Schmidt, A. (1985) *Young People's Dyirbal*. Cambridge: Cambridge University Press.

Schopenhauer, A. (1992[1891]) On language and words. In R.R. Schulte and J. Biguenet (eds) *Theories of Translation: From Dryden to Derrida* (pp. 32–35). Chicago, IL: University of Chicago Press.

Schuchardt, H. (1883a) Kreolische Studien IV: Über das Malaiospanische der Philippinen. *Sitzungberichte der Kaiserlichen Akademie der Wisssenschaften zu Wien (philosophisch-historische Klasse)* 105, 111–150.

Schuchardt, H. (1883b) Kreolische Studien III: Über das Indoportugiesische von Diu. *Sitzungberichte der Kaiserlichen Akademie der Wissenschaften zu Wien (philosophische–historische Klasse)* 103, 3–18.

Schuchardt, H. (1971[1884]) *Slawo–Deutsches und Slawo–Italienisches* [with reprinted reviews of the work by A.M. Elliott, H. Paul, and others]. Munich: Wilhem Fink.

Schuchardt, H. (1889) Zum Indoportugiesischen von Mahe und Cannanore. *Zeitschrift für Romanische Philologie* 13, 516–524.

Schulte, R. and Biguenet, J. (1992) Introduction. In R.R. Schulte and J. Biguenet (eds) *Theories of Translation: From Dryden to Derrida* (pp. 1–16). Chicago, IL: University of Chicago Press.

Scribner, S. and Cole, M. (1981) *The Psychology of Literacy*. Cambridge, MA: Harvard University Press.

Selinker, L. (1969) Language transfer. *General Linguistics* 9, 67–92.

Selinker, L. (1972) Interlanguage. *International Review of Applied Linguistics* 10, 209–231.

Selinker, L. (1992) *Rediscovering Interlanguage*. London: Longman.

Selinker, L. (2006) Afterword: Fossilization or 'Does your mind mind?' In Z. Han and T. Odlin (eds) *Studies of Fossilization in Second Language Acquisition* (pp. 201–210). Clevedon: Multilingual Matters.

Selinker, L. (2014) Interlanguage 40 years on: Three themes from here. In Z.H. Han and E. Tarone (eds) *Interlanguage: Forty Years Later* (pp. 221–246). Amsterdam: Benjamins.

Selinker, L. and Lakshmanan, U. (1993) Language transfer and fossilization: The Multiple Effects Principle. In S. Gass and L. Selinker (eds) *Language Transfer in Language Learning* (pp. 197–216). Amsterdam: Benjamins.

Shahani, A. (2016) Google announces improvements to translation system. Story on All Things Considered, National Public Radio, October 3, 2016.

Sharwood Smith, M. (1981) Consciousness-raising and the second language learner. *Applied Linguistics* 2, 59–68.

Siegel, J. (1987) *Language Contact in a Plantation Environment: A Sociolinguistic History of Fiji*. Cambridge: Cambridge University Press.

Siemund, P. (2000) *Intensifiers*. London: Routledge.

Singley, M. and Anderson, J. (1989) *The Transfer of Cognitive Skill*. Cambridge, MA: Harvard University Press.

Skinner, B. (1957) *Verbal Behavior*. New York, NY: Appleton-Century-Crofts.

Slobin, D. (1982) Universal and particular in the acquisition of language. In E. Wanner and L.R. Gleitman (eds) *Language Acquisition: The State of the Art* (pp. 128–170). Cambridge: Cambridge University Press.

Slobin, D. (1996) From 'thought and language' to 'thinking for speaking'. In J. Gumperz and S. Levinson (eds) *Rethinking Linguistic Relativity* (pp. 97–114). Cambridge: Cambridge University Press.

Slobin, D. (2000) Verbalized events: A dynamic approach to linguistic relativity and determinism. In S. Niemier and R. Dirven (eds) *Evidence for Linguistic Relativity* (pp. 107–138). Amsterdam: Benjamins.

Slobin, D. and Welsh, C. (1973) Elicited imitation as a research tool in developmental psycholinguistics. In C.A. Ferguson and D.I. Slobin (eds) *Studies of Child Language Development* (pp. 485–497). New York, NY: Holt, Rinehart & Winston.

Smith, I. (1977) Sri Lanka Creole Portuguese phonology. Unpublished PhD dissertation, Cornell University.

Smith, N. (1996) We-focus in Saramaccan: Substrate feature or grammaticalization? In P. Baker and A. Syea (eds) *Changing Meanings, Changing Functions: Papers Relating to Grammaticalization in Contact Languages* (pp. 113–128). Westminster Creolistics Series 2. London: University of Westminster Press.

Sorenson, A.P. (1967) Multilingualism in the northwest Amazon. *American Anthropologist* 69, 670–684.

Sperber, D. and Wilson, D. (1995) *Relevance: Communication and Cognition.* Oxford: Blackwell.

Stein, D. (1995) Subjective meanings and the history of inversion in English. In D. Stein and S. Wright (eds) *Subjectivity and Subjectivisation: Linguistic Perspectives* (pp. 129–150). Cambridge: Cambridge University Press.

Stockwell, R., Bowen, J.D. and Martin, J. (1965) *The Grammatical Structures of English and Spanish.* Chicago, IL: University of Chicago Press.

Sun, C.F. and Givón, T. (1985) On the so-called SOV word order in Mandarin Chinese. *Language* 61, 329–351.

Tabakowska, E. (1993) Articles in translation: An exercise in cognitive linguistics. In R. Geiger and B. Rudzka-Ostyn (eds) *Conceptualizations and Mental Processing in Language* (pp. 785–800). Amsterdam: Benjamins.

Thomas, M. (2004) *Universal Grammar in Second Language Acquisition: A History.* London: Routledge.

Thomas, M. (2006) Robert Lado, 1915–1995. In K. Brown (ed.) *Encyclopedia of Language and Linguistics. Volume 6* (pp. 301–302). Amsterdam: Elsevier.

Thomason, S.G. (1981) Are there linguistic prerequisites for contact-induced language change? Paper presented at the Annual University of Wisconsin–Milwaukee Linguistics Symposium on Language Contact, Milwaukee, WI, March 1981. ED 205054.

Thomason, S.G. (1983) Genetic relationship and the case of Ma'a (Mbugu). *Studies in African Linguistics* 14, 195–231.

Thomason, S. and Kaufman, T. (1988) *Language Contact, Creolization, and Genetic Linguistics.* Berkeley, CA: University of California Press.

Thompson, S. (1978) Modern English from a typological point of view. *Linguistiche Berichte* 54, 19–35.

Thorne, D. (1993) *Comprehensive Welsh Grammar.* Oxford: Blackwell.

Tomlin, R. (1994) Functional grammar, pedagogical grammars, and communicative language teaching. In T. Odlin (ed.) *Perspectives on Pedagogical Grammar* (pp. 140–178). Cambridge: Cambridge University Press.

Tomlin, R. (1995) Focal attention, voice, and word order: an experimental, cross-linguistic study. In P. Downing and M. Noonan (eds) *Word Order in Discourse* (pp. 517–554). Amsterdam: Benjamins.

Tomlin, R. (1997) Mapping conceptual representations into linguistic representations: The role of attention in grammar. In J. Nuyts and E. Pederson (eds) *Language and Linguistic Categorization* (pp. 162–189). Cambridge: Cambridge University Press.

Trèvise, A. (1986) Is it transferable topicalization? In E. Kellerman and M. Sharwood Smith (eds) *Crosslinguistic Influence and Second Language Acquisition* (pp. 186–206). New York, NY: Pergamon.

Tyler, A. and Ortega, L. (2018) Usage-inspired L2 instruction: An emergent, researched pedagogy. In A. Tyler and L. Ortega (eds) *Usage-inspired L2 Instruction* (pp. 3–26). Amsterdam: Benjamins.

Tymczyńska, M. (2012) Trilingual lexical processing in online translation recognition: The influence of conference interpreting experience. In D. Gabryś-Barker (ed.) *Cross-linguistic Influences in Multilingual Language Acquisition, Second Language Learning and Teaching* (pp. 151–167). Berlin: Springer.

Vainikka, A. and Young-Scholten, M. (1998) The initial state in the L2 acquisition of phrase structure. In S. Flynn, M. Gita and W. O'Neil (eds) *The Generative Study of Second Language Acquisition* (pp. 17–34). Mahwah, NJ: Lawrence Erlbaum.

Wardhaugh, R. (1970) The Contrastive Analysis Hypothesis. *TESOL Quarterly* 4, 123–130.

Weinreich, U. (1953a) *Languages in Contact.* The Hague: Mouton.

Weinreich, U. (1953b) Review of *The Study of Language* by John Carroll. *Word* 9, 277–279.

Weinreich, U. (1963) The semantic structure of language. In J. Greenbaum (ed.) *Universals of Language* (pp. 142–216). Cambridge, MA: MIT Press.

Weintraub, S. (1997) *Uncrowned King: The Life of Prince Albert.* New York, NY: Free Press.

Weiss, A. (1925) Language and psychology. *Language* 1, 52–57.

White, L. (2000) Second language acquisition: From initial to final state. In J. Archibald (ed.) *Second Language Acquisition and Linguistic Theory* (pp. 130–155). Oxford: Blackwell.

White, L. (2003) On the nature of interlanguage representation: Universal Grammar in the second language. In C. Doughty and M. Long (eds) *Handbook of Second Language Acquisition* (pp. 19–42). Oxford: Blackwell.

Whitley, M. (2002) *Spanish/English Contrasts.* Washington, DC: Georgetown University Press.

Whitney, W.D. (1881) On mixture in language. *Transactions of the American Philological Association* 12, 5–26.

Whitney, W.D. (1971[1881]) On mixture in language. In M. Silverstein (ed.) *Whitney on Language* (pp. 170–191). Chicago, IL: University of Chicago Press.

Whorf, B.L. (1956) *Language, Thought, and Reality: Selected Writings of Benjamin Lee Whorf. Edited by John B. Carroll.* Cambridge, MA: MIT Press.

Williams, P., Sennich, P., Post, M. and Koehn, P. (2016) *Syntax-based Statistical Machine Translation.* San Rafael, CA: Morgan & Claypool.

Wilson, D. and Sperber, D. (1993) Linguistic form and relevance. *Lingua* 90, 1–25.

Winford, D. (2003) *An Introduction to Contact Linguistics.* Oxford: Blackwell.

Zeldes, A. (2018) Compounds and productivity in advanced L2 German. In A. Tyler and L. Ortega (eds) *Usage-Inspired L2 Instruction* (pp. 237–265). Amsterdam: Benjamins.

Zobl, H. (1980) Developmental and transfer errors: Their common bases and (possibly) differential effects on subsequent learning. *TESOL Quarterly* 14, 469–479.

Zobl, H. (1983) L1 acquisition, age of L2 acquisition and the learning of word order. In S. Gass and L. Selinker (eds) *Language Transfer in Language Learning* (pp. 205–221). Rowley, MA: Newbury House.

Zobl, H. (1986a) Word order typology, lexical government, and the prediction of multiple, graded effects in L2 word order. *Language Learning* 36, 159–183.

Zobl, H. (1986b) A functional approach to the attainability of typological targets in L2 acquisition. *Second Language Studies* 2, 16–32.

Index

Note: References in *italics* are to figures, those in **bold** to tables; 'n' refers to chapter notes.

CPSIA information can be obtained
at www.ICGtesting.com
Printed in the USA
JSHW051047120722
28000JS00003B/44